Curriculum Considerations
in Inclusive Classrooms

Curriculum Considerations in Inclusive Classrooms

Facilitating Learning for All Students

edited by

Susan Stainback, Ed.D.
William Stainback, Ed.D.
College of Education
University of Northern Iowa
Cedar Falls

·P·A·U·L·H·
BROOKES
PUBLISHING CO.

Baltimore • London • Toronto • Sydney

Paul H. Brookes Publishing Co.
P.O. Box 10624
Baltimore, Maryland 21285-0624

Typeset by Brushwood Graphics, Inc., Baltimore, Maryland.
Manufactured in the United States of America by
The Maple Press Company, York, Pennsylvania.

Library of Congress Cataloging-in-Publication Data

Curriculum considerations in inclusive classrooms : facilitating
   learning for all students / edited by Susan & William Stainback.
      p.   cm.
Companion volume to: Support networks for inclusive schooling,
c 1990.
Includes bibliographical references and index.
ISBN 1-55766-078-6
   1. Education—United States—Curricula.   2. Handicapped children—
Education—United States.   3. Mainstreaming in education—United
States.   I. Stainback, Susan Bray.   II. Stainback, William C.
III. Support networks for inclusive schooling.
LB1570.C88393   1991
371.9'046'0973—dc20   91-18472
                                                                      CIP

Contents

Contributors

Anne M. Bauer, Ed.D.
Associate Professor
College of Education
Teachers College ML 02
University of Cincinnati
Cincinnati, Ohio 45221-002

Barb Buswell, B.A.
Co-Director
PEAK Parent Center
6055 Lehman Drive
Suite 101
Colorado Springs, Colorado 80918

Jennifer Coots, M.A.
Doctoral Student
School of Education
California State University,
   Los Angeles
5151 State University Drive
Los Angeles, California 90032

Brian Cullen, M.Ed.
Principal
St. Francis School
Waterloo Region Separate School
   Board
154 Gatewood Road
Kitchener, Ontario
Canada N2M 4E4

Linda Davern, M.S.
Coordinator
Inclusive Education Project
Syracuse University
805 South Crouse Avenue
Syracuse, New York 13244-2280

Mary Falvey, Ph.D.
Professor
School of Education
California State University,
   Los Angeles
5151 State University Drive
Los Angeles, California 90032

Dianne L. Ferguson, Ph.D.
Associate Professor
Specialized Training Program
College of Education
University of Oregon
Eugene, Oregon 97403

Sharon Field, Ed.D.
Coordinator
Transition and Employment Program
Developmental Disabilities Institute
Wayne State University
6001 Cass, Suite 285
Detroit, Michigan 48202

Alison Ford, Ph.D.
Associate Professor
Department of Exceptional Education
University of Wisconsin–Milwaukee
P.O. Box 413
Milwaukee, Wisconsin 53201

Michael F. Giangreco, Ph.D.
Visiting Assistant Professor
University of Vermont
Center for Developmental Disabilities
499C Waterman Building
Burlington, Vermont 05405

Janet L. Graden, Ph.D.
Associate Professor
School Psychology
University of Cincinnati
522 Teachers College ML 02
Cincinnati, Ohio 45221-002

Wade Hitzing, Ph.D.
Director
Society for Community Support
1335 Dublin Road
Suite 126D
Columbus, Ohio 43215

H. James Jackson, M.Ed.
Principal
Helen Hansen Elementary School
616 Holmes Drive
Cedar Falls, Iowa 50613

Lysa A. Jeanchild, M.S.
Research Assistant
Specialized Training Program
College of Education
University of Oregon
Eugene, Oregon 97403

Barbara LeRoy, Ph.D.
Coordinator
Center for Inclusive Education
Developmental Disabilities Institute
Wayne State University
6001 Cass, Suite 285
Detroit, Michigan 48202

Cathy Macdonald, M.A.
Interdisciplinary Certificate
    Coordinator
Institute on Community Integration
University of Minnesota
6 Pattee Hall
150 Pillsbury Drive, S.E.
Minneapolis, Minnesota 55455

Jeanette Moravec, M.Ed.
Support Facilitator
Helen Hansen Elementary School
616 Holmes Drive
Cedar Falls, Iowa 50613

Leslie New, B.A.
Integration Facilitator
Arapahoe High School
Littleton, Colorado 80120

Michael Peterson, Ph.D.
Director
Developmental Disabilities Institute
Wayne State University
6001 Cass, Suite 285
Detroit, Michigan 48202

Theresa Pratt, M.Ed.
Consultant
Waterloo Region Separate School
    Board
91 Moore Avenue
Kitchener, Ontario
Canada N2G 4G2

Mara Sapon-Shevin, Ed.D.
Professor
Division for the Study of Teaching
School of Education
Syracuse University
Syracuse, New York 13244

Beth Schaffner, B.A.
Integration Facilitator
PEAK Parent Center
6055 Lehman Drive
Suite 101
Colorado Springs, Colorado 80918

Roberta Schnorr, Ph.D.
Project Associate
Inclusive Education Project
Syracuse University
805 South Crouse Avenue
Syracuse, New York 13244-2280

Susan Stainback, Ed.D.
Professor
College of Education
University of Northern Iowa
Cedar Falls, Iowa 50614-0601

William Stainback, Ed.D.
Professor
College of Education
University of Northern Iowa
Cedar Falls, Iowa 50614-0601

Cindy Strully, M.A.
Director of Case Management
Centennial Developmental
    Services, Inc.
Evans, Colorado 80620

Jeff Strully, Ed.D.
Executive Director
Association for Community Living
    in Colorado
4155 East Jewell Street
Suite 916
Denver, Colorado 80122

Susann Terry-Gage, M.A.
Doctoral Student
School of Education
California State University,
  Los Angeles
5151 State University Drive
Los Angeles, California 90032

Jacqueline S. Thousand, Ph.D.
Assistant Professor
University of Vermont
Center for Developmental
  Disabilities
499 Waterman Building
Burlington, Vermont 05405

Terri Vandercook, Ph.D.
Associate Director
Institute on Community Integration
University of Minnesota
6 Pattee Hall
150 Pillsbury Drive, S.E.
Minneapolis, Minnesota 55455

Richard A. Villa, Ed.D.
Director of Instructional Services
Winooski School District
80 Normand Street
Winooski, Vermont 05404

Paula Wood, Ph.D.
Associate Dean
College of Education
Wayne State University
Detroit, Michigan 48202

Jennifer York, Ph.D.
Associate Director
Institute on Community Integration
University of Minnesota
6 Pattee Hall
150 Pillsbury Drive, S.E.
Minneapolis, Minnesota 55455

Preface

HANSEN SCHOOL IN Cedar Falls, Iowa; Winooski High School in Winooski, Vermont; Saint Francis School in Waterloo County, Ontario; Brook Forest School in Oak Brook, Illinois; and Ed Smith School in Syracuse, New York, have all attracted the attention of parents, educators, and concerned community members. They are examples of a new breed of schools—referred to as inclusive schools.

What these schools have in common is an attempt to transform educational settings into inclusive communities. The goal in inclusive schools is to be sure that all students, including those who have been labeled severely and profoundly mentally and physically disabled, chronically disruptive, typical, gifted, or at risk, are accepted, included as equal members, recognized for what they have to offer to the school community, and provided an appropriate educational program and any necessary supports needed for them to be successful learners.

Learning to care about and take responsibility for others is emphasized in inclusive schools. Particular attention is paid to ensuring that every student is welcomed, feels secure, is supported both educationally and socially, and develops mutual respect for others as well as self-respect and confidence in what he or she has to offer to the community. This is generally accomplished by involving parents, teachers, and students in the daily operation and decision making of their schools. It involves empowering and giving responsibility and a voice to all school members involved in building a positive community within the school.

While this is a relatively new approach, used by only a small but growing number of schools, the need for doing more in regard to developing inclusive school and classroom communities is widely recognized. Although inclusive schooling was generally started as an effort to welcome and support students with disabilities into neighborhood schools and general education classrooms, the need for this approach in dealing with the education of all children is important. There is a growing need for support among all students as evidenced by the increase in such incidences as suicides, gang violence, devil worship, and drug abuse. A high school student at a local school board meeting concerning the organization of gangs in one Midwest community voiced the importance of involving students in school decision making and noted that students not only need but are seeking supports. She stated, "You guys should deal with us . . . not with the public, not with the TV. Talk to us. Because if there's a problem, it's us and it's us that should be dealt with"

(Young, 1990, p. A1). The student went on to say, "Ask us why we join gangs. It's simple. People want to belong . . . they want to have someone they can lean on. In gangs, that's what happens" (Young, 1990, p. A1).

The focus of this book is on how the curriculum can be designed, adapted, and delivered in general education classrooms that are attempting to promote inclusive communities. It is essential that every student in inclusive classrooms have an educational program that is challenging yet geared to his or her abilities, needs, and interests. This text is designed as a follow-up and complement to an earlier text, *Support Networks for Inclusive Schools: Interdependent Integrated Education* (Stainback & Stainback, 1990) that focuses on providing all students and staff opportunities to support and be supported by others in schools that promote full inclusion.

The book is composed of 14 chapters divided into three sections. Section I, Introduction, includes a chapter designed to describe inclusive classrooms and outline some practical strategies for developing inclusive classrooms and schools (Chapter 1). The focus of the second chapter in Section I is on how curriculum should honor and build on differences among students. The third chapter provides some ideas for determining appropriate curriculum content to meet the needs of all students within inclusive classrooms.

Section II, Curriculum Adaptation and Delivery, consists of seven chapters that focus on curricular modifications and strategies for delivering curriculum that can be used to meet the diverse educational needs of students within inclusive classrooms. In the first chapter in this section (Chapter 4), the authors outline how curriculum can be used to actually build more inclusive classrooms. The second chapter (Chapter 5) discusses the use of a collaborative approach to curricular design and modification. The roles of support personnel and students as instructional partners in the delivery of curriculum and instructional procedures in inclusive classrooms are discussed in Chapters 6 and 7. Chapter 8 in this section addresses the need to promote or support student responsibility for maximizing successful learning in the classroom. Finally, Chapters 9 and 10 suggest some guidelines that may be useful when thinking about how to implement curricular decisions and positive ways of measuring and reporting student progress.

Section III, Related Considerations, discusses curriculum selection, modification, and delivery. Chapter 11, the first chapter in Section III, addresses the need to involve parents and other community members in curricular decisions. Chapters 12 and 13 address the issues of community-referenced and cocurricular considerations when organizing and evaluating curriculum offerings in an inclusive school. The final chapter (Chapter 14) looks to the future in regard to trends, issues, problems, and potential solutions to the curriculum needs of students within inclusive classrooms and schools.

The compilation of this text could not have been possible without the contributions of many people. The editors would like to take this opportunity to laud the outstanding contribution of each of the contributing authors. In addition, the contributions of many students, parents, educators, and other community members who offered their ideas, concerns, and moral support throughout the development of this book are acknowledged. Finally, we would like to heartily thank Joyce Broell, Cheryl Reynolds, Amy Kluesner, and Carla Loynachan at the University of Northern Iowa for their assistance in the preparation of this book, and our colleagues at Brookes Publishing Company who have encouraged and contributed significantly to the sharing of the ideas and concepts of the many authors in this book.

REFERENCES

Stainback, W., & Stainback, S. (1990). *Support networks for inclusive schools: Interdependent integrated education.* Baltimore: Paul H. Brookes Publishing Co.

Young, J. (1990, April 17). Gangs hearing: School board's policy review draws wide range of opinions. *Waterloo Courier.*

Foreword

WE ARE PRIVILEGED to write the introduction to a book on a topic vital to our hearts—inclusion. For us, inclusion is not simply a matter of placement or changes in the curriculum; it is not something one does only from 8:30 to 4:00. Inclusion is more than a method, philosophy, or research agenda. It is a way of life. It is about "living together." It is about "welcoming back the stranger" and making us all whole again.

We simply believe inclusion is a better way to live. It is the opposite of segregation and apartheid. "Inclusion" determines where we live, receive education, work, and play. It is about changing our hearts and our values.

Whether we include everyone is not a question for science or research. Inclusion is a value judgment. Our values are clear. Educators must demand and fight for a public education system that will provide *quality education and equity for all*. This challenge must be met. There can no longer be a "softening" of the issue.

TWO ROADS

Our analogy is that our society and our schooling systems are at a crossroad. There are two roads—the road of inclusion and the road of exclusion. Advocates for the exclusion route promote, if unintentionally, elitism. They suggest that some children are better off segregated or that there is neither the time nor the money to provide quality education and equity for all. The conclusion of the exclusion road option is to "educate the best, and take care of the rest." Exclusion accepts the validity of a permanent "underclass" in our society.

We reject the concept of permanent inequality. Our society is too rich. There are choices; there can be no excuses. If we can build Stealth bombers with a price tag of almost $1 billion per plane, surely we can educate all of our children to the best of their abilities. It is a values issue.

We choose the other road—inclusion. The simple starting point for this road is to include everyone. Educate *all* children in *regular* classrooms and communities. It is a better way.

THE REAL MEANING OF INCLUSION

Inclusion means welcoming everyone—all students, all citizens—back into our schools and communities. Schools are a good place to start. Historically, for reasons that seemed good at the time, we fragmented our system to ensure appropriate support to everyone (special education, intelligence quotient tests, labels). Over time, this small empire has turned into a support system for segregation. It has had unanticipated, tragic long-term outcomes for the vast majority of children who were and are labeled—often with the best of intentions. Reports, commissions, and studies confirm that once students are segregated, they are doomed to live life lonely, rejected, without friends, and without jobs. The brutal truth is that the statistical outcome of segregation is a "life" characterized by poverty, often terminating in institutions that no longer work, that are outrageously expensive, and that are devastating to the human spirit. The inclusion option signifies the end of labeling, special education, and special classes, but not the end of necessary supports and services that must be provided in integrated classrooms.

A RETURN TO BASICS

We praise efforts to include all children, not because it is good for children with "labels," but because it is better for everyone. Therefore, we must return to the "basics": the ABCs—acceptance, belonging, and community; and the new three Rs—reading, writing, and relationships.

To make this happen, we simply must reach out and ask children to help each other with real problems in the real world. Our children know these problems exist. Their struggles are not to run from challenges, but to find meaningful ways to engage themselves in today's critical issues.

Children of all ages are our most underutilized force for change. They are there in abundance—eager for involvement. All we have to do is ask; it is amazing to observe. The children with the "obvious" disabilities have a unique and profound gift to contribute—the gift of their presence and the gift of needing to be needed. In a society where it is perceived as "weak" to ask for help, excluded children's very presence challenges us to help each other. And, as if by magic, those truly in the greatest need (not those with the obvious labels) snatch this opportunity to reach out to another person, to help, and to invest energy in a constructive, supportive endeavor. Helping another person builds friendships and communities. If kids are unfulfilled in challenges and support, they make other choices, such as gangs. Our present nonfeasible alternative is to hire more "experts," build bigger and better prisons, and see more gang violence in our schools and on our streets. Inclusion is a better way.

We asked children in several California schools what they thought about inclusion—about welcoming all children into schools, and into the community as full and equal participants. One 10-year-old child incisively summed it up: "It's the right thing to do, and the best way to do it!"

Education in the future must be child centered and promote cooperative and collaborative learning that fosters interdependent living. Because our system is challenged, there is an opportunity to change and to build a new, more democratic and just future.

Some may call us and the authors in this book "naive," "idealistic," or "dreamers." Yes, we are! But we can make quality, inclusive education a reality. This book is not simply rhetoric; it is written by people slogging it out in the educational trenches. They are making inclusion a reality—classroom by classroom and school by school.

To become idealistic dreamers and to start working toward full inclusion for all, we need to ask ourselves several questions:

What do we as a society really value?

What kind of world do we want our children to live in?

Are we willing to invest resources to prevent illiteracy, poverty, segregation, and pain?

Are we willing to create a just society for all?

Inclusion is simply the first step on the road to integration. The word "inclusion" implies shutting the door after someone has come into the house. Some people still think you can speak of integration without inclusion. Integration, however, begins only when each child truly *belongs* as part of the whole school community. Inclusion is the first necessary step.

Integration is our goal. Integration means renewing or restoring wholeness. Our aim, as the aim of this book, is to see an education system where both adults and children continually renew and restore one another's wholeness and where the diversity of real communities are *welcomed* and not simply tolerated.

Most educators today agree that there are serious problems in our schools. In Chapter 9 of his book *The Classroom Crucible* (1991), Edward Pauly writes:

American education is already in deep trouble . . . most reform movements are engaged in a fruitless search for magic-bullet solutions to education's problems, even when all the evidence shows that no magic-bullets exist. While the debate continues, the nation's students are caught in an education system that is sliding from mediocrity to outright failure. (p. 197)

The move to bring children "back" from the isolation and segregation of special education, the move to see all children as "gifted" and not as "disabled," the move to create one unified (not uniform) system that truly serves all the nation's children, is one clear action to humanize and change from mediocrity to the marvel and magic education can and must be.

We are truly at a crossroad. This book is clearly on the road to a new education system—a system that will be flexible, courageous, and powerful in its invitation to ALL students to stay and participate—*not* to drop out and die either spiritually or physically. This book is part of the road that is seeking to find solutions (not magic bullets) to the complex social and educational issues of our times. It will help those who are on the inclusion road.

We congratulate all the authors on their excellent chapters and we ask all educators, parents, students, and concerned community members to remember that *the education we provide students tomorrow can be no better than what we dream today.*

Jack Pearpoint
Marsha Forest
Directors, Center for Integrated Education and Community
Toronto, Ontario

REFERENCE

Pauly, E. (1991). *The classroom crucible: What really works, what doesn't and why.* New York: Basic Books.

For Samantha Bray Stainback and all the children and surrogate children who bring happiness into the lives of families

Curriculum Considerations
in Inclusive Classrooms

I

Introduction

1

Toward Inclusive Classrooms

Susan Stainback, William Stainback, and H. James Jackson

THE CONCEPT OF inclusive schools and classrooms is introduced in this chapter to provide a structure for considering curricula content, adaptations, and delivery. It is essential that curricula considerations take place within schools and classrooms that welcome and value everyone.

INTEGRATION VERSUS INCLUSION

The authors of this chapter hope that it will soon be possible to simply talk about providing a quality education for all students. Yet, there are still students excluded from the mainstream of school and community life, so many people are now using the term *full inclusion* to refer to the education of all students in neighborhood classrooms and schools. There has been a shift away from concepts such as mainstreaming or integration toward full inclusion. There are a number of reasons for this shift. First, the concept of inclusion is being adopted because it more accurately and clearly communicates what is needed—all children need to be *included* in the educational and social life of their neighborhood schools and classrooms, not merely placed in the mainstream. Second, the term *integration* is being abandoned since it implies that the goal is to integrate someone or some group back into the mainstream of school and community life who has been excluded. The basic goal should be to not leave anyone out of the mainstream of school life in the first place, either educationally, physically, or socially.

Third, the focus in inclusive schools is on how to build a system that includes and is structured to meet everyone's needs. It does not assume that traditional schools and classrooms, which are structured to meet the needs of the so-called "normal" or majority, are appropriate and any student must fit within what was designed for the majority or else be excluded. Integration or mainstreaming implies a need to fit students previously excluded into an existing mainstream. In inclusive schooling, the responsibility is being placed on school personnel to arrange a mainstream that accommodates the needs of all students.

Finally, there has been a shift away from how to help only students with disabilities in the mainstream. The focus has been broadened to address the support needs of every member of the school (i.e., school personnel as well as all students) to be successful, secure, and welcome in the educational mainstream.

These changes have led educators, parents, and students to alter their perspective. The problem or dilemma is no longer how to mainstream or integrate some students who were previously excluded, but rather how to develop a sense of community and mutual support within the mainstream that fosters success among all members of neighborhood schools.

AN EMPHASIS ON COMMUNITY

In inclusive schools and classrooms, there is an emphasis on building community. Some of the early concepts of community are described below by Flynn (1989):

> True community is rare in today's society even though there is a natural longing in each of us to be a part of something. Scott Peck, in his book "The Different Drum" says that we humans often have a sense that in the good old days we knew more of community than we do today. For example, John Winthrop, the first Governor of the Massachusetts Bay Colony, in 1630, speaking to his fellow colonists just before they stepped on land, said: "We must delight in each other, make others' conditions our own, rejoice together, mourn together, labour and suffer together, always having before our eyes our community as members of the same body."
>
> Two hundred years later the Frenchman Alexis de Tocqueville published a book in 1835 entitled "Democracy In America." In the book he marvelled at a characteristic that he found in people throughout the United States that he described as individualism. He went on to caution however that unless this individualism was continually and strongly

balanced by "other habits," it would inevitably lead to fragmentation of American society and social isolation of its citizens.

In 1985, Robert Bellah published a book entitled ironically enough "Habits of the Heart." In the book Bellah argues compellingly that our individualism has not remained balanced and that de Tocqueville's predictions have come true and that *isolation* and *fragmentation* have become the order of the day. (p. 1)

Flynn (1989) defines community as follows:

To respond to the call "to community" we must have some understanding of what community is—what it looks like when it happens. When we describe a school as being a community what have we seen or experienced. I think that a . . . true community is a group of individuals who have learned to communicate honestly with one another, whose relationships go deeper than their composures and who have developed some significant commitment to "rejoice together, mourn together, to delight in each other, and make others' conditions their own." (p. 4)

Community is hard to define, as can be ascertained from the above extract. However, it is essential to gain a sense of what is meant by community if it is to be promoted in schools. Many successful inclusive schools and classrooms that emphasize community focus on how to operate classrooms and schools where everyone belongs, is accepted, supports, and is supported by his or her peers and other members of the school community while his or her educational needs are met.

It should be stressed that in inclusive communities everyone's gifts and talents, including those of students traditionally defined as having profound disabilities or chronically disruptive behaviors, are recognized, encouraged, and utilized to the fullest extent possible. This occurs because each person is an important and worthwhile member with responsibilities and a role to play in supporting others. This helps to foster self-esteem, pride in accomplishments, mutual respect, and a sense of belonging and self-worth among community members. This cannot occur if certain students are always receiving and never giving support. As noted by Wilkinson (1980), " . . . people are interdependent; everyone has a function and everyone has a role to play, and that keeps people together and forms a community" (p. 452).

INCLUSIVE SCHOOL COMMUNITIES IN PERSPECTIVE

Although it is not yet widespread, there is a movement toward recognizing the value of inclusive school and classroom communities (Barth, 1990; Coleman & Hoffer, 1987; Maeroff, 1990; McLaughlin,

Talbert, Kahne, & Powell, 1990). It is not just a topic of interest among those people interested in full inclusion; some educational philosophers, sociologists, and scholars have, in recent years, focused on the problems of depersonalized schools (Coleman & Hoffer, 1987; Murphy & Hallinger, 1988). There is evidence that in schools where students, parents, and educators do not establish friendships, commitments, and bonds with each other (i.e., where there is an absence of community), there are increased problems with underachievement, student drop-outs, drug abuse, and gang activity (Coleman & Hoffer, 1987; Maeroff, 1990). As a result, Coleman and Hoffer have hypothesized that some of the present day problems in general education may be due, at least in part, to the lack of community in many schools in an increasingly urban, complex, and depersonalized society.

To reestablish a sense of community, educators and community leaders in some large, impersonal schools in the United States and other countries have started dividing their schools into smaller units, each with its own principal, teachers, students, and self-identity. The idea is to organize smaller schools where teachers and students stay together for most, if not all, of the time the students attend the school. There also is a focus on these schools becoming a center of community activities that involve parents and community members. To form bonds and friendships and create more personalized and sensitive institutions, people need these opportunities to communicate with each other on a personal level.

In schools such as the Saint Francis School in Kitchener, Ontario, and the Helen Hansen School in Cedar Falls, Iowa, students traditionally classified as having severe and profound disabilities are included in the mainstream through the use of "circles of friends" and other approaches that focus on "connecting" students and teachers in friendships and caring relationships. These efforts can also lead to the entire school developing a better sense of community (Flynn, 1989; Jackson, 1990).

ADVANTAGES OF INCLUSIVE SCHOOLS

Moving toward inclusive schools has several advantages over continuing with traditional approaches that attempt to help students with disabilities or disadvantages "fit into the mainstream." One advantage is that everyone benefits from inclusive schools focusing on ways to develop supportive and caring school communities for *all* students, rather than selected categories of students. Some parents and educators have found it difficult to motivate school personnel and community members to restructure the schools to benefit one student or a selected category of students (Discover the Possibilities, 1988). Focusing on the development of inclusive school communities avoids this problem by giving everyone a reason to be involved. All children benefit when neighborhood schools and classrooms develop a sense of community, that is, when education is sensitive and responsive to the individual differences of every member of the school.

A second advantage is that all of the resources and efforts of school personnel can be spent on assessing instructional needs, adapting instruction, and providing support to students. Many of today's "special" education personnel have expressed concern that it is extremely difficult for them to find time to work in the mainstream (Bauwens, Hourcade, & Friend, 1989). The primary reason is that when only selected students are mainstreamed, "special" educators are required to spend considerable time in resource rooms and special classes with the students not in the mainstream. In inclusive schools all students are in the mainstream full time; therefore, all personnel and resources can be in the mainstream full time. In addition, valuable resources and time are not spent on classifying, labeling, and making placement decisions. "General" educators and "former" special educators are able to focus on providing every student challenging and appropriate educational programs geared to his or her unique needs and capabilities.

Another advantage is the ability to provide social and instructional supports for all students. Supports that in the past were provided to students through strong, intact family units; multiple siblings; ongoing, stable neighborhood friendships; and extended family relationships are sometimes lacking in today's world due to changes in family structure and mobility in an increasingly complex society. The increasing pressures of drugs, gangs, suicide, and increased family breakup also add to the need for acceptance and a sense of belonging. Inclusive schools can provide this support and assistance since they focus on building interdependence, mutual respect, and responsibility.

CHARACTERISTICS OF INCLUSIVE CLASSROOMS

In inclusive schools, the classroom is the basic unit of focus. Classrooms in inclusive schools are organized heterogeneously and staff and students are encouraged and empowered to support one another. Following are some characteristics that inclusive classrooms tend to incorporate.

Classroom Philosophy

Inclusive classrooms start with a philosophy that all children belong and can learn in the mainstream of school and community life. Diversity is valued; it is believed that diversity strengthens the class and offers all of its members greater opportunities for learning.

Robert Barth (1990), a Harvard professor, described the value of diversity as follows:

> I would prefer my children to be in a school in which differences are looked for, attended to, and celebrated as good news, as opportunities for learning. The question with which so many school people are preoccupied is, "What are the limits of diversity beyond which behavior is unacceptable?" . . . But the question I would like to see asked more often is, "How can we make conscious, deliberate use of differences in social class, gender, age, ability, race, and interest as resources for learning?" . . . Differences hold great opportunities for learning. Differences offer a free, abundant, and renewable resource. I would like to see our compulsion for eliminating differences replaced by an equally compelling focus on making use of these differences to improve schools. What is important about people—and about schools—is what is different, not what is the same. (pp. 514–515)

Classroom Rules

Within the rules of an inclusive classroom the rights of each member are typically communicated. For example, posted on the wall of one inclusive classroom is the rule: "I have a right to learn according to my own ability. This means no one will call me names because of the way I learn." Another rule is: "I have a right to be myself in this room. This means that no one will treat me unfairly because of my skin color, fat or thin, tall or short, boy or girl or by the way I look." (These rules were posted on the wall of an inclusive first grade class, 1990, Helen Hansen Elementary School, Cedar Falls, Iowa.) These rules should reflect the philosophy of fair and equal treatment and mutual respect among students as well as other school and community members.

Instruction that Fits the Student

In inclusive classrooms, support and assistance is provided to students to help them succeed in achieving appropriate curriculum objectives. Students are not expected to achieve a predefined, standard classroom curriculum that does not take into account their diverse characteristics and needs. The general education curriculum is adjusted and/or expanded, when necessary, to meet their needs. (See Stainback, Stainback, & Moravec, chap. 4, this volume.)

Supports in the Mainstream

Services and supports are provided in integrated, general education settings to students in inclusive classrooms. If a student needs certain types of instructional modifications or specialized tools and techniques to succeed educationally or socially, they are provided in the general education classroom, not in a system or setting outside of the mainstream. This means that instead of taking the student to the service or support, it is brought to the student. The focus is on determining ways students can get their educational and related needs met within the existing natural and normal classroom settings.

Natural Support Networking Encouraged Inclusive classrooms tend to foster *natural* support networks. There is an emphasis on peer tutoring, buddy systems, circles of friends, cooperative learning, and other ways of connecting students in natural, ongoing, and supportive relationships. There also is an emphasis on teachers and other school personnel working together and supporting each other through professional collaboration, team teaching, teacher and student assistance teams, and other cooperative arrangements.

Cooperation and collaboration with peers rather than competitive or independent activities are generally fostered among students and staff (Villa & Thousand, 1988). It is assumed that natural, supportive relationships in which individuals within the classroom and school assist and support one another as peers, friends, or colleagues are as important as providing professional support from "experts." Focusing on natural supports within the classroom helps connect students and staff in ongoing peer and collegial relationships that facilitate the development of a supportive community (Strully & Strully, 1990).

(Specific and practical strategies for building natural support networks among students as well as school personnel are discussed in Stainback and Stainback [1990] and subsequent chapters in this volume.)

Classroom Accommodation When assistance from external "experts" is required to meet the unique needs of a student, the classroom support system and curriculum are modified to help not only the student in need of specialized support and assistance, but also other students in the classroom who could benefit from similar supports. For example, if a specialist in the area of hearing impairment is in the classroom to assist and support one student, the teacher might use his or her expertise to organize the classroom and use methods and equipment so that all of the students may benefit from the auditory stimulation available. In addition, such a specialist may be helpful in developing a basic sign language curriculum for the class to help them better communicate with a range of people.

While the needs of the student or students with a hearing impairment would be the concern of the specialist, utilizing the specialist's expertise to benefit the entire classroom would be the teacher's goal. Similarly, in an inclusive classroom a school psychologist might help in the design, adaptations, and delivery of classroom assessments and evaluations appropriate to the needs of all students rather than focusing on testing, classifying, and labeling any particular student.

Empowerment   In too many classroom situations the teacher is the primary source of support, problem solving, and information dissemination. In an inclusive classroom, the focus is different—the teacher often becomes a facilitator of learning and support opportunities. There is a shift away from maintaining total control and responsibility for everything that occurs in the classroom to delegating responsibility to the group members for learning and supporting each other. It is the teacher's role to empower the students to provide support and assistance to their fellow classmates and make decisions about their own learning (see Villa & Thousand, chap. 7, this volume). The skill of all members in a class to share and accept responsibility for learning, as well as the teacher's ability to promote self-direction and mutual support among students are necessary to capitalize upon the diversity in learning and teaching potential (capabilities).

Promote Understanding of Individual Differences   Educators in inclusive classrooms make a conscious effort to guide class members to understand and utilize their inherent individual differences. This is critical to the healthy development of self-confidence, mutual respect, and a sense of community and reciprocal support in the classroom.

Activities and projects that promote an understanding of individual differences and the value of each person is one approach to creating an understanding and respect for diversity. Likewise, encouraging discussion about the individuality and contributions of people with diverse characteristics can provide a more comprehensive study of the topic. However, as noted earlier in this chapter, the focus for studying diversity should be on the positive aspects and how they can be capitalized on to enhance the functioning of the group rather than focus on individual differences such as handicaps, disabilities, or disadvantages.

Flexibility   Since inclusive schooling is a new and emerging approach to addressing the diverse needs of individuals within natural school settings, creativity and open-mindedness have been necessary among school members to achieve success. Those involved in inclusive schools and classrooms have recognized that there are no simple or universal answers that address concerns in all settings at all times. For this reason, a key element in classroom operation is flexibility. Flexibility as discussed here does not imply a lack of structure or direction, but an acceptance and adaptation to change when deemed necessary. As noted by Vandercook, York, and Forest (1989):

> Flexibility . . . is necessary as even the most thoughtfully designed strategies and plans sometimes are not successful and need revision. False starts should be anticipated and a commitment made to ongoing problem-solving and change as needed. Initial objectives for student involvement in regular classes and the support necessary to achieve individualized objectives may need to be modified after the students actually participate in regular classes. (p. 2)

We now know from experience that all children can be included in classrooms if people in the mainstream make an effort to welcome them, foster friendships, and adapt the curriculum and grading practices. However, full inclusion does not always flow smoothly. Therefore, it is vital that adults do *not* take the easy road out by excluding the child, but instead seek solutions to achieve successful full inclusion.

HOW CAN INCLUSIVE CLASSROOMS BE FACILITATED?

There are a number of practical steps that can be taken to facilitate inclusive schools and classroom communities (Berrigan, 1989; Biklen, 1985; Blackman & Peterson, 1989; Forest & Flynn, 1988; O'Brien, Forest, Snow, & Hasburg, 1989; Stainback & Stainback, 1990; Stainback, Stainback, & Forest, 1989; Villa & Thousand, 1988). A few of the major ones are reviewed below.

Gain the Teacher's Commitment

In most of today's teacher preparation programs, teachers not only fail to receive information about full inclusion, but are in many instances actually taught to reject and exclude some children. Therefore, it is critical to make every effort to gain a commitment to full inclusion from the general education teacher. This includes his or her acceptance of previously excluded students as equal and valued members of the class. If the teacher does not value the child and does not want him or her in the class, there probably will be major difficulties in achieving successful full inclusion.

It is sometimes essential to have teachers view videotapes such as *Kids Belong Together* (People First, 1990) and participate in workshops or in-service preparation classes. In addition, teachers should have opportunities for informal and formal conversations with people knowledgeable about full inclusion, and/or opportunities to become acquainted with the child (e.g., home visits, going out to eat, going to a movie). In other words, the teacher needs to understand the reasons for full inclusion and get to know and accept the child. This needs to occur in the beginning so that full inclusion starts with a positive attitude on the part of the teacher and continues after full inclusion is in operation.

Unfortunately, in addition to receiving outdated and incorrect information in their university preparation programs, most of today's teachers never attended school with students who are often excluded from general education classrooms. Therefore, they may be unsure of how to communicate with them or adapt to their learning styles and speeds. They must accept, value, and be at ease with all children. This is not always easy to achieve and may take some extra effort in the beginning. Discussions of methods and techniques such as curricular adaptations, circles of friends, McGill Action Planning System (MAPS), or professional and peer collaboration can be of little use to a teacher who simply does not value or want a particular child as part of his or her class. In addition, it is crucial that the classroom teacher serves as a role model for the students by welcoming every child and including every child in social interactions and classroom activities. When a teacher demonstrates that she or he is pleased to have a child in the class, it can have a tremendous impact on the attitudes and actions of the students. (See Strully et al., chap. 11, this volume, for a discussion of the importance of educators welcoming a child as a valued member of a classroom and school.)

It should be noted here that full inclusion should never be delayed until appropriate attitudes are developed. Full inclusion and attitude development should *both* be started immediately. It is only through daily experiences with full inclusion that teachers, parents, students, and specialists can develop realistic attitudes and expectations and overcome any real, as opposed to imagined, difficulties.

Use Special Education and Other Resources

There are billions of dollars being spent and hundreds of thousands of personnel working in segregated special and compensatory educational programs (Schenkat, 1988). All of these dollars and personnel can and should be integrated into the educational mainstream to provide specialized knowledge and assistance, reduce class sizes, and facilitate informal support networks.

More specifically, the informal and formal supports needed to operate inclusive classrooms that are responsive to the needs of all students can be facilitated by phasing out segregated special schools, classrooms, and programs. Special educators who previously worked in these schools can become classroom teachers, team teachers, resource and consulting specialists, or facilitators of support networks within general education. In addition, the wealth of resources in special and compensatory education can be integrated into general education classes.

Furthermore, teachers in inclusive classrooms should call upon reading specialists, Title I compensatory education personnel, students in the classroom or school, counselors, physical and speech therapists, school psychologists, other classroom teachers, math and science consultants, and a variety of other people to provide suggestions or work in the classroom to make it more flexible and adaptive to the unique needs of all the students. All personnel available should be utilized to contribute whatever expertise and time they have rather than only relying on one or two people (e.g., a collaborating teacher or teacher's aide).

Follow the Principles of Natural Proportions

It is advantageous when establishing inclusive classrooms to accept only those students who are a natural part of the neighborhood, zone, or district from which the school draws its students.

It is difficult for schools that serve large numbers of students with a particular characteristic, such as severe disabilities, to establish and maintain inclusive classrooms. The reason is that natural class integration is almost impossible to achieve due to the high density of students with disabilities. As a consequence, students who have often been excluded from their neighborhood schools should attend the classroom they would be assigned to if they were not classified as having a disability.

Establish an Inclusive Education Task Force

Some schools, in the process of promoting the operation of fully inclusive classrooms, have found it helpful to establish an inclusive education task force made up of teachers, parents, students, counselors, administrators, and specialists. In addition to serving as a general advocacy group for full inclusion, the purpose of the task force is to help all individuals involved with the school gain a better understanding of developing and maintaining an integrated, caring, and inclusive school community. To accomplish this, the task force is often assigned several duties.

One of these duties is to gather background information in the form of books, articles, and videotapes on the subject of inclusion. These can be recommended to and shared with school personnel, students, parents, and school board members. A special section of the school library should be designated to maintain all the materials compiled. Also, when gathering background information, key task force or other school personnel may want to visit an inclusive classroom or school in their own or a nearby school district.

A second duty of the task force is to organize and conduct information sessions for parents and school personnel where people knowledgeable and experienced in full inclusion can discuss how it might be accomplished. It is important that the key people invited to share information have direct experience in full inclusion. Usually, listening to people involved with a school that has successfully integrated its classrooms can be more "believable" and effective than just hearing from "experts." Some schools hold one information session for all people involved—parents, educators, students, and administrators—so that everyone may participate in creating an inclusive classroom.

A third function of the task force is to establish a plan that includes specific objectives for achieving full inclusion. This plan usually shows how the resources and personnel in "special" education can be utilized to reduce teacher/pupil ratios, provide team teachers, consultants, teacher aides, and/or support facilitators in the mainstream.

By establishing such a task force, community members, students, and a variety of personnel within a school can become involved and take pride in achieving an inclusive school.

Designate a Person To Serve as a Support Facilitator

In inclusive schools, special educators generally integrate themselves into general education. Some become classroom teachers or consulting specialists, others assume the role of encouraging and organizing support in general education classrooms. They have been referred to as support facilitators, collaborating teachers, or methods and resource teachers (Porter, 1988; Stainback & Stainback, 1990; Thousand & Villa, 1989). Regardless of what they are called, they work in collaboration with other school personnel to ensure that all students' needs are met in the mainstream. "Collaboration" means that the support facilitator, teacher, students, and other school personnel work together with no one assuming an expert, supervisory, or evaluator role. In this way, everyone is involved in facilitating support systems and adapting instruction to individual needs. As noted by Nevin, Thousand, Paulucci-Whitcomb, and Villa (1989):

> The collaborative process is multi-directional, since all members are considered to have unique and needed expertise. At any point in time a member of the collaborative relationship may be the giver or receiver of

consultation . . . (or) any member of a group may become a leader by taking actions that help the group complete its tasks and maintain effective collaborative relationships. (p. 21)

A number of schools have begun to designate a person to serve as a support facilitator. They can enhance efforts to educate all students in inclusive classrooms. As noted by Annmarie Ruttiman, who served as one of the first support facilitators, it requires someone who "is open, flexible, willing to take risks, work hard, accept failure and try again. . ." (Ruttiman & Forest, 1986, p. 26).

A primary objective of the support facilitator is to work side by side with classroom teachers and other school personnel to *encourage natural support networks*. Teachers, in collaboration with support facilitators, promote peer interdependence through buddy systems, peer tutoring, cooperative learning, and friendship development for students to learn how to assist each other (Stainback & Stainback, 1990).

The support facilitator or collaborating teacher also frequently functions as a *resource locator* since a classroom teacher cannot be expected to have expertise in every possible assessment, curricular, or behavior management area. This role may involve locating appropriate material and equipment, or specialists, consultants, teachers, and other school personnel who have expertise in a particular area needed by a teacher and/or student. For example, if a student displays disruptive behaviors in a classroom, a support facilitator can help the teacher locate the appropriate specialist to provide assistance. Likewise, as a resource locator, he or she can assist in the recruitment and organization of classroom assistants such as peer tutors, paraprofessionals, and volunteers.

These collaborating teachers or support personnel can also provide direct help as *team teachers*, facilitating learning in their area of expertise (see Bauwens et al., 1989). In addition they often provide support to empower teachers to adapt and individualize instruction to meet the unique needs of all class members. It is crucial to note that the teacher maintains responsibility for the education and support of all students in the class. The support facilitator should not assume the role of the student's personal teacher in the general education class. The collaborating teacher or support facilitator acts as a resource to the teacher, family, principal, and the class as a whole to build support networks and adapt instruction to individual needs.

Any one of a number of school personnel (e.g., counselors, school psychologists, teachers) could be designated as a support facilitator to ensure that networking does occur. Sources for support facilitators are former special education teachers, consultants, or other school members who have gained expertise in the development and maintenance of support networks within a school.

CONCLUSION

The development of inclusive schools and classrooms can be expected to pose new and challenging questions as its implementation proceeds, such as: What should the curriculum be in inclusive schools? How can curricular content be modified or adapted, when necessary, and delivered to students with diverse characteristics and needs? What evaluations, grading systems, and report card practices can be used in inclusive classrooms that are fair to everyone? In the following chapters, people who have faced these questions and have been struggling with them for several years will share what they have experienced and learned.

REFERENCES

Barth, R. (1990). A personal vision of a good school. *Phi Delta Kappan, 71,* 512–571.
Bauwens, J., Hourcade, J., & Friend, M. (1989). Cooperative teaching: A model for general and special education integration. *Remedial and Special Education, 10,* 17–22.
Berrigan, C. (1989). All students belong in the classroom: Johnson City Central Schools, Johnson City, New York. *TASH Newsletter, 15*(1), 6.
Biklen, D. (Ed.). (1985). *The complete school.* New York: Teacher's College Press.
Blackman, H., & Peterson, D. (1989). *Total integration—neighborhood schools.* LaGrange, IL: LaGrange Department of Special Education.
Coleman, J., & Hoffer, T. (1987). *Public and private high schools: The impact of communities.* New York: Basic Books.
Discover the Possibilities. (1988). Colorado Springs: PEAK Parent Center.
Flynn, G. (1989, November). *Toward community.* Paper presented at the 16th Annual TASH Conference, San Francisco, CA.
Forest, M., & Flynn, G. (Directors). (1988). *With a little help from my friends.* [Videotape]. Toronto: Center for Integrated Education.
Jackson, J. (1990, March). *Full inclusion at Hansen.* Paper presented to the University of Northern Iowa's Educating All Students in the Mainstream course, Cedar Falls, IA.
Maeroff, G. (1990). Getting to know a good middle school. *Phi Delta Kappan, 71,* 505–511.
McLaughlin, M., Talbert J., Kahne, J., & Powell, J. (1990). Constructing a personalized school environment. *Phi Delta Kappan, 72,* 230–236.
Murphy, J., & Hallinger, P. (1988). Equity as access to learning: Curricular and instructional treatment differences. *Journal of Curriculum Studies, 21,* 129–149.
Nevin, A., Thousand, J., Paulucci-Whitcomb, P., & Villa, R. (1989). Collaborative consultation: Empowering public school personnel to provide hetero-

geneous schooling for all. *Journal of Educational and Psychological Consultation, 1,* 41–67.

O'Brien, J., Forest, M., Snow, J., & Hasburg, D. (1989). *Action for inclusion.* Toronto: Frontier College Press.

People First Association of Lethbridge. (1990). *Kids belong together.* Niwot, CO: Expectations Unlimited.

Porter, G. (Producer). (1988). *A chance to belong.* [Videotape]. Ontario, Canada: Canadian Association for Community Living.

Ruttiman, A., & Forest, M. (1986). With a little help from my friends: The integration facilitator at work. *Entourage, 1,* 24–33.

Schenkat, R. (1988, November). The promise of restructuring for special education. *Education Week, 8,* 36.

Stainback, S., Stainback, W., & Forest, M. (Eds.). (1989). *Educating all students in the mainstream of regular education.* Baltimore: Paul H. Brookes Publishing Co.

Stainback, W., & Stainback, S. (Eds.). (1990). *Support networks for inclusive schooling: Interdependent integrated education.* Baltimore: Paul H. Brookes Publishing Co.

Strully, J., & Strully, C. (1990). Foreword. In W. Stainback & S. Stainback (Eds.), *Support networks for inclusive schooling: Interdependent integrated education* (pp. ix–xi). Baltimore: Paul H. Brookes Publishing Co.

Thousand, J., & Villa, R. (1989). Enhancing success in heterogeneous schools. In S. Stainback, W. Stainback, & M. Forest (Eds.), *Educating all students in the mainstream of regular education* (pp. 89–103). Baltimore: Paul H. Brookes Publishing Co.

Vandercook, T., York, J., & Forest, M. (1989). *MAPS: A strategy for building a vision.* Minneapolis: Institute on Community Integration.

Villa, R., & Thousand, J. (1988). Enhancing success in heterogeneous classrooms and schools: The power of partnership. *Teacher Education and Special Education, 11,* 144–153.

Wilkinson, J. (1980). On assistance to Indian people. *Social Casework: Journal of Contemporary Social Work, 61,* 451–454.

York, J., & Vandercook, T. (1989). *Strategies for achieving an integrated education for middle school aged learners with severe disabilities.* Minneapolis: Institution on Community Integration.

2

Celebrating Diversity, Creating Community

Curriculum that Honors and Builds on Differences

Mara Sapon-Shevin

CREATING AN INCLUSIVE school where all students are acknowledged, valued, and respected involves attending to what is taught as
well as to how it is delivered. Not only must teaching strategies be
designed and curriculum determined to respond to a range of student differences, but the curriculum must address the many ways in
which students differ.

All members of inclusive communities have a sense of belonging. Students cannot become a community or be comfortable if they
believe that they must ignore their own differences and those of their
classmates in order to belong. The goal cannot and should not be to
become oblivious to differences, to not notice the diversity in society.
The same child who observes that Rumpelstilskin is wearing a hat on
page 4, but not on page 5, certainly realizes that she has classmates
who are larger, smaller, use wheelchairs, have different skin colors,
speak different languages, celebrate different holidays, or come from
nontraditional families. Not attending directly to differences, not acknowledging the many ways in which people are different (as well as
the many ways people are similar) gives children the message that
differences cannot or should not be discussed. If teachers do not address differences, children's discussions about how they each differ
will go underground, become topics that are seemingly forbidden and

must be whispered. The goal must be the honest exploration of differences, the chance for students to experience and understand diversity within a community that is safe and supportive.

THINKING INCLUSIVELY ABOUT INCLUSIVE TEACHING

Children differ along many dimensions, and each child's identity is shaped by membership in many groups. To only describe 6-year-old Jonas as a child who is "physically challenged" is to ignore the fact that he is also Jewish and an only child. To simply discuss Carmen as a child who requires extensive enrichment materials because of her accelerated performance may mask the fact that she comes from a single-parent, Spanish-speaking family. Just as single labels are not sufficient to determine adequate educational needs, making certain aspects of the curriculum inclusive without attending to the child's whole identity or whole life is also inadequate. For example, adapting a Christmas craft activity so that Jonas is able to make decorations with the other children does not address the fact that the project may be inappropriate or insensitive to his or other children's religious differences. Similarly, providing Carmen with a book at her reading level is important, but since all of the classroom textbooks and reading materials show only white, middle-class, traditional families, the reality of a Spanish-speaking child who lives with her mother in an apartment is not taken into consideration.

The increasing racial and ethnic diversity of our society and our schools has made it imperative that school programs and curricula be responsive to children's differences. Ramsey (1987) describes eight goals for teaching from a multicultural perspective that are applicable to the concept of full inclusion. These goals are:

1. To help children develop positive gender, racial, cultural, class and individual identities and to recognize and accept their membership in many different groups.
2. To enable children to see themselves as part of the larger society; to identify, empathize, and relate with individuals from other groups.
3. To foster respect and appreciation for the diverse ways in which other people live.
4. To encourage in young children's earliest social relationships an openness and interest in others, a willingness to include others, and a desire to cooperate.
5. To promote the development of a realistic awareness of contemporary society, a sense of social responsibility, and an active concern that extends beyond one's immediate family or group.
6. To empower children to become autonomous and critical analysts and activists in their social environment.
7. To support the development of educational and social skills that are

needed for children to become full participants in the larger society in ways that are most appropriate to individual styles, cultural orientations and linguistic backgrounds.
8. To promote effective and reciprocal relationships between schools and families. (pp. 3–5)

As Sleeter and Grant (1988) argued, education that is multicultural may not be adequate enough to create a just society unless it directly addresses issues of inequality, power, and oppression in the social structure. They argue that society must move beyond simply "celebrating diversity" by teaching students to understand social inequalities and empowering them to work actively to change society. Teaching must make a point of being antiracist and antisexist in order to overcome the predominant messages children receive elsewhere in society.

Teaching children to be knowledgeable about differences, supportive of others, and active in changing structures that are oppressive to various groups can all begin within inclusive classrooms. It is within a classroom that openly and directly addresses the interests, needs, and possibilities of all its members that students may best experience democratic structures that empower and support all participants.

The goal must be to create a community that embraces differences, uses children's differences as part of the curriculum, and respects children's differences throughout all aspects of the school program. This chapter explores some of the areas of diversity that teachers must address if they are to create classroom communities that reflect and respect the multicultural, multifaceted nature of their students. It also provides strategies for teaching students to respond effectively to injustice and inequality.

TRANSFORMING OUR CLASSROOMS

Learning About Racial Differences

Learning about racial differences cannot be separated from the rest of the curriculum. For example, a one-day, multicultural fair may be an interesting learning experience for children, but it does little to communicate the message that there have been people of color throughout history, and that the contributions of men and women of color are not separate from the standard curriculum. A positive respect and acknowledgment of racial differences can permeate everything from the social studies lessons to the bulletin boards, the books in the book corner, and the songs learned in music class.

Teachers' goals may vary depending on the racial differences represented in the classroom. Derman-Sparks (1989) suggests that in classes that consist primarily of children of color, the primary task is to build knowledge and pride in physical characteristics and to counter the influences of racism that have left some children believing that being "white" is better than having a darker skin color. In classrooms where all the students are white, children can be guided to see the many ways in which they differ, including skin shades, hair color, or freckles. Teachers in predominantly white communities have a particular responsibility to teach about racial diversity in an accurate and respectful way. In classes where there are only a few children of color, it is important that teachers talk about the ways in which all children are different, rather than implying that "we're all the same except for Michael."

Derman-Sparks (1989) offers the following cautions about promoting a "tourist curriculum" (one that presents diversity as something foreign, exotic, and isolated from the rest of the classroom). She urges teachers to avoid the following:

Trivializing: Organizing activities only around holidays or only around food. Only involving parents for holiday and cooking activities.

Tokenism: One Black doll amidst many White dolls; a bulletin board of "ethnic" images—the only diversity in the room; only one book about any cultural group.

Disconnecting cultural diversity from daily classroom life: Reading books about children of color only on special occasions. Teaching a unit on a different culture and then never seeing that culture again.

Stereotyping: Images of Native Americans only from the past; people of color always shown as poor; people from cultures outside the U.S. only shown in "traditional" dress and rural settings.

Misrepresenting American ethnic groups: Pictures and books about Mexico to teach about Mexican-Americans; of Japan to teach about Japanese-Americans; of Africa to teach about Black-Americans. (p. 63)

There are many excellent resources available to help teachers include racial differences in everything they teach; these include curriculum guides on multicultural education, sources for children's books about children of color, and curricula for teaching about differences. (Some of these are included in a list of resources at the end of the chapter.)

History lessons are ideal for presenting multiple perspectives. For example, the truth behind Columbus and his "discovery" of America includes stories about the destruction of native people, the slave trade Columbus initiated, and the effects of greed and colonialism on other people and cultures. Discussions of this era in history should include why many native people consider Columbus Day to be a day of mourning. Inclusive history means encouraging students to read standard textbooks critically and not limiting the study of historical events to a single perspective. Students can go beyond studying racial differences to understanding racism (prejudice plus power) and the ways people are able to be allies to those discriminated against on the basis of race.

Teachers can also use children's direct experiences to discuss instances of prejudice, discrimination, and injustice related to cultural or racial differences. Carl Burk, a social studies teacher at Gompers Middle School in Madison, Wisconsin, used the local hunting rights and spear fishing controversy to engage his students in a discussion of Native American rights and traditions. Students had read graffiti such as "Spear an Indian, Save a Fish" and began asking questions. Some of them were aware that many hunters and sportsmen were complaining about the "Indians taking our fish, our deer, and our land," but many had never met or talked with a Native American. Burk challenged the students' prejudices and stereotypes and answered their questions by inviting members of various tribes to talk to his class about their traditions and beliefs (Staff, 1989).

Virtually every activity or curriculum project can be redefined so that it is inclusive. For example, an activity on American painters can be expanded to include the paintings of Ben Shahn and Raphael Soyer, both white immigrants from Russia; Diego Rivera and Antonio Garcia, two Mexican artists who worked in the United States; and Allan Crite and Charles White, both African-American artists (Grant & Sleeter, 1989).

Music activities can also be implemented inclusively by listening to music from all over the world and learning songs in sign language, authentic songs from other cultures (not those written about the culture), and family songs that relate to various rituals or holiday celebrations. One Chanukah song included in the traditional Christmas program is an example of tokenism and may actually discourage children from understanding the cultural diversity of their classmates. A range of music activities should be included throughout the year.

Learning About Cultural Differences

Everyone has a culture, a background, a history, and customs that inform his or her daily life, beliefs, attitudes, and behaviors. Although it may be tempting to believe that only the most visible "minority" groups have a culture, it is not true. Even within a class that appears to be homogeneous, there will be many differences in cultural backgrounds. Therefore, it is best to approach teaching about cultural differences from the perspective that everyone has a culture, all cultures are valuable and deserving of respect, and that diversity enriches the classroom. Whaley and Swadener (1990) explain that "early multicultural education is not a curriculum; it is a perspective and a commitment to equity, sensitivity and empowerment" (p. 240).

One interesting and useful way to begin a discussion of different backgrounds and cultures is to talk about the children's names. When children are asked to share the background of their full names, many exciting details of cultural background and history emerge. Rebecca is named after her Jewish great-grandmother Rivka who came to the United States from Russia at the turn of the century. Why would Rebecca's grandmother have come then? What was happening in the world? What kind of a name is Rebecca? What does it mean? Richard Flying Bye is Native American. What tribe is he from? Who gave him his name and why? What are some Native American customs related to names and naming? Jenna, who was adopted at age 2, is Korean. What is the meaning of her middle name, Mei-Wan, and how did she get it? Why do some people call Richard "Ricardo"? Which name does he prefer? An exercise such as this makes it clear that all children have a culture and a unique background; this allows children and adults to take pride in their own heritage and to see similarities and differences.

Language differences present another excellent way to learn about diversity. For example, in one class several students speak Spanish; two children are studying Hebrew after school; LaMont has cerebral palsy and everyone must listen closely to understand him; one child speaks Japanese to her mother at home and to her grandmother whom she visits in California; Carla uses sign language; and Dustin uses a talking computer. These children have in common the need to communicate, to be understood, and to be connected to other people. Inclusive classrooms encourage children to become as multilingual as possible. All children can learn basic sign language, the braille alphabet, and important phrases in other languages. The teacher can emphasize the values of these various languages by making some classroom posters in other languages, telling stories in sign language, or inviting a Spanish-speaking parent to share a story with the class in her language. The message is important—there are many ways to communicate and if people want to they can learn how to talk to each other.

Learning About Family Differences

There are many kinds of families. Some children live with single parents; others in extended families with cousins, aunts, and uncles in the same household; some in blended families; some with adoptive parents; and others in foster families. How do we communicate to children that there are many ways to be a family, many ways in which people can give each other support and love?

One method for very young children is to assist them to make posters or books such as "The People in My Family." The diversity of this project provides a model of full and complete acceptance of various family arrangements for the teacher to discuss: "Tara's father lives in California, but she put him in her picture because he's still part of her family; Zach drew two mothers in his picture because Mama Alice and Mama Kate are both part of his family—they both love him and take care of him."

Older children may engage in more sophisticated lessons about stepparents, half-brothers and sisters, adoption and foster care, lesbian parenting, or joint custody arrangements. Teachers must remember that they are not raising difficult or uncomfortable issues with students; rather, they are acknowledging and validating situations that students are already experiencing, and making it clear that it is okay to talk about such differences.

Teachers must be careful in implementing projects or activities that assume all children come from traditional, nuclear families. Father—son hockey games, mother—daughter teas, and even grandparent visiting days can all be painful for children whose parents or grandparents are not alive, available, willing, or able to be involved in such activities. Teachers can create more inclusive opportunities such as "Bring Someone You Love To School Day" (this might be a member of their church, their little sister, or their next door neighbor). Various creative solutions will show that there are many kinds of families and many ways of being closely connected to other people.

Teachers must also exercise caution in assigning projects related to family trees, baby pictures, and other activities that presume children are living with their biological parents and/or have access to information about their early years. Alternative assignments can be presented that preserve the intent of the lesson and still honor children's varying situations and experiences. For example, teachers could ask the students to interview someone in their community who is more than 60 years old to find out what things were like in the town when they were a child. Students could also bring a picture of themselves at a different age, or a picture of someone else in their family, and let the class guess who the person is.

Learning About Gender Differences

As with other aspects of diversity, the goal in learning about gender differences should be for children to acknowledge and accept sex differences, and yet, at the same time, not be limited by those characteristics. Two specific goals in this area might be: 1) to free children from constraining, stereotypical views of what "girls can do" or what "boys can be," thus opening up greater options for growth and development; and 2) to encourage children to interact with and understand what is unfortunately referred to as "the opposite sex."

In order to meet the first objective, teachers must be attentive to their own language and behaviors in the classroom as well as the materials and activities they provide for students. Admonitions that "big boys don't cry," or attempts to redirect a boy away from the housekeeping corner and into the block area clearly communicate that there are certain things boys just don't do. Similarly, studying only male authors, male inventors, and the history of "mankind" disenfranchises girls from full understanding or pride in women's accomplishments and their own potential.

Teachers must continually examine their materials and their activities to ensure that all children sense that they are included and welcome. There are many children's books available that challenge stereotypical sex roles. *William's Doll* (Zolotow, 1972), for example, can help all children explore the role that loving and nurturing plays in their lives. Older children should read books that have female protagonists, and be encouraged to find out about the many women who have been omitted from history books. Children can also be encouraged to become critical consumers and challengers of sexism in their lives and the materials they use. Teachers should help even young children explore the assumptions in the books they read—"In this book I noticed that only the women were doing the cooking. Can men cook, too? Do you know men who cook?" Story time can then be followed by a cooking activity that involves all students. Looking at toy catalogs and noticing how the toys are designated for boys or girls can lead to discussions of which toys look interesting to them and why and how parents and other adults often make decisions about buying toys marketed for a particular gender.

If a teacher notices that the girls in the class rarely choose science projects, for example, he or she might want to address this issue by assigning girls to specific projects that build their competence and confidence in this area. If a boy is teased because he mentions that he is learning to crochet, the teacher can talk about the history of men knitting or net-making, and teach all of the students to crochet winter hats and scarves.

Prompting children to play and interact "across gender lines" can be approached in the same way as other integration strategies. Teachers must ask: "How can I arrange my classroom and my activities so that boys and girls are comfortable working together and choosing one another as partners?" Again, teachers must be careful to avoid perpetuating artificial distinctions by having a "girls' line" and a "boys' line," or by having a girl and boy leader of the week. More intervention may be required in order to counteract the prevailing practices and attitudes that tend to separate girls and boys and keep them from forming meaningful relationships. Teachers can assign children to work with partners or in groups that are heterogeneous in gender as well as race and/or ability. Random assignments of tasks and responsibilities can also make gender less of an issue in the classroom. For example, if children's names are randomly selected for daily math partners, then some pairs will be two boys, some two girls, or some a boy and a girl. If teachers notice teasing or ridicule based on gender issues (e.g., "Ha, ha, Michael chose pink for his drawing," or "Marina's reading a boy's book."), he or she should intervene and address the issue directly. The teacher should at least explain that teasing is not allowed and will not be permitted. Optimally, there should be a discussion of why people think pink is a girl's color or rocket books are for boys. There are plenty of opportunities for children to engage in projects that cross traditional gender lines (e.g., cooking, woodcrafts, science, arts and crafts). One third grade teacher taught all of her students to do counted cross-stitch. She reported that none of the boys or their parents objected, and all were pleased with the beautiful samplers the children made. A fifth grade teacher had all of his students build and launch rockets; it was not presented as only a boys' activity while girls, for example, built bird feeders.

Because cultural norms regarding sex roles differ considerably, Derman-Sparks (1989) cautions that teachers must be careful not to act in racist ways by trying to be antisexist. She proposes that teachers present gender roles as offering multiple choices, rather than assigning superior values to some roles. In addition, teachers should find ways of providing options that promote children's full development while respecting their background. She states that if, for example, parents object to their daughter wearing pants or to their son being encouraged to cry, then the teacher can develop alternatives such as having certain periods of the day when pants are worn for large motor activities, or encouraging the boy to write his feelings down or dictate them in a story.

Learning About Religious Differences and Holidays

Although the United States Constitution describes the importance of the separation of church and state, the reality is that many schools and teachers behave as though all children are Christian. Many teachers organize their classrooms and activities according to holidays—October is Halloween, November is Thanksgiving, and December is Christmas. Bulletin board decorations, stories, music, art projects, and curriculum often revolve around these holidays. Teachers tend to structure their curricula around holidays because they provide an excellent way to present many subject areas around a theme. The holiday symbols are recognizable and known to many children, and many of the typical holiday activities (parties, plays, singing, and community-building projects) represent a welcome source of social and affective development opportunities (Sapon-Shevin, King, & Hanhan, 1988).

However, children who are Jehovah's Witnesses may not celebrate holidays at all, Native American children may be uncomfortable with traditional presentations of Thanksgiving, and Christmas celebrations may not be appropriate for children whose families do not observe the holiday. Learning about religious differences can be closely related to learning about cultural, racial, and family differences; teachers must find ways to teach about religious differences and honor the ways children differ without fragmenting the class or destroying the sense of community. As with other areas of difference, it is important for teachers to avoid the terms *us* and *them* (e.g., "While we're having our holiday, Naomi and her family are having their holiday"). The message must not be that most of us are the same and only some of us are different; instead, it should be that we all have unique backgrounds and characteristics.

To teach about religious differences, teachers can de-emphasize traditional holidays so that they occupy less school time and activity. Children will have opportunities to celebrate Christmas with their families and in their churches; school time should be devoted to other areas of study and involvement. The holidays that teachers *do* choose to celebrate should be presented with multicultural perspectives. For example, Davids and Gudinas (1979) of the Madison, Wisconsin Public Schools' Department of Human Relations prepared and disseminated a "Thanksgiving Holiday Packet" for use by elementary teachers in the district. The packet included: "Thanksgiving: A New Perspective," an article describing recent research on the "first Thanksgiving" and its implications; "Indians and Pilgrims," a simulation story to help children experience what it would feel like to have been a Native American when Europeans arrived and settled in North America; "Thanksgiving: A Multicultural Approach," an activity that emphasizes how the concept of gratitude is expressed by people around the world; and "Teaching About Hunger," a list of suggestions for helping children think about hunger and responses to hunger problems. Other states such as Oregon have also implemented statewide curricula regarding Thanksgiving and Columbus Day that present a variety of viewpoints and respect the history and traditions of Native Americans.

Teachers can also make a serious effort to learn and teach about other religious and nonreligious holidays. Kwanza, Chinese New Year, Sukkot, and Buddha's birthday all present opportunities to talk about different religions, nationalities, and beliefs. Often, one of the major barriers for instructors as they teach about religions and customs is their own inexperience and relative ignorance; although parents and children can provide wonderful resources, teachers must take the responsibility to read, listen, and become informed so that they can easily and comfortably discuss religious differences.

It is also possible to organize instruction around nonholiday themes. One teacher organized a month's curriculum around bears. Children read stories about bears, learned bear songs, studied about bears in science, did plays and fairy tales about bears, and created art projects related to bears. The unit culminated with a "Bear Party" to which children brought stuffed bears and feasted on goodies made with honey! Another teacher organized a unit around oceans, implementing activities related to water, tides, animal and plant life in the ocean, and myths and legends about the sea. Such units preserve the benefits of organizing instruction topically, include all children, and stretch the limits of curriculum past routine songs, stories, and art projects.

Holiday celebrations also tend to be popular because they provide opportunities for children to think empathetically about their classmates and the greater community (e.g., schoolwide food drives and Secret Santas [children picking secret friends to do favors for]). However, such opportunities need not be limited to holiday time. Local food cupboards need food all year, and environmental concerns such as recycling are ongoing. A long-term commitment by a particular class to such a project would be a valuable demonstration of the importance of caring about other people all the time, not just at holidays. Singing, preparing food, doing favors for friends, making gifts, and being friendly can all be implemented on a year-round basis. Community-building activities are most effective when they are seen as important and valued throughout the school year, not just occasionally.

Learning About Skill and Ability Differences[1]

Although some differences in skills and abilities may be more apparent within an inclusive classroom—Dalia does not hear well and

[1]For further explanation of this topic, see Sapon-Shevin, M. (in press). Ability differences in the classroom: Teaching and learning in inclusive classrooms. In D. Byrnes & G. Kiger (Eds.), *Differences in common: Anti-bias teaching in a diverse society* (pp. 168–192). Washington, DC: Association for Childhood Education International.

wears hearing aids, Everett finishes his math before anyone else, Carlos can't walk and uses a wheelchair—the reality is that all children have strengths and weaknesses. To contradict and challenge some of the typical hierarchies that establish themselves in classrooms based on children's performances (e.g., the highest reading group, the fastest runner) teachers can see to it that children are engaged in a range of activities and projects, thus sharing and validating many kinds of excellence. One teacher created a classroom Yellow Pages that listed children's names, their areas of "expertise," and the ways they were willing to provide assistance to classmates. The guide included entries such as:

LaDonna Smith; jump rope songs and jingles; willing to teach double-dutch jumping and crossing over to anyone interested.
Miguel Hernandez; baseball card collector; can show interested people how to start a collection, special cards to look for, and how to figure batting averages and statistics.

By encouraging students to look beyond some of the typical school subjects that they may use to rank and evaluate themselves and each other, this teacher created new areas of interest, promoted peer interaction, and broke existing stereotypes about who was "smart" and who was not.

Teachers can also engage students in a discussion of "helping" behaviors. Students can generate and practice appropriate ways of offering and receiving help (e.g., "Can I help you?" rather than, "Let me do that, you're too short/dumb/slow") and ways of gracefully accepting and declining help (e.g., "No thanks, I'm doing fine," rather than, "What do you think I am, dumb or something?"). These are repertoires that all people need, not only those whose skills are more limited. Teachers can help students reflect on questions such as the following:

What are three things I'm really good at?
What are three things I have trouble with?
What are some ways I can provide help to people?
What are some things I need help with, and what kind of help would I like?

By generating answers to these questions, students and teachers can see that everyone has skills and abilities and that everyone needs help in certain areas. Karen may be a "whiz" as a reader, but she may need help being accepted into playground games. Carmen may struggle with math, but she excels in remembering things and getting people and activities organized. Classrooms can become communities of mutual support if teachers promote respect for differences and provide multiple opportunities for students to view each other in many ways.

Competitive teaching and evaluation structures are incompatible with accepting and inclusive school communities. Star charts indicating to all who enter the classroom who is doing well and who is not, choosing the best artist or the quietest group, or rewarding children for finishing first, are not conducive to creating classroom communities that respect diversity. Competition is not only damaging to the student who does poorly (e.g., "We don't want Miguel on our math team, we had him last week"), but also to students who consistently do well (e.g., "She thinks she's so smart just because she finished faster than everyone else").

In cooperative classrooms, children help one another, provide each other with instructional help and peer support, and discover that by working together they can accomplish far more than working alone. Children with different strengths and repertoires can all be functioning, contributing members of groups when skills and expertise are shared. Cooperative classrooms use the motto, "None of us is as smart as all of us."

Teachers in inclusive classrooms who individualize instruction may initially be asked questions such as "How come LaVonne doesn't do the same math we do?" or "When will I get to work on the computer like Kari does?" Responses to these and similar questions set the tone of the classroom. Generally, honest, forthright answers seem to be best. For example, "LaVonne works in a different book because she's working on addition, and she's not ready for multiplication yet," or, "Let's find a time when you can work with Kari on the computer." After a short period of time, most children accept the fact that they each do different work.

When the need for help is not stigmatized, but is seen as a common, natural occurrence, and when giving help is regarded as a valuable, also natural occurrence, then children can be very accommodating of one another's challenges and appreciative of their accomplishments.

Teachers must be careful not to stress differences at the cost of allowing students to see the many ways they are similar. In order for students to find their common ground, teachers must make sure they demonstrate that all students are in school to learn, that all people have skills and areas of weakness, and that all people need encouragement and support. One teacher created a lesson to teach students that although all children have various characteristics, such as owning pets, being good runners, liking spinach, or speaking another language, *all* of them have feelings that can be hurt and *all* children want friends.

Learning About Challenging Stereotypes and Discrimination

To create and maintain truly inclusive schools and communities, children and teachers must see themselves as active change agents, willing and able to confront and challenge stereotypes and oppressive, discriminatory behavior. Depending on the age of the students, different levels of social activism and response will be possible and appropriate, but even young children can recognize and respond to stereotypes and prejudices.

One first grade teacher explained the difference between a "dislike" and a "prejudice" in a unique way. She allowed students to express a dislike for something, that is, have a negative reaction to it (e.g., a food, an activity) after they had extensive experience with it, but she did not allow them to prejudge people and things without sufficient experience. Children learned to discriminate legitimate dislikes (e.g., "I tasted broccoli and I hate it," or, "Jared hits children and I don't want to play with him") from prejudices (e.g., "I don't want to taste that, it looks yucky," or, "Children with dark skin are mean.").

A preschool teacher taught her class the difference between terms that are exclusive, pushing people away, and terms that are inclusive, bringing people together. "You can't play with us" and "There's no room here for you" are examples of exclusive terms. "Do you want to be in our group?" and "Move over and make room for Micah" are examples of inclusive terms.

Children can also become critical consumers of their own environments and the materials they encounter. There are numerous checklists that enable readers to examine materials for evidence of discrimination, misinformation, and omission of people of color, women, people with disabilities, or nontraditional families. Young children can recognize that there are not any people of color in many children's books or that the mommies in the books stay home and the daddies go to work in suits, even though their mommy is a waitress and their daddy is a farm laborer.

Older children can engage in more sophisticated analyses of classroom materials. In an article about sensitizing children to Native American stereotypes, Califf (1977) shared her experiences teaching children about Native American values and traditions and how to recognize misrepresentations and stereotypes of Native people in the media. At the culmination of her teaching, she shared a book about Christopher Columbus with the class. She was delighted that the children detected many stereotypes and distortions. Thirteen of the children wrote letters of response to the editor at the publishing company. One of the children wrote that he thought the book portrayed Indians as dogs and that it did not make it clear that Indians have their own language. A second child explained that the book should not have said that Columbus invited the Indians to Spain because he learned that Columbus stole the Indians. When the editor wrote back to the students and responded that she agreed with the criticisms and would stop carrying the book, the children experienced the importance of being an ally and confronting racism.

Students can also learn to confront racism, sexism, and discrimination in their own settings. One seventh grade social studies teacher asked his students to complete an accessibility checklist of their school (Sapon-Shevin, 1988). Students set out with guidelines and tape measures to assess whether the students who could not hear, used braille, and used wheelchairs had full access to the building and its programs. These students then wrote letters to the principal sharing their results, and their anger, about some of their findings.

They discovered, for example, that the elevator would go up, but it did not come down. They realized that this meant that students using wheelchairs could not take classes on the second floor. Their insights into full inclusion and their indignation about injustice were promising indicators of their growing ability to recognize and challenge discrimination and exclusion.

At the most basic level, children can also learn how to respond to name-calling and exclusion of children based on differences. The Madison Public Schools (1989) have articulated a specific policy in this area that reads: "In accordance with the District's nondiscrimination policy, racial name-calling will not be tolerated. This includes all derogatory language, gestures and behaviors with racial overtones" (not paginated).

The district's handout goes on to state that children need to know that racial names and slurs represent a form of verbal abuse and are unacceptable. They suggest that when racist language is used, the following statements could be useful:

Racial name-calling is not allowed in this school.
Racial name-calling is demeaning.
I find that word offensive.
We value all people in our room and in our school and we do not use that language.

In addition, children can come to recognize and interrupt racist, sexist, and ethnic humor. Teachers should explore with students the ways that such jokes perpetuate stereotypes and are damaging to people, even though they may be intended as humor. Students can learn ways of firmly interrupting such humor (e.g., "I don't think that's funny") and can be encouraged to find and share jokes and stories that are funny, but not at the expense of another group. One teacher told her class that the first 5 minutes of class would be devoted to joke sharing, with the provision that the joke not be offensive to any group. This offer challenged students to listen critically to the jokes they heard and to analyze humor for its potential negative overtones and consequences.

It is important that children believe they can make a difference. Classrooms that are inclusive work to empower all children to improve their own situations and those of their classmates. Students who feel powerful and effective in grade school are far more likely to become adults who believe they *can* make a difference. The typical school day or year provides multiple opportunities to problem solve issues of inclusiveness. When one fifth grade class that included a vegetarian child, a child who only ate Kosher foods, and a Muslim child, wanted to plan refreshments for their party, the children brainstormed food choices that would allow all of the children to participate. Another class became involved in a fitness and muscle-building unit to improve upper body strength so they could assist a child in a wheelchair who was not strong enough to lift himself out of his chair. The messages in these classrooms are consistent—we are a community, we are all in this together, we will take responsibility for one another, and we won't abandon people because of their differences or difficulties.

CONCLUSION

Creating classrooms that honor and respect all children and all of their differences is an ongoing, time-consuming challenge. Despite our best efforts, we will continue to struggle with our own language, teaching, and curriculum in our attempts at inclusiveness, fairness, and respect. The most important thing teachers can do is explore their own understandings, values, and beliefs about diversity. When did you first learn about racial differences and what was communicated? When you were growing up, which groups did you have ongoing contact with and which groups did you never interact with? How comfortable are you with people of color? Lesbians? Single parents? African-Americans? Hispanics? Jews? Latinos? Only by exploring our own personal histories and experiences can we attempt to understand and challenge the effects of our upbringing so that we may create inclusive classrooms that model social justice and equality.

Swadener, Gudinas, and Kaiser (1988) suggest that teachers respond to the following quotes from parents:

Chinese-American Parent: "My four-year-old son asked me, When I grow up can I be blond? It's better to be blond, Dad! I feel . . ."
Adoptive parent of Korean child: "We had to remove our child from the day care when other children kept teasing her about not being a real American¡ and the teacher didn't take this seriously. I feel . . ."
Hmong parent: "In our Hmong tradition, masks have spiritual significance. My child was expected to do an art project making scary masks and was very upset by this. I feel . . ."
Low-income parent: "It is so hard to just tell my six-year-old that we cannot afford the things that other kids at school take for granted—you know, the brand name jeans and Cabbage Patch stuff. I feel . . ." (p. 5)

Discussing our own responses to such parental concerns and classroom dilemmas can help to sensitize us to the many kinds of diversity that our children present, and to the need to develop caring, inclusive responses. The task is a difficult one, but it is critical to our ability to shape the kinds of schools we envision.

REFERENCES

Califf, J. (1977). Sensitizing nine-year-olds to Native American stereotypes. *Interracial Books for Children Bulletin,* 8(1), 3–7.
Davids, D.W., & Gudinas, R.A. (1979). *Student activities and teacher materials for use during the Thanksgiving season.* Madison: Department of Human Relations, Madison, Wisconsin School District.
Derman-Sparks, L., & the A.B.C. Task Force. (1989). *Anti-bias curriculum: Tools for empowering young children.* Washington, DC: National Association for the Education of Young Children.
Grant, C.A., & Sleeter, C.A. (1989). *Turning on learning: Five approaches for multicultural teaching plans for race, class, gender and disability.* Columbus, OH: Charles E. Merrill.
Madison Public School's Department of Human Relations. (1989). *Racial name-calling: Strategies, activities and resources.* Madison, WI: Author.
Ramsey, P.G. (1987). *Teaching and learning in a diverse world: Multicultural education for young children.* New York: Teachers College Press.
Sapon-Shevin, M. (1988). Countering prejudiced beliefs and behaviors: A minicourse for junior high students. *Social Education,* 52(4), 272–275.
Sapon-Shevin, M., King, R., & Hanhan, S. (1988). The holiday-centered curriculum. *Education and Society,* 1(3), 26–31.
Sleeter, C.E., & Grant, C.A. (1988). *Making choices for multicultural education: Five approaches to race, class, and gender.* Columbus, OH: Charles E. Merrill.
Staff. (1989, November). *The Teachers' Workshop Newsletter.* Madison, WI: Emerson Elementary School.
Swadener, E.B., Gudinas, R.A., & Kaiser, R.B. (1988). Parent perspectives: An activity to sensitize teachers to cultural, religious and class diversity. *Journal of School Social Work,* 2(2), 1–7.

Whaley, K., & Swadener, E.B. (1990). Multicultural education in infant and toddler settings. *Childhood Education,* 66(4), 238–240.
Zolotow, C. (1972). *William's doll.* New York: Harper & Row.

RESOURCES

There are many excellent resources available for teaching children about differences, implementing education that is multicultural, and helping students and teachers to challenge racism, sexism, and other forms of oppression and discrimination. Teachers are also encouraged to seek out and identify children's books that are inclusive and present diversity in a positive light. Following is a list of resources:

Barnes, E., Berrigan, C., & Biklen, D. (1978). *What's the difference: Teaching positive attitudes towards people with disabilities.* Syracuse, NY: Human Policy Press.
Byrnes, D. (1987). *Teacher, they called me a . . .* New York: Anti-defamation league of B'nai B'rith.
Children's Book Press. 1461 Ninth Avenue, San Franciso, CA. 94122 [publishers of multicultural literature and audiocassettes for children].
Council on Interracial Books for Children, 1841 Broadway, New York, N.Y. 10023 [publishers of book lists, film strips, and other media about unlearning racism].
Cummings, M. (1977). *Individual differences: An experience in human relations for children.* New York: Anti-defamation league of B'nai B'rith.
Derman-Sparks, L., & the ABC Task Force. (1989). *Anti-bias curriculum: Tools for empowering young children.* Washington, DC: National Association for the Education of Young Children.
Froeschl, M., & Sprung, B. (1988). *Resources for educational equity: A guide for grades pre-K–12.* New York: Garland.
Grant, C.A., & Sleeter, C.A. (1989). *Turning on learning: Five approaches for multicultural teaching plans for race, class, gender and disability.* Columbus, OH: Charles E. Merrill.
Kendall, F. (1983). *Diversity in the classroom: A multicultural approach to the education of young children.* New York: Teachers College Press.
Ramsey, P.G. (1987). *Teaching and learning in a diverse world: Multicultural education for young children.* New York: Teachers College Press.
Ramsey, P.G., Vold, E.B., & Williams, L.R. (1989). *Multicultural education: A sourcebook.* New York: Garland.
Schniedewind, N., & Davidson, E. (1983). *Open minds to equality: A sourcebook of learning activities to promote race, sex, class and age equity.* Englewood Cliffs, NJ: Prentice-Hall.

3

Inclusive Education

"Making Sense" of the Curriculum

Alison Ford,
Linda Davern,
and Roberta Schnorr

AS MORE SCHOOLS and classrooms promote the inclusion of *all* students as full and valued members, an important step is taken toward better preparing students for a world rich in diversity. Yet, as we move away from sorting and separating learners, classroom teachers are faced with new challenges. Students—particularly those who have been educated in separate schools and classes—often come to regular classrooms with a separate curriculum; at least it may seem that way to the teachers who review the individualized education programs (IEPs) and try to determine how to best include the students in a regular class setting. How does this process of inclusion work? How will teachers "make sense" out of curriculum when the needs of the students seem so diverse?

Initially, many teachers are likely to view the curriculum needs of their diverse learners in a "parallel" fashion; that is, the "regular" curriculum is followed for most of the students (although it may need to be adapted for some), and a "functional" curriculum is used for the few students who have extensive educational needs. In time, however, these two curricular paths may seem less distinct, not because the goals of each are de-emphasized, but because the teachers are beginning to understand the diverse needs of students within a common framework. The sections that follow offer five strategies that, in combination, can contribute to a teacher's understanding of a planning approach for all students. These are: 1) being mindful of the broad outcomes of education, 2) creating a common curriculum framework, 3) offering a curriculum rich in meaning, 4) measuring outcomes that are individualized and performance based, and 5) acknowledging the power of the "implicit" curriculum (Goodlad, 1984).

BEING MINDFUL OF THE BROAD OUTCOMES OF EDUCATION

As noted by one teacher, "I have to remind myself that schooling is much more than passing competency exams in content areas such as math, English, social studies, and science." Many educators share the same sentiment. It is easy to lose sight of the broad goals of education when a single outcome (acquiring the knowledge measured by standardized achievement tests) receives so much attention and others receive so little.

What Do Students Need To Learn?

It is generally accepted that students should leave school with a solid, basic level of knowledge. Traditionally, this has meant helping students to develop at least "minimal proficiency" in language (the ability to read, speak, and listen), computations, and general knowledge about their world. To accomplish this, education has been translated for many years into the teaching of a variety of subject areas, each having their own scope and sequence of knowledge and skills (e.g., language arts/English, mathematics, science, social studies). Other major outcomes (e.g., physical well being, creative expression through the arts, success in work life) have been referred to as physical education, art, music, and vocational and career education.

Most educators, however, contend that they strive for more than the mastery of information typically contained on the scope and sequence charts. In an age when people struggle to keep pace with the growing body of worldwide information available, the ability to find strategies and processes for retrieving and utilizing this information is viewed as a critical outcome of education. Recently, for example, we have been reminded that learning basic operations is not a substitute for common sense problem-solving ability. Students have received endless criticism from the media for their lack of this ability.

Where American students fall down is in thinking. Take the division problem . . . "An Army bus holds 36 soldiers. If 1,128 soldiers are being bused to their training site, how many buses are needed?" Only 70 percent of secondary-school students who were given this problem in a national assessment performed the right operation—dividing 1,128 by 36 to arrive at 31 with the remainder of 12 (or 31⅓). Worse, of those who go that far, only one in three went on to draw the conclusion that to move all the soldiers, a total of 32 buses were needed. The rest, accustomed to the sterile, self-referential world of school math courses, did not stop to question an answer involving one third of a bus. (Adler, 1990, p. 18)

Therefore, while the concern remains about graduates acquiring a solid knowledge base, as much attention, if not more, is being placed on the ability to integrate it (integrated subject areas), apply it (critical thinking and problem-solving skills), manage it (computer literacy), expand upon it (learning to learn; self-directed learning), and use it with other people (building interpersonal skills through cooperative structures).

Other social forces have entered into the discussion of what is wanted from today's students and tomorrow's adult citizens. There is a great deal of concern about the large percentage of students who do not graduate from high school. Many of these "at-risk" students feel alienated and disengaged from school activity. Terms such as *fostering connectedness*, creating a *sense of community*, and developing *social responsibility* are now becoming a part of school vocabulary.

Global economy and worldwide communications have strengthened the need for graduates with a deeper knowledge of other languages and cultures. In the United States, the growing mix of racial and ethnic groups in schools and the continuing insensitivities to differences have heightened the need for students to understand and value the differences in their own country.

Finally, there is a continuing concern about the readiness of our graduates to enter the job market and become responsible citizens. As dependence on the work force increases with fewer workers contributing to the social security system, there is a realization that every potential worker is needed (including people with disabilities who, until recently, had little preparation to enter the work force). In addition, as teenage pregnancy rates continue to rise, more attention is being focused on learning about the responsibilities associated with family life. Educators are also becoming concerned with preparing young people to deal with health risks, such as drug use and AIDS.

To account for these and other societal forces, the mission statements of school systems are necessarily broad. In one large, urban school district, the superintendent succinctly describes the mission of the school district as providing "each student with a positive attitude toward self and learning, as well as the ability to think creatively and critically, communicate effectively, welcome diversity in people, appreciate the arts and contribute to society" (Staff, 1990). In another district (Johnson City, NY), five major outcomes of education mo-

...vate the system: 1) cognitive skills, 2) self-esteem, 3) concern for others, 4) self-directedness, and 5) process skills. For the purpose of this chapter, the following list of outcomes is given, which is similarly broad in scope, but perhaps a bit more descriptive:

1. Cognitive skills
   To read, write, listen, speak, and use math
   To use scientific principles and methods
   To think creatively and critically
2. Personal development
   To achieve physical well-being
   To express oneself artistically
   To have a positive attitude toward self and learning
3. Preparation for citizenship and future roles
   To show concern and respect for others
   To work cooperatively
   To become knowledgeable and appreciative of people and society, other cultures, and history
4. To show awareness of and preparation for community participation, career possibilities, domestic responsibilities, and constructive use of free time

All students can and should work toward these *same* broad outcomes of education. What will differ is the level at which these outcomes are achieved and the degree of emphasis placed on each of them.

A Matter of Emphasis

Presumably, each teacher makes a contribution to the overall outcomes of each district. A teacher in the primary grades, for example, may be expected to place greater emphasis on developing basic knowledge and process skills, such as reading, writing, and basic math, whereas teachers in the upper grades are to build on this knowledge by developing more advanced analytical and reasoning skills across various disciplines. Some teachers may be expected to concentrate on the development of creative expression, physical well-being, career awareness, and community participation. Logically, all teachers must assume the responsibility for outcomes such as thinking creatively and critically, developing a positive attitude toward self and learning, and showing concern and respect for others. These are not areas of development that can be parceled out. They must be emphasized in each learning situation throughout every student's school career.

Judgments about which outcomes should be priorities for an individual student are made every day by classroom teachers. It is not uncommon to hear a teacher say, "If I can just get Suzette to *want* to learn, then I will have accomplished something." For this teacher, all outcomes are important, but the highest priority for Suzette is to instill self-motivation and self-directedness.

The desired outcomes carry different weights depending upon the student. For a student with a very low opinion of herself, the most important goal is to help strengthen her self-esteem. For a student who remains isolated from or rejected by peers, there can be no more important goal than developing a supportive peer group. For a student who does not have speech, one clear priority would be the development of a communication system that is useful in a variety of settings.

In addition, some domains of education may be weighted differently for individuals. Special emphasis may be placed on science or a foreign language depending on the particular career the individual is interested in pursuing. Another student's program may include community participation as a priority if he or she has limited proficiency in community functioning.

The commonalities (and the differences) among learners may be better understood and appreciated when evaluated against a common set of outcomes. In the next section, we take this notion one step further when we examine the use of a common curricular framework.

CREATING A COMMON CURRICULAR FRAMEWORK

To provide clarity for everyone involved in planning for an individual student, it may prove helpful to develop a common curricular framework from which to address educational priorities. Unfortunately, in most cases, *all* students have not been considered when school districts lay out their goals and articulate the curriculum sequences through which students will need to progress from year to year. Generally, special educators accept this and develop their own sequences using another framework (e.g., life skills) for students classified as having disabilities. Thus, under present circumstances, classroom teachers and special educators face the task of determining how the goals of previously excluded students interface with the broad spectrum of school curricula. This process can be aided when a common curricular framework is used in the development of an IEP.

Unfortunately, many IEPs are written as if the needs of the individual bear little or no relationship to those of the student's peers. For example, below are some of the goals that may appear on the IEP of a student, Zachary, who had previously attended a segregated special school:

1. Zach will select the appropriate line drawing from an array of three when presented in a horizontal pattern (within 5 seconds, on four consecutive opportunities).

2. Zach will indicate a preference between two familiar leisure activities by pointing to a picture that represents the activity or reaching for the object.
3. Zach will wear a palmar splint for 10 minutes during various instructional sessions and will maintain a pincer grasp to successfully handle small objects.
4. Zach will partially participate in preparing a simple snack including spreading, pouring, and cutting with a butter knife.

After reviewing the contents of some IEPs, it is perhaps understandable that conclusions such as the following are made: "How could his needs be met in a third grade class? He appears to have very little in common with his peers. This may be too much diversity to effectively manage." Or, "Are you sure Zachary doesn't need a special 'functional' program to meet his needs—like the one offered at Westwood school (a segregated, special school)?"

When a student's educational plan bears little resemblance to the content areas addressed within a general education structure, teachers are likely to be apprehensive about meeting the needs of the student. A teacher who is already overwhelmed with the "regular" curricular demands (and there are many), will have a difficult time incorporating new ones. She or he may believe that the only manageable solution is to send the student out for special instruction (and run the risk of fragmenting his or her day); or else include the student, but believe that meaningful learning is being sacrificed.

The demands of addressing diverse needs can be eased in several ways. Certainly many of these concerns can and should be addressed by adjusting staffing patterns and ratios. In a team arrangement, for example, instructional staff would be better able to accommodate the range of student needs. Managing the curriculum is also influenced by the way it is structured (a topic that is addressed in the following section). Yet another influencing factor involves how the goals are stated from the onset. It does appear that Zachary has very little in common with his third grade peers by the way his goals are stated. This is not to suggest that he must forsake these goals to be included in a third grade class. However, much can be done at the stage of writing the goals so that they are better understood within the context of an inclusive classroom.

First, the use of special education jargon could be minimized. Second, the focus could be on the broader activities or contexts that are important to the learner instead of long lists of precise skills and objectives that only have meaning once the daily routines have been established. Third, a framework for writing IEPs that all students have in common could be utilized.

By writing these goals, it should be easier to see the similarities as well as the differences that will need to be accounted for when developing the class schedule. With these considerations in mind, Zach's needs have been "reframed" and presented in Table 1. In the first column, the relationship between Zach's needs and the overall outcomes of education previously discussed are shown. The second column of this table contains a summary of Zach's IEP (his actual IEP would be written in much more detail, but would be framed within these types of headings that emphasize activities or contexts of instruction).

In response to the comment, "He still needs a functional program," it does appear that Zach will require more direct instruction in areas that affect his day-to-day functioning than most of his peers. This need should not be dismissed simply because he is in a third grade class. However, it does *not* mean that he needs a separate, functional "program," which generally means separate goals, methods, and often, locations. Nor does he need a full day comprised of functional routines such as preparing meals, purchasing groceries, or learning leisure time activities. Instead, he needs a functional *component* to his school program. He also needs components such as art and music, and those that would allow him to develop valuable communication and social skills and a sense of membership with his class, as well as exposure to "academic" information that is meaningful to him.

Initially, a functional component may seem difficult to incorporate into an existing class routine. Most students have already mastered the skills that Zach needs to improve. How, then, can the teacher justify setting aside time for him to work on such things? It is important to recognize that many functional activities already exist in the routines and schedules of students. For example, students engage in many self-management tasks throughout their school careers (taking care of personal belongings, taking off and putting on outdoor clothing, using the restroom, and eating lunch). Thus, while a special time is not set aside to work on these activities, they do exist in students' everyday routines. The difference, as mentioned, is that Zach requires direct and more intensive instruction in these areas whereas most of his peers may only need a reminder once in a while. In Zach's case, these functional parts of the school routine are not taken for granted, but are planned for and taught in systematic ways.

Typical school routines may not offer opportunities to teach all of the functional skills targeted for a particular student. In this case, it is a matter of working them into logical places in the schedule. For example, the third grade routine could be modified to accommodate several activities that are considered important for Zach—a snack time, classroom jobs, and walking to the neighborhood store to prac-

Table 1.   Using a common framework to understand Zach's needs

Educational outcomes and emphases for Zach	A summary of Zach's IEP goals
To read, write, listen, speak, and use math -- To use scientific principles and methods[a] To become knowledgeable and appreciative of people and society, other cultures, history[a] To think creatively and critically[a] --	*Reading*—listening to a story; interpreting pictures and words in language experience stories and everyday routines *Writing*—keeping a picture journal; marking his name on papers *Listening*—listening to announcements, directions; following cues in environment; understanding basic requests and comments *Speaking*—using line drawings paired with speech to make requests, comment, answer, greet, and express feelings; indicating preferences *Math*—handling money for purchases; counting in a meaningful context
To achieve physical well-being	*Physical education and motor development*—performing exercise routines; engaging in individual and team games and sports; climbing stairs (alternating feet); refining pincer grasp; gaining accuracy in pointing; becoming more adept in manipulating objects; using fork for cutting and eating; opening milk carton
To express oneself artistically	*Art and music*—gaining experience with various art media; further developing skills in drawing; moving rhythmically to music; playing the keyboard
To show awareness of and preparation for community participation, career possibilities, domestic responsibilities, and constructive use of free time	*Self-management, school jobs, and leisure*—checking and correcting appearance; dressing and undressing (outerwear) and using locker; following the cafeteria routine; purchasing snack items in grocery store; traveling to locations in the school and surrounding community (crossing streets safely); managing belongings; performing a classroom or school job; engaging in individual and small group leisure activities

(*continued*)

Table 1. (*continued*)

Educational outcomes and emphases for Zach	A summary of Zach's IEP goals
To have a positive attitude toward self and learning To show concern and respect for others To work cooperatively	*Social*—developing close relationships with several peers; watching and imitating positive actions of peers; following classroom rules and routines; participating in partner and group activities

[a]The fact that a student's IEP does not emphasize these particular outcomes does not mean that a student would be excluded from class activities related to these outcomes. For example, Zach participates in science and social studies lessons that are project based and allow him to work on communication skills, working cooperatively, and grasping and handling materials.

tice street crossing and to purchase familiar items. Some of Zach's classmates will participate in these activities, but not with the same goals or the degree of frequency as Zach.

Figure 1 provides an example of a "Routine Chart" that shows how Zach's curriculum needs are being addressed within one common structure. Similar charts could be designed for the middle and high school classes beginning with the parts of the routines that students have in common (even if the instructional intensity varies), and then gradually building in those components that are unique.

OFFERING A CURRICULUM RICH IN MEANING

Curriculum reform is underway in districts throughout the country. Many districts are heeding the advice of Jeanie Oakes and Martin Lipton (1990), among others, who have called for a curriculum rich in meaning:

> We refer to a curriculum that helps all children make sense of their experiences as a curriculum rich in meaning. That is our shorthand expression for lessons that are concept- and theme-based and much more. This curriculum emphasizes knowledge worth taking time to probe and explore—perhaps a week, a month, or longer. (p. 82)

Oakes and Lipton (1990) contrast a rich, experiential approach with "traditional curriculum hallmarks" (p. 84). First among these hallmarks is the drive to keep the curriculum standardized, sequential, and measurable. In doing so, we confine our measures, and hence many of our practices, to the "smallest possible teachable and testable units" (p. 84). This approach teaches students that the details and basic facts are of primary importance and the larger, more significant

Classroom activities and routines	Zach's activities and routines
8:10 A.M. Entering school/locating classroom	8:10 A.M. Entering school/locating classroom
8:15 A.M. Using bathroom/lockers	8:15 A.M. Using bathroom/lockers— This routine will require more instructional time for Zach. Fifteen minutes will be devoted to this routine, then he will join his classmates for "Journal Writing."
8:20 A.M. Getting organized/ announcements	
8:30 A.M. Writing journals	8:30 A.M. Writing journals— Zach keeps a picture journal. A key event in his day is depicted with a picture that the teacher (peer or assistant) helps him cut out. He glues it in his journal and is encouraged to say a few words about it. These words are written in the journal for him to copy and read.
8:50 A.M. Journal sharing/class meeting	8:50 A.M. Journal sharing/class meeting— Like his classmates, Zach takes his turn "reading" an entry from his journal (i.e., holding up the picture and pointing to the words read by his partner).
9:30 A.M. Reading groups Group 1—teacher-directed Group 2—reading partners	9:30 A.M. Getting organized for the day— This is when Zach will empty the contents of his knapsack, organize his belongings (e.g., lunch money, notes from home), and set up his daily schedule cards.

(continued)

Figure 1. A "routine chart" depicting Zach's involvement in his third grade class.

Classroom activities and routines	Zach's activities and routines
	10:00 A.M. Break— Zach prepares a simple snack (e.g., crackers with peanut butter). At 10:10 A.M. he joins his classmates for a break. Many of them bring a snack.
10:10 A.M. Break	
10:15 A.M. Reading groups (continued) Group 1—reading partners Group 2—teacher-directed	10:15 A.M. Reading partner and library— Zach has a different reading partner for each day. He and his partner go to the school library and select a book to read. They return to the classroom and read their books to each other. (Zach is learning to listen, follow along, point out pictures, and turn the pages.)
11:00 A.M. Lunch and recess	11:00 A.M. Lunch and recess— Zach sits with his classmates. He also receives some support from an assistant.
11:50 A.M. Getting organized	11:50 A.M. Getting organized
12:00 P.M. Monday—Thursday: Math Friday: Science/social studies (project-based instruction)	12:00 P.M. Monday—Thursday: Buying program Friday: Science/social studies (project-based)— Mondays through Thursdays Zach participates in the "Buying Program." Students in this class have a chance to buy school supplies and go to the neighborhood store to purchase items for snack time. Zach always receives instruction in the "Buying Pro-

(continued)

Figure 1. *(continued)*

Classroom activities and routines	Zach's activities and routines
	gram." Other students rotate based on a predetermined schedule. Tuesdays and Thursdays are the days that Zach (and one or two other students) go to a neighborhood grocery store.
1:30 P.M. "Specials" (Monday and Wednesday: Physical education; Tuesday: Art; Thursday: Music)	1:30 P.M. "Specials" (Monday and Wednesday: Physical education; Tuesday: Art; Thursday: Music)— Zach fully participates in these sessions. The activities are adapted on an "as needed" basis
2:15 P.M. Current events/sharing	2:15 P.M. Class meeting/current events— Zach joins his classmates for this last activity. He listens, comments (nonverbally), and observes during this time. Sometimes he leaves the group early to begin to gather his belongings for home.
2:40 P.M. Dismissal	2:40 P.M. Dismissal

concepts are secondary. In another, related, hallmark, Oakes and Lipton discuss how the traditional curriculum favors learning about something rather than learning to do it. The experience of learning is lost in much of what is taught. For example, the desire to convey one's ideas in writing may be lost to the overemphasis on discrete lessons of spelling, correct punctuation, and proper grammar. Math, as illustrated in a previous example, can be perceived as a set of formulas and rules with little or no attempt on the part of the learner to relate his or her answer to his or her life.

Many schools are gradually incorporating curricular approaches that offer a more experiential, personalized learning experience to students. The increasing use of methods such as whole language instruction, hands-on activities, cooperative learning, and thematic instruction make it possible to accommodate a much wider range of learners while providing a richer experience for all children.

Whole Language

There is a rapidly increasing interest in using a whole language approach to instruction, particularly in the elementary grades. In this approach, the story, the literature, and the written expression are central to the lesson. Reading, writing, speaking, and listening are not taught in isolated lessons as discrete sets of skills, but are viewed as interconnected and taught as natural parts of every lesson. This approach is child-centered and seeks to take advantage of individual interests and needs. Students involved in whole language instruction actually write (as opposed to *practicing* writing) and read literature (as opposed to using basal readers).

Microsociety

Since 1981, the City Magnet School in Lowell, Massachusetts, has been operating as a *microsociety*—making schoolwork resemble the real world (Corbo, 1990). The goal is to give students an early and accurate sense of the real world by teaching how institutions work through participation, thus empowering students for active roles as adults.

Students attend classes (grades kindergarten through eight) for 4 hours a day. Then, every afternoon, students run their own society with faculty guidance. In this society, each student has a job, earns money, and pays tuition and taxes. The "micro," as it is referred to, has its own government (legislature), judicial system, banks and currency, and businesses. As workers in the micro, student legislators adopt budgets, levy taxes, and enact laws. Student lawyers, judges, and jury members hear their peers' cases related to discipline and other problems, determine guilt or innocence, and decide on consequences. Business workers manufacture and market products including buttons, posters, and crafts, as well as do their own accounting—keeping ledgers of expenditures and profits. In the "newsroom," student workers write, edit, lay out, produce, and market newspapers, magazines, and a yearbook. Bank employees handle student and teacher deposits and loans in the micro currency, paying or charging their customers interest. Lessons taught during classroom time in the morning are related to students' experiences in "micro." In addition to learning and applying academic skills in situations that closely approximate real life, supporters note that students also acquire a range of "people" skills such as negotiation, communication, and problem solving.

Cooperative Approaches

Cooperative learning approaches are gaining increased popularity as schools look toward increasing students' achievement as well as social skills. Cooperative learning teaches children how to work with each other in order to achieve common goals. These methods greatly increase the ease of including students with diverse characteristics as active learners in the class. Given the characteristics of cooperative approaches (small group structures, face-to-face interaction, assigned roles, emphasis on pro-social skills as well as individual accountability), teachers can structure roles to suit individual abilities (Johnson, Johnson, Holubec, & Roy, 1984). Materials can also be adapted to better include children. Individualized goals can be addressed within the cooperative group structure—even for students with very extensive needs.

Thematic and Project-Based Approaches

The terms *thematic* and *project-based* are sometimes used to describe learning activities that emphasize the application of children's emerging skills in "informal and open-ended activities which are intended to improve their understanding of the world they live in" (Katz & Chard, 1989, p. xii). Projects are indepth studies of topics of interest to children and young adults. Investigation of topics may continue for days or weeks depending on the student's age and other factors. Projects can be undertaken by the entire class, small groups within the class, or individuals. These approaches hold great promise because they can be directly related to children's lives, experiences, and interests; thereby lessening the refrain so often heard in the corridors of our schools that school is "boring."

Similar to cooperative learning, projects can be structured so that children with various characteristics may make a contribution to the group effort. Project activities may include investigation (use of library and other sources of information), management (running the school store), construction activities, and dramatic play. Since students are "doing" as opposed to solely talking and reading, the opportunities for an individual with special needs to be actively involved are greatly increased.

Such approaches are more accommodating than the traditional practices of lectures, seatwork, and textbook-based instruction. When the curriculum content is organized around the larger, more meaningful activity, students can be challenged at different levels.

Many teachers in schools and classrooms working on greater inclusion have already begun to incorporate some of these practices into their classrooms. It is a matter of continuing to build upon the steps that have already been taken to provide a richer, more personalized approach to learning.

MEASURING OUTCOMES THAT ARE
INDIVIDUALIZED AND PERFORMANCE-BASED

The method schools use to measure educational outcomes has a profound impact on the curriculum—what teachers teach and what students learn. The overreliance on standardized achievement tests as the primary measure of student, teacher, and district outcomes has been under criticism for quite some time. One of the primary criticisms is that standardized tests are inadequate measures of many, if not most, of the outcomes people value.

> They tell us something about a child's neatness, facility for guessing and ability to work well under a time limit. [But] the tests tell us little about a child's ability to learn, to analyze or to reason—and nothing of the child's judgement, originality, imagination, or creativity. (Henry, as cited in Hall, 1990, p. 7)

Other concerns include increasing the amount of instructional time used to teach "test-taking" skills, and the fact that content not addressed by standardized tests is often de-emphasized. Counter trends are emerging that emphasize a shift from standardized tests to alternative forms of assessment that would measure student performance (Hall, 1990). This is especially promising for teachers who are beginning to make a greater investment in experiential learning, but have had to use traditional testing measures that are not consistent with this approach.

Performance Tests and Portfolios

"If tests could be composed of tasks that we valued . . . then the very act of preparing for the test would be educationally sound" (Grant Wiggins, as cited in Corbo, 1990). "Performance tests" are one alternative method of assessment that fit Wiggins's criteria. These are designed to measure student performance on a series of tasks that may take several weeks or months to complete. "Students may work as individuals or in groups to frame problems, collect data, and analyze and report their results. The final product may be shared through exhibitions, portfolios, or a written report" (Berla, Henderson, & Kerewsky, 1989, p. 75).

California's statewide assessment effort is based on the belief that students need to be taught in ways that enable them "to do things in the real world" (Susan Bennett as cited in Corbo, 1990). One part of this goal is using assessment methods that support this kind of instruction. Performance tests in science were piloted in 1,000 sixth grade classrooms where students (some working in teams) conducted experiments to answer open-ended questions by interpreting real data and applying scientific principles. Performance tests in social studies were also given to groups of California high school students.

Another strategy that is being implemented in California, Vermont, and other areas is the use of portfolios. Vermont, for example, has just begun a pilot program in approximately 135 schools to use portfolios, in addition to standardized tests, to measure students' abilities in mathematics and writing (Rothman, 1990). The portfolios will include material collected during the course of the year (e.g., a poem, play, or personal narration; a personal response to an issue or event; a solution to a problem assigned as homework; a problem made up by the student; perhaps even a videotape of a problem-solving activity). This material is then evaluated according to a set of criteria that should provide a broader picture of the student's ability than that measured by conventional tests.

Although performance-based measures and portfolio systems are offered as alternatives or supplements to the annual standardized achievement tests, they can also serve as valuable periodic checks on student performance. Together, students and teachers can review portfolios and determine which areas of development to emphasize during the next quarter. These, along with other ongoing measures (e.g., pretests and posttests, individualized checklists, comments on papers, daily informal feedback) would provide the information necessary to ensure continuous progress.

The following is an example of the use of a portfolio:

> Ms. B. and Mr. L. are team teaching a third grade class of students with diverse needs. They have decided to compile portfolios for all of their students. Emily, who was formerly served in a resource room program, might have several writing samples in her portfolio by December. Each sample is dated and has a brief description of the activity (including questions the teacher asked to prompt her). The samples range from one sentence of five words to one story that has four sentences. Each story is accompanied by a picture Emily drew. Words with inventive spellings are translated in parentheses by the teacher to communicate what Emily read aloud. Also included is a list of books that Emily has read and a copy of two passages that were used as an informal reading inventory at the end of the first 10 weeks. These passages are coded as a way of assessing reading strengths and difficulties.
>
> Zachary is the third grader who transferred to Harrison Elementary School from a special segregated school. Like Emily, his portfolio would include samples of his work based on individual goals and participation such as dated copies of picture symbols he uses (e.g., his daily schedule, symbols of menu items in the school cafeteria, symbols for places in the school) and descriptions of how and when he uses them. There would also be dated copies of two

sample stories (with pictures) that Zachary listened to and responded to questions about. His responses are recorded (and described) for each question (e.g., "Where did the children go?" Zachary pointed to the picture of the house.).

Ms. B. and Mr. L. may worry about the amount of time that portfolio systems will require (compiling them, individualizing them, meeting about them). The time spent on this activity, however, must be seen in terms of its full instructional value. Students are actively involved in developing their portfolios—they help to evaluate and choose the "best pieces." By doing so they learn how to set their own standards and evaluate their own work, and they are much more likely to assume responsibility for their learning (Rothman, 1990). Developing a sense of responsibility and becoming a self-directed learner are educational outcomes well worth the expenditure of time.

Individualizing the Measures

Teachers generally experience considerable difficulty when it comes to evaluating and grading their students. This difficulty is likely to become even more pronounced when the range of diverse learners in the class widens as a result of including all students. The situation depicted below is one that many teachers will recognize:

> A class recently completed a 3-week science unit on the solar system. At the beginning of the unit each student took a pretest. Katie, a previously excluded student, had only two correct responses on the pretest, while one of her classmates, Elliott, had 16 of the 20 items correct. Throughout the unit's projects and activities, Katie was an enthusiastic learner. She clearly enjoyed the topic, sharing the new facts and vocabulary she was learning with her family and writing about it in her journal.
>
> When the posttest was given at the end of the unit, Katie answered 13 of the 20 items correctly. Her classmate Elliott had 18 of the 20 items correct this time.

How should these two students be graded? In many classes, Elliott would receive an "A" for scoring 90% and Katie a "D" for her 65%. However, one could certainly argue that Katie's score is the more impressive of the two. She achieved much more than was expected; from 10% on the pretest to 65% on the posttest, and she was enthusiastic about the material. How do we justify giving her a "D"? Then again, would it be appropriate to give her an "A"? After all, many of her classmates scored much higher than she. Isn't it misleading for her to receive the same grade without achieving the same results?

This example raises important questions about our willingness to evaluate students according to individual rather than normative methods. The use of normative methods, curved grades, or universal grading criteria for all students emphasizes a narrow focus on academic outcomes, and encourages student judgments about some class members' "superiority" (and of course, others' "inferiority"). Normative assessment will always negatively affect some students' self-images and attitudes toward school by setting them up for failure. These methods may also send false messages to so-called "bright" students who receive high scores, but are in fact inadequately challenged. Normative methods can also reduce teacher expectations for some students and lead to inequitable practices such as "tracking."

Yet, without schoolwide or districtwide policies empowering teachers to change grading practices, many will be hesitant or unable to do so. Some flexibility does exist for students with IEPs. These students should be evaluated on the basis of individualized learning objectives and criteria. Thus, if grades are to be given they should reflect the student's ability to meet individualized goals, not classroom norms. In this case, a student such as Katie might receive an "A" on her report card in science with the understanding that it reflects her IEP goals.

ACKNOWLEDGING THE POWER OF THE "IMPLICIT" CURRICULUM

Learning, for any student, is never limited to only those items designated on an IEP or in a curriculum guide. What a teacher explicitly "plans" to teach is only part of what a student experiences during the school day. School staff create climates in their classrooms and throughout their schools. These climates have a powerful influence on children's educations, determining a significant part of "what" they learn. These climates can make the difference between students learning to:

Trust themselves and one another—or be fearful and suspicious.
Deal with problems through communication—or be silent, avoidant, or aggressive.
Support one another—or strive to outdo one another.
Respect one another—or ridicule and ostracize one another.
Consider the perspective of others—or view their own perspective as the only one with legitimacy.
Direct their own learning—or become dependent on those "in authority" for motivation and discipline.

This climate is reflected, for example, in the classroom that only acknowledges the accomplishments of the students with the highest achievement levels, or the classroom where children previously excluded spend most of the day in the back of the room with a teaching assistant—at a table never used by other children. Then, there is the classroom where teasing is ignored by adults "since that's the way kids are," or the classroom where children spend significant parts of their day trying to outdo each other (e.g., math contests, spelling bees). What lessons, however unintended, are these children learning about themselves? It is likely that some children are learning that they are unimportant because of their learning characteristics, that they need to be separated from their classmates, that they are (and always will be) "losers."

Conversely, teachers can consciously create classroom activities that provide opportunities for students to develop characteristics such as a strong sense of self-worth, concern and respect for others, an ability to work interdependently, and other outcomes that have to do with personal development and responsible citizenship. These teachers and their students create and experience a sense of "community" in their classrooms.

> To build a sense of community is to create a group that extends to others the respect one has for oneself. . . . to come to know one another as individuals, to respect and care about one another, and to feel a sense of membership in and accountability to the group. (Lickona, 1988, p. 421)

To attain this sense of community, conscious efforts are made to ensure that students feel safe (both physically and psychologically). Students are actively taught to work in cooperation with each other —to be concerned with each other's success. They learn that they do not have to measure themselves against each other to feel a sense of accomplishment. Students are affirmed for who they are as well as what they accomplish. In addition, they are given a voice in decision making—learning to consider the needs of the class as well as their own preferences. The discussion in this section is based upon a framework developed by the Boston Area Educators for Social Responsibility (1984).

Creating Classrooms that Are "Safe" Places

When students feel "safe" in their classrooms, they do not have to invest energy in being concerned about their physical well-being and personal property. Class members learn to assist each other and share their resources, rather than focusing on defending themselves and protecting their belongings.

Psychologically, feeling safe means that students believe they "belong" and that they can express themselves freely. In these safe settings, children and young adults learn to take risks and to try, rather than avoid, challenges or new situations due to fear of failure or ridicule. They learn that mistakes are a "natural" part of the learning process. Creating a safe environment will enhance the success of all students and will be particularly important if we seek the successful involvement of students with diverse needs as members of regular classes. For example:

Jason is a member of Mr. Owens's social studies class at Mill Valley Middle School. The course content focuses on American history and current events. Mr. Owens has been concerned with de-emphasizing the pursuit of "right" and "wrong" answers for questions where many ideas or perspectives have validity. One strategy he uses in class is to have students work in small groups and use a structured problem-solving process to discuss issues related to course content.

The first step in this process is for group members to generate at least five possible ideas for a given challenge or problem. No evaluation is allowed on any ideas at this stage and all contributions are recorded. Students are expected to focus on encouraging participation and rewarding each other for contributions.

The second step is for the group to choose three ideas from their list that seem to best address the problem. The group must justify why each one was chosen and how these ideas could lead to resolving the problem.

The brainstorming allows students to think and contribute ideas freely. It also provides practice in responding respectfully to different ideas. This structure has been appropriate for Jason who participates enthusiastically, but sometimes suggests ideas or answers that seem "way out" or not fully developed. His participation is encouraged. Among other things, Jason is learning to solve problems with others and express his ideas with less fear of humiliation. His groupmates are learning similar skills, in addition to respecting each member's contribution, and listening and asking clarifying questions if a person has difficulty with communication.

Another aspect of a safe learning environment is the "openness" with which students are encouraged to discuss what is troubling them:

Some members of Felicia's drama class are upset because Felicia tends to make repetitive sounds during the teacher's instructions. Mr. Thomas has noticed that several students are starting to make sarcastic comments about her. They also seem to be talking to her less. Rather than avoiding this problem, Mr. Thomas has pulled the group aside and asked them to talk about what is bothering them. He has created a climate where students understand that it is okay to express themselves. He welcomes their ideas as to how they might help Felicia learn when it is okay to be loud and when it isn't. Mr. Thomas pointed out that she seems to like being with them.

Since Felicia arrives at class just as the bell rings, little time is available for interaction. Some of the students offered to meet Felicia in her homeroom and accompany her to class. Three of the students also decided that they should sit next to her and remind her to listen by touching her arm and gesturing if she begins to make loud sounds.

Felicia is learning what the expectations for behavior are in this environment, and her classmates are learning that there are alternatives to anger and ostracism when they are having problems with a classmate. They are learning that they can be part of a solution. They are also learning that the teacher is open to their concerns and will not dismiss them. He is creating a climate where talking about problems is okay.

In a closed atmosphere where conflicts are ignored or punished, students learn that their opinions and feelings have little value. In an open atmosphere, students learn that their concerns are worthy of respect and that they can work together to solve problems.

Working Cooperatively with Others

True communities are characterized by a spirit of cooperation. Students learn how to set and pursue goals with classmates, how to assist peers and receive assistance from them, and how to use interpersonal skills such as listening, negotiating, and sharing. Children learn that each member of the class can make a contribution to the group effort.

Making the transition from a competitive to a cooperative environment is critical to building a sense of community in the classroom; however, it is not an easy task. Most of us—adults and children—have been socialized into competitive ways of thinking and acting.

Structuring activities in a competitive manner is extremely tempting for teachers. Children do become excited about contests and competitive games. It is important to be aware in this situation that the child is not excited about math or social studies, but about the prospect of *beating* her or his classmate. There are ways to achieve excitement and interest that arise directly from the learning experience.

Ms. B. and Mr. L., for example, are making a gradual shift in the way they structure activities in their third grade classroom. Their schedule includes a math contest every Friday. They divide the class into two teams; one member of each team goes to the board and the teacher poses a problem. The first student to write the answer correctly wins a point for their team. During their discussion of how to involve students with diverse needs (which was proving to be a challenge), they uncovered some general discontent with the activity.

They were pleased because teams studied together before the contest, and they seldom heard complaints about Friday's math class being "boring." Yet, they were uneasy with the level of competition this activity inspired. Since the focus was on "winning," students became very upset at individual team members when they made a mistake or performed slowly. One fight in the hall was traced back to a student who was called a "dummy" after the contest. It was also a challenge to incorporate the students who did not perform on "grade level."

They began to consider how they could meet similar objectives using a cooperative structure. The students were interested in games and having fun, so they began to list ways to incorporate cooperative games to help students learn the math skills. The class was divided into five groups and each group could pick a cooperative game; each game has a "group challenge." For example, one group's activity involved memorizing multiplication facts. A packet of cards was distributed to each member and the group's challenge was to try to use up all of the cards by putting together those that would result in the products 12, 36, and 48. Each member of the group needed to be involved in order to achieve the goal of using all of the cards.

It is important to note that teachers who are building cooperative classrooms diligently strive for each child to achieve at the highest possible level, but the tone and approach are different. Students learn that they do not have to measure themselves against each other to do well.

Affirming Each Student's Identity

To affirm students means to validate them for *who* they are—individuals and valued members of the classroom community. "They are validated not only for the qualities they have in common, but also for their uniqueness" (Boston Area Educators for Social Responsibility, 1984, p. 12). Attention and displays are not limited to the most outstanding work—all students are consciously and continuously affirmed for their efforts and contributions. As a result, students learn that each member's participation is important. Class members learn to "appreciate all levels of performance and to accept different kinds of contributions as significant" (Boston Area Educators for Social Responsibility, 1984, p. 13).

> Ms. L., a middle school English teacher, has been very successful in addressing the diverse educational needs of the range of students in her classroom. She has developed a climate that is very affirming. That is, she begins with the attitude that each student has unique qualities and positive characteristics and can make a contribution. She allows no put-downs in her class, and has discussed the issues of put-downs with the students. Ms. L. has begun to incorporate community-building exercises into her class. Students are given structured opportunities to play cooperative games and develop role plays related to the topics they are studying.
>
> They have a class meeting each Friday for 15 minutes. The agenda changes from week to week. One week they chose to talk about the pressure they may feel to act "tough." Another week the

focus was on becoming at ease with talking about qualities they like or admire in one another. Since several of the students who are new to regular classes had sometimes been the target of put-downs, they are able to relax and contribute in this class. The bonds that have been established have extended beyond English class.

Students learn self-respect by experiencing affirmation of their individuality. Frequent opportunities to acknowledge and celebrate differences teach children to get to know each other as *individuals* rather than relying on negative or limiting stereotypes. Children learn to place importance on characteristics beyond the superficial. They can learn to appreciate each other's positive attributes such as humor, helpfulness, and friendliness rather than what classmates wear or own, or their physical features.

Having a Voice in Decision Making

As educators pursue community-building, they seek opportunities to teach students how to be thoughtful decision makers. Giving students a voice in decision making is active preparation for democracy. "We teach reading, writing, and math by doing them, but we teach democracy by lecture" (Berman, 1990, p. 2). By using a "doing" approach, students learn to share roles and responsibilities to ensure that the class functions well. Class members learn that their actions, both individually and collectively, can have an influence on their environment.

Each homeroom at Mill Valley Middle School picks one school or community improvement project that it will address throughout the school year. This is done in a democratic fashion. Students develop the rules that will prevail during the homeroom period as well as during their project. As active members of the school community, they are encouraged to look for ways to contribute to and improve this community. The students in one eighth grade homeroom were concerned with drug use. They decided to gather information to share with younger students.

In cooperative small groups, students began to investigate the drug issue. They developed a plan to teach others about the effects and dangers of using drugs. After one month of preparation, pairs of eighth graders were matched with third graders (Mill Valley Elementary School is located on the same campus). Once a week during homeroom, they tutored the third graders on the issue.

Several eighth graders who had previously been in special classes are now members of the participating homeroom. Each contributed to the project by helping their partners gather resources and share them with the younger students.

Projects such as this can help all students develop a sense of social responsibility. Students learn that there are answers to many problems and that there are ways to work toward solutions (Berman,

1990). They learn to take the perspective of others and develop a sense of empowerment in addressing problems.

Classroom activities such as those described throughout this section can help students learn to be comfortable with human differences and to accept a range of people into their current and future lives as friends, neighbors, and co-workers. Careful attention to the features of the classroom environment will be important regardless of whether there are class members who have diverse needs and characteristics (e.g., cultural, physical, intellectual, emotional); however, it becomes critical with the presence of these students. Yet, it is important to note that building a sense of community is not an "add-on" to what busy teachers are expected to do. Teachers *do* create a classroom environment—it is a matter of how consciously they build in the positive features that result in "community." The informal lessons that students learn from the classroom environment may be as influential in their development as any "formal" lessons drawn from the curriculum guide.

CONCLUSION

How will teachers "make sense" of the curriculum provided to their diverse groups of learners? It is suggested in this chapter that they will find themselves placing an increased emphasis on helping all students to attain outcomes such as developing a positive attitude toward self and others, working cooperatively, and showing respect and concern for others. Attention to these broad outcomes of education is likely to have positive effects on outcomes that we have traditionally valued, including academic and process skills. Teachers may also find more ways to incorporate the functional goals of some students into a common planning framework so that they don't seem so distinct from the needs of other students in the class. These teachers, who already have some rich and meaningful ways to teach the curriculum, will probably see the need to incorporate more of these strategies in their daily schedules. They will also be more at ease with individualizing their measurement systems. Finally, teachers will become increasingly aware of the role of the classroom climate in the creation of powerful learning experiences for and with students.

REFERENCES

Adler, J. (1990, Fall/Winter). Creating problems. *Newsweek* (Special Edition-Education: A Consumer's Handbook), pp. 16–22.
Berla, N., Henderson, A.T., & Kerewsky, W. (1989). *The middle school years: A parents' handbook.* Columbia, MD: National Committee for Citizens in Education.

Berman, S. (1990). The real ropes course: The development of social consciousness. *Educators for Social Responsibility Journal, 1,* 1–18.

Boston Area Educators for Social Responsibility. (1984). *Taking part: An elementary curriculum in the participation series.* Cambridge, MA: Author.

Chandler, R., Werb, S., & Freedman, G. (Producers). (1990). *Learning in America: Schools that work.* New York: MacNeil/Lehrer Productions.

Corbo, D. (Producer). (1990). *America's toughest assignment: Solving the education crisis.* New York: CBS News.

Goodlad, J. (1984). *A place called school: Prospects for the future.* New York: McGraw-Hill.

Hall, S. (1990). High scores vs. high achievement: Concern about testing in America's school improvement movement. *NETWORK for Public Schools, 16*(1), 1–9.

Johnson, D.W., Johnson, R., Holubec, E., & Roy, P. (1984). *Circles of learning.* Alexandria, VA: The Association for Supervision and Curriculum Development.

Katz, L.G., & Chard, S.C. (1989). *Engaging children's minds: The project approach.* Norwood, NJ: Ablex Publishing.

Lickona, T. (1988, February). Four strategies for fostering character development in children. *Phi Delta Kappan, 69* (6), 419–423.

Oakes, J., & Lipton, M. (1990). *Making the best of schools: A handbook for parents, teachers and policy makers.* New Haven, CT: Yale University Press.

Rothman, R. (1990, October 10). Large 'faculty meeting' ushers in pioneering assessment in Vermont. *Education Week,* 1,18.

Staff. (1990, October 7). Quotation by Superintendent Peterkin regarding the Milwaukee Public Schools. *Milwaukee Journal.*

II

Curriculum Adaptation and Delivery

4

Using Curriculum To Build Inclusive Classrooms

William Stainback,
Susan Stainback,
and Jeanette Moravec

We do not have to choose between socialization and friendships in regular classes and a quality education in segregated special classes. We can provide a quality education in regular classes. (Strully, in Stainback, Stainback, & Forest, 1989, p. 77)

GROWING NUMBERS OF previously excluded students are being integrated into the mainstream of general education (Berrigan, 1988, 1989; Biklen, 1988; *Discover the Possibilities*, 1988; Forest, 1987; Porter, 1988; Stainback & Stainback, 1988, in press; Stainback, Stainback, & Forest, 1989; Strully, 1986; Villa & Thousand, 1988; York & Vandercook, 1989). However, these students need more than mere placement in the mainstream. They also need to be *included* as an equal and valued member of the classroom. In recent years, there has been considerable emphasis on how to include all students in the social life of the classroom (see Stainback & Stainback, 1990), but significantly less attention has been given to how all students might be involved in actively learning what is important to them in inclusive classrooms.

Portions of this chapter are based on an article by Stainback, W., Stainback, S., & Stefanich, G. (in press). Learning together in inclusive classrooms. *TEACHING Exceptional Children.* Used with permission of the Council for Exceptional Children.

The authors' purpose in this chapter is to suggest some strategies that general educators, in collaboration with support facilitators and other specialists, can use to make classroom curricula an asset to the inclusion process. The strategies presented are based on a review of the professional literature and research regarding curriculum in education (e.g., Bangert, Kulik, & Kulik, 1988; Cox & Kelly, 1989; Doll, 1986; Falvey, 1989; Glatthorn, 1987; Miller, 1983; Pallas, Natriello, & McDill, 1989; Smith, 1986) and the authors' experiences working in general education classes.

BACKGROUND

Curriculum in Perspective

When discussing what students should learn, care must be exercised not to overemphasize predefined curriculum concerns. Although learning math, history, geography, daily life (e.g., dressing, cooking), and vocational skills are all important, these are not the only or necessarily the primary goals for students. Strully and Strully (1985) clearly stated this point:

> Our daughter, Shawntell, is not going to one day wake up with all the competencies and skills that she needs in order to live independently. The reality is that we have been working on teaching Shawntell to use the bathroom for the last nine years. At this point in time, Shawntell is approximately 58% toilet trained. This is a significant increase in her accuracy, but Shawntell may never achieve complete success. The same is true for lots of other areas such as eating independently, walking, and communicating. Though Shawntell has learned important things and will continue to do so, the issue that we face is, will the skills our daughter has learned keep her in the community? The answer, we are afraid, is no!
>
> Yet imagine if you will, that she did achieve all these competencies, would that make everything perfect? Again, the answer is no! One's ability to know things or master skills is not a litmus test of the person's capability to be an active member of the community and to have friends. What matters, we believe, is trying to be the best person you can and having people accept you for who you are, with all of your strengths and weaknesses. If we can accept people for who they are and not for who we want them to be, our communities will have moved a considerable distance. In the final analysis, whether or not Shawntell obtains all the competencies and skills in the world, it really isn't that significant. What is important is being cared about by another human being. If Shawntell is really going to be an integral member of her community, she will need to rely on her friends who want to be involved with her because they are her friends. (pp. 7–8)

As is evident in this statement, socialization and friendships are among the major educational goals to enable students to become active members of the community. When adults focus on and foster buddy systems, circles of friends, and other friendship facilitation activities, children start to gain what will be most important to them in their lives—a range of people who genuinely care about them as individuals. Thus, if a child never learns any math, history, or other subject, it is still critical that he or she be included so that all students can learn about mutual respect, caring, and support in an integrated society.

This focus on friendship does not mean, however, that teachers and administrators should not be concerned about fostering curricular goals in daily life, and academic or vocational skills for all students. It is important that all students learn as much as possible in these areas. Yet, specific curricular goal achievement is not always the only, or even the major, concern to ensure success and happiness in life.

The authors have observed a number of classrooms and schools that have been successful and some that have been unsuccessful when a full inclusion policy was implemented. The successful ones tend to focus on students being secure, accepted, and friends of the teachers and students, while developing feelings of belonging, positive self-worth, and success. In some cases, the primary goal is for the student to be accepted by his or her peers and teachers while developing friendships and supportive relationships. The focus on predefined curricular goals for some students is not a priority until acceptance and friendship development is addressed, although major efforts are made to keep them actively involved with their peers in classroom activities. That is, these students are generally included in the activities of their peers even if the long-term benefits are not always clear. Being accepted, welcome, and secure in a learning setting with peers is considered prerequisite to the success of students in focused learning tasks. Gradually, as students become accepted, ways are worked out for them to be involved in classroom activities that address daily life, academic, and vocational objectives.

In contrast, the classrooms and schools that are unsuccessful with full inclusion tend to focus almost exclusively on assessing previously excluded students' competencies in daily life, academic and vocational skills, and designing specific curricular objectives and activities for students (regardless of what a particular student is interested in or is secure doing). They also put too little emphasis on relationships, acceptance, and friendships. This is not to imply that previously excluded students should initially focus only on socialization in an inclusive classroom. From the first day, all students should be involved in interesting and worthwhile learning activities, and be included as much as possible with their classmates in ways they can be successful. Only concentrating on isolated, boring, or frustrating activities can lead to any child's dislike of the setting, disruption, and initial rejection by peers and educators.

The focus should be on friendships. As friendships are developed, numerous opportunities for meaningful learning will begin to emerge. It is through socialization with a diversity of peers in mainstream settings that children may learn, find meaning and purpose, and gain a greater understanding of many of the subject areas covered in school. Perhaps more important, the socialization process, if properly organized, can provide opportunities for students to get to know, respect, care about, and support each other, as well as learn academic, daily life, social, and other critical skills (e.g., sharing, communicating, initiating, responding, making choices, acting appropriately). That is, we all learn many of the critical and practical communication and social skills needed to live happy, productive lives through a socialization process with peers (Johnson & Johnson, 1987). Students do not just learn from teacher–student interactions, it is clear that much of what is learned in school is through student–student interactions. Therefore, while involving students in the process of learning specific curricular objectives, it is important to keep socialization activities in perspective with regard to the overall educational experience.

In summary, teachers, specialists, and classmates can and should focus on helping students become involved as much as possible in subject areas such as history, math, and daily life and vocational skills. In school, all children should learn as much as they can and grow toward independence as well as interdependence with others. Students also should be actively engaged from the first day of class in doing something academic or vocational that is interesting and potentially beneficial to them. However, acceptance, belonging, caring, and friendships should be given priority. As friendships develop and grow, numerous opportunities for teaching and learning will emerge.

Basic Premises of Classroom Curriculum

In general, curriculum has long been perceived and implemented from a perspective that general education classrooms have a standardized set of curriculum requirements that every student must achieve to successfully complete the "grade." This is based on the assumption that there are predefinable bodies of knowledge or information that when achieved in sequence result in a successful postschool life (Poplin & Stone, in press). It is this type of sequenced information that has been used in many classrooms as "the curriculum."

It is often delivered through lectures from the teacher, reading the textbook, or completing worksheets to learn and practice the terms, concepts, and skills needed to understand the subject. For the most part, if a child cannot learn "the curriculum," he or she fails and in some cases is excluded from general education classrooms.

Fortunately for the inclusive school movement, this method is becoming increasingly disfavored among many progressive general educators (Smith, 1986). Some of the reasons are listed below:

1. There is a growing recognition that in a rapidly changing, complex, and dynamic society there is no longer (if there ever was) a single, discrete, stagnant body of information that can be provided to students that will result in a successful adult life (see Giangreco, chap. 14, this volume). Instead, a more productive approach is to teach students a learning process—a process that involves how to learn or become adept at discerning: 1) what is needed to adapt to and become proficient in a new situation, and 2) how and/or where to go about locating and accessing any needed information.

2. A standardized curriculum does not accommodate the inherent diversity in background experiences, learning speeds, styles, and interests of all students. This diversity exists not only among students who have been labeled retarded, at risk, or gifted/talented, but also among the "average" or "normal" group.

3. When the curriculum is predefined, educators start with the curriculum instead of the child. In recent years, there has been an emphasis on building the curriculum around the child's experiences, perceptions, and current knowledge while firmly keeping in mind what history and life experiences have shown people generally need to know to live happy and productive lives.

4. Standardized curriculum and delivery approaches have proven to be boring, uninteresting, and lacking in meaning or purposefulness for many students whether classified as having disabilities or as not having disabilities (Smith, 1986). A standardized curriculum often does not evolve from or relate to what is currently occurring in students' lives and the world around them.

5. The "standard curriculum" often disempowers those individuals directly involved in the learning process. That is, "the curriculum" is generally predefined by such individuals as consultants in state departments of education and curriculum specialists who compile, for example, basal readers, math and history textbooks, or national standardized examinations. The concerns of the teachers and students who use the materials often go unrec-

ognized, and their advice concerning the best way to learn the material remains untapped.

As a result of the shortcomings of a standardized, lockstep curriculum, greater attention to a more holistic, constructivistic perspective on learning is gaining attention and acceptance in general education. There are a number of common elements that tend to emerge in the holistic perspective, such as recognizing the student as the center of learning (Lipsky & Gartner, in press). It starts with the student and builds on his or her strengths (what the student already knows) to facilitate learning and success. There is little or no focus on remediating deficits and weaknesses—these are addressed or compensated for as children become excited about learning and engage in real-life, purposeful projects and activities.

A holistic or constructivistic perspective to curriculum recognizes that: 1) the content to be learned must take into account the dynamic nature of what is needed to successfully live and work in a community (the focus on learning how to learn), and 2) for information to be learned, used, and maintained it must be meaningful and make sense to the learner (the focus on considering the child's background of experiences, interest, and understanding). Within a holistic, constructivistic perspective, the teacher is viewed as a facilitator of students who become actively involved in the process of learning information that is meaningful and of interest to them, rather than the teacher being the dispenser of "the curriculum" (a predefined, discrete, unchanging set of facts and information) (Smith, 1986). The teacher may teach or share his or her knowledge or "tricks of the trade" with students through "mini-lessons" or by other means, but the focus is on facilitating students to become actively engaged in their own learning. The classroom is often filled with real-life, purposeful projects and activities. For example, reading and discussing interesting books and stories rather than learning fragmented, isolated reading skills (e.g., diphthongs) by completing worksheets. Keeping a diary or journal and writing letters, memos, stories, books, and editorials constitute other typical activities. There is little focus on practicing skills such as punctuation, capitalization, or noun-verb identification in isolated ways—these are learned in the context of writing activities. It should be noted, especially in regard to the purpose of this book, that a holistic, constructivistic perspective to learning encourages all children to read (or listen, discuss) stories or information of interest to them at their ability level, or write (or communicate in some other way) information that is meaningful and functional to them. It does not advocate a lockstep, standardized curriculum that all children must master at the same age and time regardless of their individual backgrounds, learning characteristics, interest, and experiences.

The underlying theory or philosophy of the holistic, constructivistic perspective leads one away from teaching isolated skills in isolated settings and toward children learning while engaged in purposeful, real-life projects and activities as they interact and cooperate with each other (see Smith, 1986, for the concept of learning clubs). An example of this shift in thinking is illustrated in an exchange between a junior high music teacher and a support facilitator as they collaborated to determine what a new seventh grade student who had been labeled nonverbal, autistic, and severely retarded might learn in the music class. In this particular classroom, the teacher engaged the children in listening to music, reading about the basics of music, learning to play various musical instruments, and composing their own musical pieces. That is, she facilitated them in becoming involved in real-life music projects and activities as much as possible. While there were some traditional lectures and textbook readings, the focus was on how the children could become actively involved in enjoying and engaging in purposeful music activities while learning more about music and how it is created.

The initial exchange between the teacher and support facilitator occurred as a result of the teacher's question, "What am I supposed to teach this student?" When the teacher was asked what she wanted the other children to learn, she answered that she wanted the children to learn to enjoy music and become familiar with the scale, notes, and symbols basic to music knowledge. When she was asked if everyone was required to master all the content to pass, initially the teacher said "yes," but then reconsidered her answer. She stated that students are expected to learn varying amounts, some students will enter the class with considerable knowledge and appreciation of music through their past experiences with music lessons, while other students will be totally unfamiliar with the material.

After further discussion, it was the consensus of the two educators that all students, including the new student labeled severely disabled, could be expected to achieve varying degrees of appreciation and involvement with music, and mastery of terms and concepts in the music class. However, it was agreed that mastery of the curriculum was not the ultimate objective of the class. Rather, the curriculum or content of music, as other curriculum areas (e.g., history, science), simply provides a vehicle for students to learn to better understand, appreciate, adapt to, and use to the best of their ability what is available in the world around them (in this case music) to live a positive, productive life as a member of their community. The teacher uses the curriculum to challenge every class member to achieve as much as possible. From a holistic, constructivistic perspective, all children simply engage in a process of learning as much as they can in a particular subject area; how much and exactly what they learn will depend upon their backgrounds, interests, and abilities. This perspective allows all students to gain from learning opportunities offered in classrooms rather than using the curriculum to define some students as successes and others as failures.

STRATEGIES

The following section includes strategies that might be helpful when using curriculum to foster the diverse abilities of class members in inclusive classrooms. Although some of the examples used in the strategies described are holistic, others are more traditional in an attempt to cover the range of teaching styles typically found in today's classrooms and schools. However, it now appears that more classrooms will move toward a holistic, constructivistic perspective in the near future. This will not only make learning more interesting and meaningful for all students, it will also make it easier for all students to actively participate in the curriculum activities of general education classrooms.

Flexible Learning Objectives

The diversity of students included in the mainstream makes educators take a critical look at what is being required of each student. Although the basic educational goals for all students may remain the same, the specific curricular learning objectives may be individualized in some instances to fit the unique needs, skills, interests, and abilities of students (Villa & Thousand, 1988). For example, a basic goal in a language arts class, such as preparing students to communicate effectively, can be appropriate for all students, but the specific learning objectives under the goal may not be the same for all students. For many students, an objective for a lesson may be to learn to write letters to friends. Yet, for other students a more appropriate objective might include dictating a letter into a tape recorder or expanding picture board vocabulary options to be able to communicate with friends.

When what is required of students is *not* considered on the basis of individual abilities, apathy toward schoolwork may result. Persistence is a by-product of success and when success is repeatedly out of reach of the student, he or she learns to stop trying (Seligman,

1975). Since this attribute of learned helplessness is exhibited by some students when a good match between learning objectives and student attributes does not exist, one single set of standardized objectives should not be used to meet the unique learning abilities of all students in inclusive classrooms. However, care must be exercised when considering individual abilities. Individual abilities can and should be considered in light of what is occurring within the classroom peer group. Developing separate or different objectives for one or a few students can lead to their isolation and/or segregation within the classroom. Activities that address the diverse abilities of students while maintaining a group context and/or having a number of class members address differing objectives at various times can help offset this potential problem.

An illustration of individualizing learning objectives occurred in a third grade science class. The need for choosing learning objectives that were appropriate to individual students resulted in the classroom teacher and the support facilitator teaming together to develop a plan. While the basic curricular goal of the third grade science unit called "Understanding the physical world around us—what is temperature?" was considered appropriate for all students, individual students had different skills and knowledge that required them to focus their energies on different learning objectives. Most of the students were learning to use Fahrenheit and Celsius temperature scales, while a few others were working with molecular movement at different temperatures. One student was learning to recognize and use hot and cold items. In this general education science unit, each student was called upon to contribute to real-life science projects involving temperature and engage in activities appropriate to the objectives he or she was responsible for learning. That is, while all the students were pursuing the same basic educational goal (What is temperature?) and learning together in the same class activities, it was necessary that they focus on and be evaluated according to different curriculum objectives.

It should be noted that everyone benefited from the diversity in the class. The activities of the student learning to differentiate and use hot and cold items, for example, gave the other students who were learning temperature scales opportunities to construct many practical hot and cold situations and practice measuring various temperatures. In addition, the student who needed experience in differentiating and using hot and cold items received many opportunities and ample assistance in learning to do so.

Another example occurred in a fourth grade classroom during a math lesson. This example is centered around a classroom situation cited by Ford and Davern (1989), but has been modified to illustrate several points about curriculum adaptations. The class was learning how to multiply and divide 3- and 4-digit numbers. The teacher used a traditional teaching approach of lecturing and asking the students questions about how to multiply and divide such numbers, working several problems at the chalkboard to illustrate the concepts and procedures, assigning worksheets for the students to practice, and toward the end of the class discussing and asking the students questions about some "real-life" math problems involving multiplying and dividing 3- and 4-digit numbers.

Since there were students with diverse abilities and achievement levels in the class, not all of them were ready to learn how to multiply and divide 3- and 4-digit numbers. One of these students, Shawn, was reviewing number recognition, learning how to count from 1 to 100, and matching coins to money cards (graphic representation of a coin).

The support facilitator assisted by analyzing the math lesson to see how students who are at different levels in math could be included. For example, in Shawn's case, questions such as the following were explored: Could the teacher ask Shawn to identify some of the numbers (e.g., six) in the multiplication and division examples given on the chalkboard in the same way that other students are asked what eight × nine equals or how to regroup numbers? When worksheets are handed out, could Shawn receive one that requires number recognition and coins to be matched with graphic representations of coins rather than a work sheet with multiplication and division problems? When discussing real-life math problems involving 3- and 4-digit multiplication and division problems, could the teacher ask Shawn which number is larger—three or five—in the problem written on the chalkboard in the same way another student may be asked what needs to be done to solve the problem? The danger with this situation is that Shawn could have been perceived as separate or different from the rest of the class since he was involved in different math activities. However, in this particular class a variety of students were often involved in different activities so it was not perceived as strange to the other students that Shawn was working on number recognition.

The classroom teacher, with assistance from the support facilitator, also organized a class activity that allowed *all* of the students to participate in a practical, real-life experience that applied what they had been learning in the math class. In the illustration provided by Ford and Davern (1989), a "hot chocolate business" was organized. For 6 weeks, each day during math, the class operated the business. Groups of students—five or six at a time—were assigned a rotating schedule devised by the classroom teacher and support facilitator.

On Mondays, Tuesdays, and Thursdays, the business was held in the classroom and on Fridays the class opened the hot chocolate business for sales during recess to other students in the school. On Wednesdays, the students walked two blocks to a grocery store where they purchased the supplies needed for the business.

Planning the business, keeping records, and figuring expenses, prices, and profits provided many opportunities to practice a range of math skills and to learn community-based skills (e.g., traveling to the grocery store, locating and purchasing the goods). A typical classroom lesson was outlined to accomplish a variety of objectives, including learning the application of the multiplication and division concepts and procedures that many of the students were currently working on in the fourth grade curriculum. Objectives also included learning skills that Shawn and other students needed such as how to count money, how to match real coins to graphic representations of coins on money cards, and some community-based skills. In addition to the math skills all the students learned, it is important to acknowledge that this activity also presented opportunities for the students to develop social and communication skills, daily living skills (e.g., shopping, going to the store, cooking), and for some students such as Shawn, motor skills.

Finally, the hot chocolate business is a better way to include all students since it does not set any particular student apart from his or her peers, unlike in the first part of the example when it may be more evident that Shawn is engaged in learning different objectives.

Activity Adaptation

Teachers also may need to modify the activities in which a particular student participates or the way he or she achieves objectives. Activity adaptation was implemented in one high school history class where the students had a general goal of "understanding the Civil War." One among several primary objectives of the students was to learn the key people involved in the war through readings, library research, and class discussion. There was one student who had a strong artistic talent but could not read or write and had considerable difficulty expressing himself verbally. While most students were given reading assignments for homework, this student was given homework assignments of drawing poster size portraits of the key people being studied from their pictures in the textbook. Subsequently, his drawings were used as the stimulus for class discussion about the people being studied. The students were requested to share with this student and others what they learned from reading the textbook and outside research concerning the person (e.g., personality, consequences of key decisions made during the war).

For evaluation, most of the students wrote an essay about one of the Civil War characters who had been studied. However, this student, along with some of his classmates, conceptualized and constructed a Civil War mural that depicted the characters being studied. The mural formed a basis for culminating essay sharing and discussion of these historic individuals. In this way, the talents of a student who did not have the skills necessary to learn and share information about historic figures of the Civil War in the same way as the majority of the students was nevertheless involved with his peers in classroom curriculum activities.

In this example, the student was contributing to the class by producing poster size pictures and a mural that were used to stimulate class discussions. At the same time, he had opportunities to improve his skills in drawing, group participation, volunteering information (e.g., pointing to his pictures), and listening to and responding to classmates (e.g., showing the picture of Robert E. Lee). In addition, he had an opportunity to share and learn with his classmates information about key people in the Civil War.

Multiple Adaptations

In addition to curricular variations that accommodate diverse student abilities in terms of a single element (e.g., adapting objectives, pursuing different objectives, adapting activities), several such modifications can be implemented simultaneously. Multiple adaptations were used at the junior high school level in an integrated English literature class where the students were studying the concept of courage. Activities of the unit included becoming familiar with the story *My Friend Flicka* by Mary O'Hara, being able to demonstrate or explain how courage was an important element in the story, and how such courage might relate to the students' own lives. A range of student abilities, interests, and knowledge exhibited within the class influenced the selection of diverse learning objectives, from simply recognizing characters and what was meant by the word courage to analyzing, synthesizing, and forecasting events in the story.

In order to pursue the individual learning objectives of the students, the classroom teacher and support facilitator worked together to organize a series of activities designed to present and explore the elements of the story in a variety of ways. Students read the story silently, listened to tape recordings of the story, arranged picture sequences, and/or wrote summary reports. This variety of activities allowed students with diverse abilities to participate in some way. One student who could not read listened to a brief tape recording of the basic ideas of the story and shared the rudimentary elements in discussions with peers. Some students made a picture book and a tape-recorded explanation of the pictures summarizing what was learned while other students wrote a traditional book report.

After initial exposure to the story, the teacher divided the class into small groups consisting of students of differing abilities and assigned the task of reviewing the story and sharing and explaining facts, concepts, and insights about the characters and plot with one another. With prompting and support from classmates, each student shared his or her knowledge of the main character and explained what courage meant to him or her. Some students helped their group analyze and synthesize events in the story.

Another example of multiple adaptations occurred in the study of plants in a high school biology class. The goal was for the class members to learn and understand various plant characteristics and aspects of growth. Class members visited a plant nursery and participated in growing plants in the classroom. In addition to the traditional class textbook, the teacher and support facilitator arranged a variety of materials on plants, such as books with pictures of plants in various stages of development, simple how-to-grow plants pamphlets, books containing stories about plants, and textbooks containing elementary to college level material about plants. Many of the students were responsible for the learning objectives of knowing and understanding types of plants (e.g., vascular and nonvascular), technical terminology of plant parts (e.g., herbaceous stems), and technical plant life processes (e.g., photosynthesis).

Students had their own specific objectives while engaging in group activities with their classmates. For instance, one student in the class was unable to read or comprehend the technical words describing plants, but she still participated by concentrating her studies on labeling the parts of the plants in everyday language. She also learned with her peers how to put seeds, cuttings, roots, and young plants into the dirt and be responsible for their care. The teacher asked her basic questions about plants and practical procedures for growing plants in the same way he asked other students questions about technical terminology and growth processes.

All of the students not only learned about plants, but also worked cooperatively together and contributed to the class by growing and nurturing a number of different plants in the classroom. Everyone benefited. One student learned practical plant parts and how to grow plants as well as a few of the technical words and aspects of the technical growth process by listening to and observing her classmates; other students related the technical terminology, concepts, and ideas they were learning in the biology class to real plants.

IMPLEMENTATION CONSIDERATIONS

A Team Approach

At this time, some educators have had little or no experience in providing and/or adapting a general education curriculum to meet all students' needs. Thus, it may be viewed as an overwhelming or intimidating task. This problem generally can be overcome by having a team of people (teachers, parents, classmates, administrators, occupational and physical therapists, communications experts, school psychologists) meet to brainstorm and provide suggestions in regard to objectives for children and how the objectives can be fostered in general education classrooms. Once everyone has experience and practice in curricular design and adaptations, it becomes fairly easy and routine for the teacher, collaborating with one or more colleagues, specialists, students, and parents, to develop onging curricular procedures or accommodations that can allow even the most challenging students to participate in the classroom.

Peer Involvement

Students can help teachers implement curriculum flexibility. In fact, the involvement of students in their own learning and in the planning and implementation of purposeful and meaningful learning experiences for their classmates is increasingly critical to inclusive classrooms (see Villa & Thousand, chap. 7, this volume). Students can help propose activities, gather materials, and organize and implement the curriculum for themselves and their classmates. The authors of this chapter have observed a circle of friends volunteer a portion of their free time to engage in gathering materials and organizing an activity for a classmate and help the classroom teacher implement the activity. The students believed that becoming involved in helping someone else was a valuable learning experience and did not see it as a distraction from their studies or a drain on their time. (For an example of the concept of a circle of friends, see the video tape *Kids Belong Together* [People First Association of Lethbridge, Alberta, Canada, 1990].) The chapter authors would like to note here that all students should be involved in helping each other rather than one or two students always being the recipient of assistance.

Functional Skills

Curricular concerns, such as daily life and vocational skills, that were traditionally addressed because of their practical utility for students who were in segregated learning settings, need not be eliminated when students are included in general education classrooms. Students who require opportunities to learn practical living, working, and social skills can be provided guidance and opportunities to do so at natural times throughout the day. Lunch, snack times, and home economics can provide opportunities for class members to learn food preparation and eating and dining skills; dressing and grooming skills can be fostered when students naturally do this before and after school or in gym class; and bus riding skills can be taught when students need to travel back and forth to school or in the community. With guidance from and interactions with peers and adults, many daily life skills are learned naturally by students as they observe and share recreational and work activities in mainstreamed settings. In one junior high school, students taught a classmate how to comb her hair, wear make-up, and dress in "style" without prompting from adults. Within several weeks, the student was dressing and looking like any other junior high school student. This occurred after years of failure to teach, collect "hard data," and program "generalization" of such skills in "systematic" ways in isolated settings. Similarly, skills such as ordering and/or eating in fast food restaurants, going to the movies, and "hanging out" and shopping at the mall have been learned while spending free time with parents and/or peers in such locations.

In addition, community-referenced and vocational skills can be taught in general education work-study and cooperative education programs. One parent described how her daughter (a student with Down syndrome) gained her most valuable vocational skills in a supervised after school and summer jobs program for teens in her community (Sylvester, 1987). Summer, weekend, and after school jobs are natural, normal ways of developing vocational skills for all students when varying degrees of support are provided.

It should be stressed here that it is a major mistake to take elementary or high school students who have been classified as having disabilities into the community during school hours to learn "functional, community-referenced, or vocational skills" unless other students in general education classes are also doing this. It decreases these students' opportunities to become integrally involved and make friends in general education classes. This is not to imply that instruction in daily life, functional skills, or vocational skills are unimportant; it is obviously critical to facilitate the development of these skills. However, as noted above, functional community-referenced and vocational skills can be learned at natural times in after school jobs, weekend shopping trips with family and friends, and in integrated, regular education work-study programs, home economics, or other classes.

It also should be stressed that care must be taken *not* to assume that the general class curriculum is nonfunctional for some students. For example, each morning during the first 15 minutes of a sixth grade class, the classroom teacher asked the students to report on a news story they had seen on television or read in the newspaper. The support facilitator and general class teacher had doubts as to whether this was a functional activity for a 12-year-old student classified as having severe mental retardation and autism. In their best judgment he would never fully understand or become fluent in a discussion of current affairs. However, because they were committed to full inclusion, they went ahead and arranged for him to participate. They recommended that his mother have him watch a television news story each night and/or look at pictures in the newspaper while she explained them to him. She also was asked to coach him on one story each night that he could share with the class. (He was particularly fond of sports so the content of the stories often related to sporting events.) By learning a news story each night, the student had something to say when the teacher asked for volunteers to report on a story. Prompting from the teacher and his classmates was often necessary, but the student gradually became an active participant in class.

After careful consideration, both the general class teacher and support facilitator concluded that what the student did was functional. He learned something that allowed him to participate with other students his age, which opened up opportunities for socialization and potential friendships. It also provided him an opportunity to become more aware of his environment (news stories); increase his vocabulary; learn skills in taking turns and interacting with his peers; and practice remembering, listening to, and sharing ideas. These were all considered functional and useful skills.

The definition of the term *functional* needs to be broadened to include science, art, music, history, English literature, and other subjects taught to students in public schools. All students need to master as much as possible in these academic areas to be able to use their knowledge to improve their quality of life with their peers in the community. Contrary to the arguments of some (e.g., Brown et al., 1990), learning history, geography, science, and math with classmates is functional and in the long-term interest of all students, including those classified as having severe and profound intellectual disabilities. While not everyone can learn the same amount and/or the same things in these academic areas, whatever knowledge can be gained is of value and is worthwhile. There is more to life for anyone than only learning to make a sandwich or sweep a floor. It is also worthwhile for any of us, regardless of individual characteristics, to have a sense of who we are and who our ancestors were, and an appreciation of the environment and world around us. It is a serious mistake to underestimate or place limitations on some students by assuming that the only things they can learn that are useful to them are how to tie their shoes or ride a bus. In addition, it is critical to guard against educating a subgroup of students in such a way that they share few common experiences and understandings with people they are expected to live, recreate, and work with in the community.

The arguments about learning practical living and vocational skills versus academic instruction are likely to wane somewhat in the near future. The reason for this is that many people are beginning to see the need to integrate them both into the eduation of *all* students. It has been found that although academic learning can lead to better vocational competence, vocational learning can provide more context and motivation for learning academic subjects and higher-order thinking skills (Rosenstock, 1991; Wirt, 1991).

Educationally Challenge All Students

Another implementation consideration is that it is essential to be *cautious* while adapting curricular goals, objectives, or activities. It is a disservice to the student to make curricular objectives or activities easy when the student is able, with persistence or different learning methods, to master more challenging learning opportunities. Research has shown that students are more successful educationally and socially when school personnel maintain high expectations for them (Jones & Jones, 1986). Thus, the curriculum provided all students should challenge them to stretch as far as possible and to always surpass previous achievements, *while being provided any necessary adaptations and supports.* That is, although the goals and methods of educational programs should be adapted to meet the unique needs of each student, high expectations and challenges based on students' unique capabilities and needs are essential to providing all students with a quality education.

CONCLUSION

In closing this chapter, it should be stressed that the major reason for full inclusion is *not* that previously excluded students are necessarily going to become proficient in socialization, history, or math facts, although it is obvious that there are more opportunities for everyone to grow and learn in integrated classrooms. Rather, inclusion of all students teaches the student and his or her peers that all persons are equally valued members of this society and that it is worthwhile to include everyone. The previously accepted mode of dealing with differences among people was segregation, which communicates the message that either we do not want to accept everyone or that some people are not worth the effort to make the necessary accommodations to include them. As stated by Forest (1988), "If we really want someone to be part of our lives, we will do what it takes to welcome that person and accommodate his or her needs" (p. 13).

Fortunately, mainstreamed education is moving toward a child-centered and holistic perspective regarding learning for all students. Forward-looking teachers are increasingly working to promote cooperative learning groups among students instead of lecturing, basing instruction on individual needs rather than arbitrary standards, and facilitating students' learning through purposeful, real-life projects and activities. This has and will continue to allow for more natural inclusion of all students in inclusive classrooms. Inclusion will help all students receive a better education and the diversity among class members will enhance learning opportunities for everyone.

REFERENCES

Bangert, R., Kulik, J., & Kulik, C. (1988). Individualized systems of instruction in secondary schools. *Review of Educational Research, 53*, 143–158.
Berrigan, C. (1988, February). Integration in Italy: A dynamic movement. *TASH Newsletter*, pp. 6–7.
Berrigan, C. (1989, October). All students belong in the classroom. *TASH Newsletter*, p. 6.
Biklen, D. (Producer). (1988). *Regular lives* [Video]. Washington, DC: State of the Art.
Brown, L., Schwartz, P., Udvari-Solner, A., Kampschroer, E., Johnson, F., Jorgensen, J., & Gruenewald, L. (1990). *How much time should students with severe intellectual disabilities spend in regular education classrooms and elsewhere?* Madison: University of Wisconsin.
Cox, J., & Kelly, J. (1989). Nurturing talent in 2000 A.D. *Gifted Children Today, 12*, 24.
Discover the Possibilities. (1988). Colorado Springs: PEAK Parent Center.
Doll, R. (1986). *Curriculum improvement: Decision making and process* (6th ed.). Newton, MA: Allyn & Bacon.
Falvey, M. (1989). *Community-based curriculum: Instructional strategies for students with severe handicaps* (2nd ed.). Baltimore: Paul H. Brookes Publishing Co.
Ford, A., & Davern, L. (1989). Moving forward with school integration: Strategies for involving students with severe handicaps in the life of the school. In R. Gaylord-Ross (Ed.), *Integration strategies for students with handicaps* (pp. 11–31). Baltimore: Paul H. Brookes Publishing Co.
Forest, M. (1987). *More education integration.* Downsview, Ontario, Canada: G. Allan Roeher Institute.

Forest, M. (1988). Full inclusion is possible. *Impact, 1*, 3–4.

Glatthorn, A. (1987). How do you adapt the curriculum to respond to individual differences? In A. Glatthorn (Ed.), *Curriculum renewal* (pp. 99–109). Alexandria, VA: Association for Supervision and Curriculum Development.

Johnson, D., & Johnson, R.T. (1987). *Joining together: Group therapy and group skills* (3rd ed.). Englewood Cliffs, NJ: Prentice-Hall.

Jones, V., & Jones, L. (1986). *Comprehensive classroom management.* Newton, MA: Allyn & Bacon.

Lipsky, D., & Gartner, A. (in press). Achieving full inclusion: Placing the student at the center of educational reform. In W. Stainback, & S. Stainback (Eds.), *Critical issues confronting special education* (pp. 122–158) Newton, MA: Allyn & Bacon.

Miller, J. (1983). *The educational spectrum: Orientations to curriculum.* New York: Longman.

Pallas, A., Natriello, G., & McDill, C. (1989). The changing nature of the disadvantaged population: Current dimensions and future trends. *Educational Researcher, 18*(5), 16–22.

People First Association of Lethbridge. (1990) *Kids belong together* [Videotape]. Alberta, Canada: Producer.

Poplin, M., & Stone, S. (in press). A holistic, constructivistic perspective. In W. Stainback & S. Stainback (Eds.), *Critical issues confronting special education.* Newton, MA: Allyn & Bacon.

Porter, G. (Producer). (1988). *A chance to belong* [Video]. Downsview, Ontario, Canada: Canadian Association for Community Living.

Rosenstock, L. (1991). The walls come down: The overdue reunification of vocational and academic education. *Phi Delta Kappan, 72*, 434–436.

Seligman, M. (1975). *Helplessness: On depression, development and death.* San Francisco: Freeman.

Smith, F. (1986). *Insult to intelligence.* New York: Arbor House.

Stainback, S., & Stainback, W. (1988). Educating all students with severe disabilities in regular classes. *Teaching Exceptional Children, 21*, 16–19.

Stainback, S., Stainback, W., & Forest, M. (Eds.). (1989). *Educating all students in the mainstream of regular education.* Baltimore: Paul H. Brookes Publishing Co.

Stainback, W., & Stainback, S. (Eds.). (1990). *Support networks for inclusive schooling: Interdependent integrated education.* Baltimore: Paul H. Brookes Publishing Co.

Stainback, W., & Stainback, S. (Eds.). (in press). *Critical issues confronting special education.* Newton, MA: Allyn & Bacon.

Strully, J. (1986, November). *Our children and the regular education classroom: Or why settle for anything less than the best?* Paper presented to the 1986 annual conference of The Association for Persons with Severe Handicaps, San Francisco.

Strully, J., & Strully, C. (1985). Friendship and our children. *Journal of The Association for Persons with Severe Handicaps, 10*, 224–227.

Sylvester, D. (1987, October). *A parent's perspective on transition: From high school to what?* Paper presented at Vermont's Least Restrictive Environment Conference, Burlington.

Villa, R., & Thousand, J. (1988). Enhancing success in heterogeneous classrooms and schools: The power of partnership. *Teacher Education and Special Education, 11*, 144–153.

Wirt, J. (1991). A new federal law on vocational education: Will reform follow? *Phi Delta Kappan, 72,* 425–433.

York, J., & Vandercook, T. (1989). *Strategies for achieving an integrated education for middle school aged learners with severe disabilities.* Minneapolis: Institution on Community Integration.

5

Using a Collaborative Approach To Support Students and Teachers in Inclusive Classrooms

Janet L. Graden and Anne M. Bauer

AS SCHOOL PERSONNEL begin to implement inclusive classroom models, they realize that a key underlying feature necessary for success is collaboration among teachers, other school personnel, parents, and students. In fact, without this collaboration, inclusive education cannot be successful since inclusion is predicated on professionals working *together* for the purpose of enhancing the education of all students in the school.

The focus of this chapter is to describe the *process* by which educators work together to develop, implement, and evaluate the adaptations that will occur in classrooms. The process is founded on two basic principles: 1) it must be *collaborative*—educators must work together as equal partners (not in a hierarchy) to provide learning opportunities for students, and 2) it must be based on a specific problem-solving sequence to provide a mechanism for deciding when and how to make adaptations. Collaborative problem solving provides the support network by which interventions, adaptations, and accommodations are implemented in inclusive classrooms.

The collaborative problem-solving process described in this

chapter is based on extensive literature involving the process in schools and other settings (cf. Gutkin & Curtis, 1990), and on the authors' experiences and those of colleagues in implementing the approach in several schools. It has been the authors' experience that if the fundamental processes of collaboration and problem solving do not form the foundation of the approach, then classroom adaptations will not occur with any success or in any systematic fashion.

RATIONALE FOR COLLABORATION IN INCLUSIVE SCHOOLS

As described by Stainback, Stainback, and Jackson in Chapter 1 of this volume, inclusive schools tend to build upon the notion that the school is a *community* of learners and educators. This sense of community is based on the commitment that all educators are responsible for the success of all students, rather than being responsible for a category of students (e.g., "special" and "regular" educators are responsible only for their particular students). Educators share the philosophy that every student can learn and that educators are there to facilitate each student's educational attainment and personal and social adjustment. This philosophy is also implicit to collaboration. For example, in a school in Michigan where personnel are prepared in the use of collaborative problem solving, teachers and support personnel work together to adapt and provide learning experiences for every student in the school, without regard to labels or designation. They named their collaborative process "Helping Hands" (Curtis & Safranski, 1991). In this schoolwide process, teachers and other school personnel (classroom teachers, support personnel, principal, school psychologist) offer "helping hands" to each other and to students and parents through collaborative problem solving.

Related to this notion of a "community" is an understanding of individual differences and the needs of different learners. There is ample research on these differences and how they are shaped by complex environmental factors (cf. Saxe, Cross, & Silverman, 1988). Yet, because of real and perceived constraints such as regulations, insufficient time, training, and attitudes, education often does not focus on accommodating individual differences by changing the educational environment (e.g., teaching strategies, grouping patterns), but on attempting to "fit" students into existing structures (e.g., through categorical placements and/or retention). Teachers have been reported to believe that most children are educationally more alike than they are different (Reynolds, Martin-Reynolds, & Mark, 1982). In addition, there is a growing recognition that educators need to structure schools to accommodate for diverse learners—students who are or were labeled disabled, students "at risk" due to poverty or family factors, and students with diverse cultural backgrounds. The growing numbers of students who are in need of accommodation and adaptation have forced educators to develop structures to meet the needs of all students. Strategies such as heterogeneous grouping, cooperative learning, and nongraded elementary classrooms are being implemented in several schools nationwide, with growing evidence of their success (cf. Graden, Zins, & Curtis, 1988). All of these strategies emphasize individual differences.

There is a need to recognize the effect of environmental factors on children's learning and adjustment. Teachers should recognize that students are active participants in the educational process and that as they participate they generate their own meaning of classroom management and instructional activities (Pinnel & Galloway, 1987). When educators focus only on child variables and assume that their problems are due to internal causes, such as a disorder or a disability, the important contribution of environmental factors (e.g., teaching strategies, peer interactions, parenting) is diminished or even ignored. Yet, these environmental factors are important because educators can control how they interact with and provide learning experiences for students, but they cannot alter internal student factors. Thus, a focus on what can be altered in relevant natural environments (classroom, home) provides a sense of empowerment to educators, students, and parents.

IMPLEMENTING COLLABORATIVE
PROBLEM SOLVING IN SCHOOLS AND CLASSROOMS

There are many practical issues that are fundamental to implementing a collaborative problem-solving approach in inclusive classrooms and schools. Some of these considerations include developing an integrated approach to collaborative problem solving that incorporates both individual problem solving among teachers, school personnel, students, and parents as well as schoolwide assistance teams.

Collaboration

Collaboration is a word commonly used in educational literature, but its core characteristics are usually not discussed. Thus, many educators may believe they are collaborating, when they may actually be engaging in activities that undermine true collaboration. One example is the current trend to develop teacher assistance teams aimed at providing intervention support to classroom teachers. Although these teams typically strive to be collaborative, in practice they often turn into expert "advice-giving" sessions and no real support is offered to ensure that the team's ideas are workable and will be implemented. This seems to occur when the team is under time constraints, when there is perceived pressure to be helpful to many teachers requesting assistance, and when members are not attentive or are not prepared to engage in collaboration. Another example of an effort to achieve collaboration that often falls short of its goal is the suggestions offered to classroom teachers by special educators on how to teach a mainstreamed student. Without meaningful collaboration in which the two teachers engage in shared problem solving to understand how that student could learn under the particular conditions of the classroom, the ideas generated by the consulting teacher will not be implemented. Thus, collaboration is not a new educational buzzword, but a fundamental way of working together in a true partnership.

Some critical concepts fundamental to collaboration have been described in detail by Gutkin and Curtis (1990) and are discussed on the following pages. Many of these concepts are well supported by research literature in the social sciences. Attention to these concepts can help ensure that educators are engaging in true collaboration.

Indirect Service Delivery to Students   When teachers or other educators collaborate to develop strategies to help students succeed, they are working together toward the goal of improving outcomes for the student. Often, only one of these individuals (e.g., the classroom teacher) is directly responsible for the student. The other person assists by problem solving with the person directly responsible to help him or her accommodate and intervene with the student. Thus, collaboration is an indirect service delivery model, and is different from the familiar model of sending students to various individuals for direct services (e.g., speech pathologists, special education teachers, physical therapists). In collaboration, the focus is on collaborating and intervening in natural settings (the classroom and the home) with educators working together to enhance functioning in these environments. Because this is a different method of providing services, it will take adjustment, support, and reinforcement to implement the approach successfully.

In moving from direct services to indirect services, the change must be supported at all levels and those who receive the indirect services must benefit and be reinforced. Therefore, school personnel should be supported in learning just as students are. There is evidence that teachers who participate in a collaborative approach to indirect services prefer it (e.g., Gutkin, 1986), so it is important to apply positive steps in working toward this goal.

The Collaborative Relationship   Central to effective collaboration is the development and maintenance of a positive, trusting relationship among the collaborators. The individuals involved in a collaborative approach must operate as equals and have coordinate, as opposed to superordinate and subordinate, status. This partnership refers to the relationship between individuals, not the titles or roles they carry. For example, some proponents of collaboration (Chalfant, Pysh, & Moultrie, 1979; Pugach & Johnson, 1989a, 1989b) emphasize professional roles, suggesting that collaboration should occur among classroom teachers. They believe that specialists cannot readily engage in collaboration with classroom teachers because of role differences. However, others (Graden, 1989) argue that collaboration is not a function of one's role or title, but a function of one's interpersonal behaviors. For example, some classroom teachers can slip into an "expert" role and some specialists can operate in collaborative ways; that is, specific skills and behaviors such as clarifying problems, listening effectively, and suggesting alternatives in a sensitive way, are more important in determining who is an effective collaborator than are one's role or title. It is important in inclusive schools not to focus on labels of students or educators and not to restrict individuals by role distinctions.

Voluntary Relationship and Right To Reject   Another core concept described by Gutkin and Curtis (1990) is that collaboration, by definition, must be voluntary, and the person engaging in collaboration must retain the right to reject or accept the ideas generated. This concept is important because the literature on treatment acceptability (e.g., Martens, Peterson, Witt, & Cirone, 1986) demonstrates that the extent to which practices are implemented is affected by teacher perceptions of their acceptability in the classroom. The educator's preparation, willingness, and comfort in implementing a practice and confidence in its effectiveness all affect his or her ability to employ it successfully (Shea & Bauer, 1987). In addition, research, as well as practical experience, has shown that if individuals are not invested in a practice, they can easily disrupt the "agreed upon" plans. Thus, the ultimate decision regarding accommodations to be made in a classroom must rest with the teacher responsible for that classroom. Ideas will not be forced on teachers as passive recipients of expert advice; rather, classroom teachers will be the key individuals involved in the decision making. Effective collaborators recognize the importance of involvement and motivation of all people engaged in collaboration.

Active Teacher Involvement   Collaboration does not involve an active facilitator and a passive recipient. Instead, collaboration involves active participation of everyone involved as well as empowerment of teachers. Teachers retain ownership of their classrooms and students in terms of making important teaching decisions. Collaborators work with them to generate alternatives, but the teacher is very active in describing the current classroom environment and in selecting adaptations that easily fit into the natural environment of that classroom. Evidence suggests that teachers do become actively involved in collaboration when they are trained in problem solving (e.g., Anderson, Kratochwill, & Bergan, 1986).

Another reason for active teacher involvement in collaboration comes from the literature on self-efficacy (Bandura, 1982) as it relates to empowerment. When individuals perceive that their actions will be successful in changing a situation, they are more likely to persevere. Thus, if teachers learn that adaptations can be successful, they will have an increased sense of self-efficacy to attempt further modifications. It also has been shown that by increasing teachers' sense of efficacy, their preferences for collaborative problem solving for students will increase (Gutkin & Hickman, 1988).

Goals of Collaboration   Collaboration has two distinct goals. The first is to remediate the current concern related to the student's performance or functioning. The second goal, perhaps more important, is not only to help the student who is the target of the current concern, but to prevent future problems for that student and others. Prevention is achieved when accommodations and alterations: 1) improve the future functioning of the student, and 2) improve the functioning of other students in the classroom, both now and in the future.

This second goal of collaboration is exceedingly important because it is the way in which educational outcomes are improved for most students. Research shows that classroom teachers have been able to increase their skills, problem-solving ability, and confidence and tolerance for dealing with individual diversity following collaborative problem solving (Gutkin & Curtis, 1990). For example, classroom teachers have implemented a new instructional technique intended to increase the learning of one student, then reported later that they continued to use the technique for the benefit of many other students in the class.

Confidentiality and Trust   A trusting, positive relationship underlies successful collaboration. A high level of trust is essential for the open discussion and sharing that needs to take place to explore environmental factors that can be altered and alternative approaches that can be implemented. Teachers need to trust that others are working with them as collaborators and not judging their teaching. Discussion of instructional options needs to be a collaborative exploration of possible factors to alter, not an attempt to judge or blame teachers.

Problem Solving

While collaboration describes the relationship among the individuals, problem solving describes the systematic tool used to guide the process. The specific problem-solving sequence described here provides a structure for moving through the collaboration process. This structure allows some flexibility for adapting to particular situations.

Problem solving as a process has been extensively researched in psychology and organizational literatures. The specific process described here is adapted for use in an intervention assistance approach to enhance all students' success in classrooms. These steps are described in Gutkin and Curtis (1982, 1990) and in Zins, Curtis, Graden, and Ponti (1988). The seven basic problem-solving steps in the sequence are listed below and described in more detail on the following pages:

1. Define and clarify the problem.
2. Analyze the problem.
3. Explore alternatives.
4. Select strategy.
5. Clarify strategy.
6. Implement strategy, provide support.
7. Evaluate outcomes.

Problem Definition and Clarification   The first step in problem solving is a critically important one—to obtain a clear behavioral and operational definition of the problem or issue. Global, nonspecific terms or terms that are not alterable should not be used. For example, if the definition of the problem is "this student cannot function in the regular social studies class because of her learning disability," effective problem solving is precluded because: 1) there is no defined problem to address, and 2) attributing the problem to an intrinsic disability puts the focus on an internal child attribute (a presumed learning disability). This latter focus on internal child attributes is referred to as a "medical model" approach. It has been shown to provide a barrier to effective problem solving since it is not seen as modifiable. Teachers reported a lower sense of efficacy in terms of their optimism about the intervention and their ability to intervene when medical model terms were used (Bergan, Byrnes, & Kratochwill, 1979; Tombari & Bergan, 1978). Effective problem solving must start with a specific definition of a problem that is modifiable.

In addition, the problem needs to be clarified in terms of its component parts and related factors. This clarification cannot be rushed. Research shows that individuals classified as low-skilled consultants moved too quickly through problem solving, taking an unclarified view of the problem, and progressing to quick recommendation of potential strategies (Curtis & Watson, 1980). This approach leads to unsatisfactory resolution of the concern. However, consultants characterized as highly skilled in problem solving actually increased teachers' problem clarification skills (Curtis & Watson, 1980). Adequate problem definition and clarification is related to a high probability of resolving the concern (Bergan & Tombari, 1976).

Relevant environmental factors must also be considered in problem solving. For example, classroom organization, teaching strategies, students' goals and objectives, methods for evaluating mastery of goals and objectives, teacher–student interactions, peer–student interactions, and parent–child interactions all could be relevant depending on the focus of the issue to be addressed. Effective problem solving operates from a systems perspective and uses a funnel approach to sift through a range of environmental variables to more specific ones.

In addition to a specific statement of the concern (current performance level), this step of problem solving needs to include specific goals (desired performance level). In this way, the discrepancy between what the student is doing now and what the student needs to be doing to be successful can be determined. Factors that could be related to that success can then be examined.

Problem Analysis   Three major concepts should be applied after defining and clarifying the problem. The first is to continue to use the systems framework and funnel approach to analyze possible contextual variables that relate to the concern and could be modified to help the student succeed. The second issue is to conduct a functional analysis of the contextual variables (e.g., Shapiro, 1989). Academic task structure (those constraints on the lesson related to the nature of the academic task) and social participation structure (the social context and interactional process involved in teaching and learning) must both be considered (Erickson, 1982). In a functional analysis, possible antecedent factors as well as events that appear to follow the behavior are examined. This functional analysis is completed to understand the sequences of a student's performance in the natural setting of the classroom and how classroom variables seem to be related to that performance. For example, if a student is completing only 20% of his or her seatwork, a problem analysis needs to delineate the task demands of the seatwork and determine if the student has the prerequisite skills to do the work. The wrong plan could be implemented without this analysis. For example, if a motivational plan (a reward system contingent on a specified level of seatwork completion) was attempted, but the student did not have the basic skills to complete the work independently, the plan would be unsuccessful. Or, if a peer tutoring intervention was attempted, but the student already had the basic skills that were the focus of the tutoring, the plan would be misguided and inefficient. These examples illustrate how problem analysis is needed to match a viable plan with a relevant concern.

The third important consideration in problem analysis is to treat the process as generating possible hypotheses to be tested. Problem analysis should result in questions to be answered and hypotheses to be tested in the classroom without the expectation that "the answer" will result. This process of hypothesis generation and testing is used in effective inclusive classrooms, in which problem solving is continually occurring to accommodate the needs of all students.

In applying a systems approach, functional analysis, and hypothesis testing in problem analysis, effective problem solvers will use whatever tools and strategies are required to collect the information necessary to adequately analyze the concern. Some examples of tools that could be used in this stage include skillful questioning, direct classroom observation, direct evaluation of student skills through curriculum-based assessment, and collection of permanent products (e.g., work samples). It is important to note that problem analysis should be efficient, only using the tools needed for the situation. For example, classroom observations do not need to be routinely conducted; they should be completed only when direct information on classroom variables and student performance is seen as useful in problem analysis. If an observation is appropriate, then the use of a framework to guide the assessment according to relevant instructional and classroom variables, such as that developed by Ysseldyke and Christenson (1987), can be extremely useful. There are other direct behavioral observation techniques and assessment strategies that are also useful (see Shapiro, 1989). In all cases, the techniques should be directly linked to providing relevant information on how to plan for the student in the classroom. Care also needs to be taken to ensure that observations occur within a collaborative problem-solving process so that the purpose of the observation is not to "validate" the presence of a concern or to question teachers' judgments but to provide additional information for problem solving. Any observation data collected should be openly shared with the teacher in the problem-solving process.

Exploration of Alternatives   After the problem has been clarified and an indepth analysis has occurred, the next step is to consider a range of options for addressing the concern. At this point, it is often helpful to brainstorm. When brainstorming, it is important to think creatively, to acknowledge that there is more than one way to approach things, and to evaluate the brainstormed options only after many have been generated. In addition, it is helpful to have a variety of resources and options available in the school. In Chapter 1 of this volume, Stainback, Stainback, and Jackson describe how a support facilitator can help to generate ideas to be implemented, compile materials and resources to be used, and link individuals with other personnel who could provide some specific assistance relative to that concern. There are extensive resources that school personnel can tap for specific examples of interventions and adaptations. Excellent examples of instructional and curricular adaptations are included in this volume and in other sources, including Falvey, Coots, Bishop, and Grenot-Scheyer (1989); Ford and Davern (1989); Giangreco and Meyer (1988); Johnson and Johnson (1989); Stainback, Stainback, and Slavin (1989); Thousand and Villa (1989); Villa and Thousand (1988); Wang (1989); and Wang, Reynolds, and Schwartz (1988).

Selection of Strategy   After examining possible alternatives, a specific strategy is selected. At this step of problem solving, a foremost consideration is to ensure that the strategy to be implemented is selected by and acceptable to the classroom teacher. The strategy should be unobtrusive and fit into the natural context of the classroom. Teachers prefer practices that can be easily employed and that only minimally disrupt normal classroom routines (Martens et al., 1986). As described in Chapter 4 of this volume, adaptations should occur only as needed, with preference given to group instructional techniques that blend easily into the classroom routine as opposed to individual interventions. Teacher, task, and classroom variables may be adapted to meet the needs of students within the conventional classroom setting. The potential positive and negative side effects of any practice or plan should be explored. A good source for examples of classroom-level strategies is Paine, Radicchi, Rossellini, Deutchman, and Darch (1983).

Clarification of the Strategy   Often, strategies are ineffective because the person responsible for their implementation did not clearly understand the basic aspects of the procedure—the who, what, when, where, and how. All of these aspects of the strategy should be clarified to ensure that all parties involved understand the fundamental aspects of the plan.

Implementation of the Strategy   The most critical aspect in implementing a strategy is to provide ongoing support in the classroom. The lack of follow-up support is often a primary reason for intervention plans not being implemented. The importance of follow-up and systematic support has been demonstrated by research on intervention assistance programs (Graden, 1988). Collaboration implies that the individuals continue to work together to support the plan and do what is necessary to ensure that the student is successful.

Evaluation of Outcomes   Central to any problem-solving process is evaluating its success. In this regard, the collection of data is recommended to assist in evaluating outcomes. This can be as easy as keeping track of completion rates or collecting work samples. Direct observational data can also be obtained if necessary. Again, efficiency is important in doing what is most natural in the classroom context. Teacher, student, and/or parent ratings of outcomes are very revealing data. Although these ratings are subjective, they have real value in terms of the perceptions of the individuals closest to the situation.

In closing the discussion of the problem-solving steps, it must be emphasized that progression through these steps does not always occur in a simplistic fashion and it may be appropriate to return to a previous stage of problem solving. For example, after a potential strategy is tried and doesn't seem to be working, the problem solvers may decide to move back into problem analysis to consider other factors that could be used to develop strategies.

PRACTICAL CONSIDERATIONS IN COLLABORATIVE PROBLEM SOLVING

When implementing the collaborative problem-solving approach to accommodate all students in inclusive classrooms, a number of practical considerations need to be addressed. A comprehensive overview of the approach and discussion of practical issues is provided in Zins et al. (1988). Some key issues are discussed briefly here. These issues include: roles of various educators in collaboration, developing an integrated approach incorporating the use of one-to-one collaboration as well as a schoolwide problem-solving team, and enhancing the process of schoolwide change toward collaboration for inclusive classrooms.

Roles in Collaboration

Collaborative approaches in inclusive schools should diminish existing role distinctions to make the best use of expertise in problem solving. The goal in collaboration is to share knowledge and perspectives and therefore arrive at better strategies than would be obtained by working alone. For example, classroom teachers can share expertise on indepth knowledge of students in their classroom, group instructional processes, and curriculum; special educators can share expertise on adapting instruction and specific intervention strategies; school psychologists can share expertise about individual differences and human learning and behavior; curriculum consultants can share expertise of the specific curriculum area and learning objectives; and parents can share considerable expertise about their own children and how they function in other environments. The challenge is to make the best use of all the potential expertise in schools without becoming involved with "turf" issues across professions. It is the authors' experience that when collaboration occurs, there are more than enough students who could benefit from problem-solving efforts; therefore, there is a need for even more personnel.

An Integrated Approach Using Individual Collaboration and Teams

The current literature on collaboration and problem solving recommends many approaches to collaboration. These approaches range from teachers collaborating with teachers (e.g., Pugach & Johnson, 1989a, 1989b), special educators collaborating with teachers (e.g., Idol-Maestas, 1983; Idol, Paolucci-Whitcomb, & Nevin, 1986), school psychologists collaborating with teachers (e.g., Rosenfield, 1987), to collaboration occurring through teams (e.g., Chalfant et al., 1979). In the authors' experience, an integrated approach that employs all levels of collaboration (teacher–teacher, teacher–other school personnel, specialist–specialist, team collaboration) is preferable. In this integrated approach, described in Curtis, Curtis, and Graden (1989) and Zins et al. (1988), the most logical, natural, and efficient collaboration occurs flexibly and as needed. Thus, team collaboration is not the sole source of support, but is used only when problem solving and collaboration by a large number of educators is required. In schools that have implemented this approach, the largest amount of collaboration occurs at the teacher–teacher level, with progressively less collaboration occurring between teachers and specialists or with a team (Curtis & Safranski, 1991).

Schoolwide Change To Support Inclusive Schools and Classrooms

It is essential that a schoolwide philosophy valuing collaboration and inclusion be adopted and that processes be in place to support a schoolwide change. Although a comprehensive discussion of this issue is beyond the scope of this chapter, it is vital to recognize the importance of a supported change process. This issue is discussed in this volume and in other volumes (cf. Gaylord-Ross, 1989; Graden et al., 1988; Henning-Stout & Conoley, 1988; Stainback & Stainback, 1990; Stainback, Stainback, & Forest, 1989; Zins et al., 1988).

CONCLUSION

Collaborative problem solving is an activity that is central to the success of inclusive schools. To be most effective, both components of the approach, collaboration and problem solving, must be considered simultaneously.

A systems approach provides further insight into effective collaborative problem solving. This approach allows participants to consider a specific, modifiable concern in the context in which it occurs. The complexity of the context is apparent in generating hypotheses, rather than searching for cause and effect relationships.

The "collaborative ethic," a schoolwide acceptance regarding the nature and importance of collaborative relationships, is an essential component of inclusive schools. As Phillips and McCullough (1990) suggest, the collaborative ethic empowers professionals to assist each other in solving problems, motivates them to action, and provides the opportunity for skill enhancement. Perhaps more important, it provides a collective endorsement of the rights of teachers, as members of a community of learners, to assistance and support from colleagues and the school.

REFERENCES

Anderson, T.K., Kratochwill, T.R., & Bergan, J.R. (1986). Training teachers in behavioral consultation and therapy: An analysis of verbal behaviors. *Journal of School Psychology, 24*, 229–241.

Bandura, A. (1982). Self-efficacy mechanism in human agency. *American Psychologist, 37*, 122–147.

Bergan, J.R., Byrnes, I.M., & Kratochwill, T.R. (1979). Effects of behavioral and medical models of consultation on teacher expectancies and instruction of a hypothetical child. *Journal of School Psychology, 17*, 306–316.

Bergan, J.R., & Tombari, M.L. (1976). Consultant skill and efficiency and the implementation of outcomes of consultation. *Journal of School Psychology, 14*, 3–14.

Chalfant, J.C., Pysh, M.V., & Moultrie, R. (1979). Teacher assistance teams: A model for within building problem solving. *Learning Disability Quarterly, 2*, 85–96.

Curtis, M.J., Curtis, V.A., & Graden, J.L. (1989). Prevention and early intervention through intervention assistance programs. *School Psychology International, 9*, 257–264.

Curtis, M.J., & Safranski, S. (1991, March). *Promoting effective services for all children: A case study for building-level change.* Paper presented to the National Association of School Psychologists, Dallas, TX.

Curtis, M.J., & Watson, K. (1980). Changes in consultee problem clarification skills following consultation. *Journal of School Psychology, 18*, 210–221.

Erickson, F. (1982). Classroom discourse as improvisations: Relationships between academic task structure and social participation structure in lessons. In L.C. Wilkinson (Ed.), *Communicating in classrooms* (pp. 153–181). New York: Academic Press.

Falvey, M.A., Coots, J., Bishop, K.D., & Grenot-Scheyer, M. (1989). Educational and curricular adaptations. In S. Stainback, W. Stainback, & M. Forest (Eds.), *Educating all students in the mainstream of regular education* (pp. 143–158). Baltimore: Paul H. Brookes Publishing Co.

Ford, A., & Davern, L. (1989). Moving forward with school integration: Strategies for involving students with severe handicaps in the life of the school. In R. Gaylord-Ross (Ed.), *Integration strategies for students with handicaps* (pp. 11–32). Baltimore: Paul H. Brookes Publishing Co.

Gaylord-Ross, R. (Ed.). (1989). *Integration strategies for students with handicaps*. Baltimore: Paul H. Brookes Publishing Co.

Giangreco, M.F., & Meyer, L.H. (1988). Expanding service delivery options in regular schools and classrooms for students with severe disabilities. In J.L. Graden, J.E. Zins, & M.J. Curtis (Eds.), *Alternative educational delivery systems: Enhancing instructional options for all students* (pp. 241–268). Washington, DC: National Association of School Psychologists.

Graden, J.L. (1988). *Prereferral evaluation studies: A research synthesis.* Unpublished manuscript, Office of Special Education Programs, Washington, D.C.

Graden, J.L. (1989). Redefining "prereferral intervention" as intervention assistance: Collaboration between general and special education. *Exceptional Children, 56,* 227–231.

Graden, J.L., Zins, J.E., & Curtis, M.J. (Eds.). (1988). *Alternative educational delivery systems: Enhancing instructional options for all students.* Washington, DC: National Association of School Psychologists.

Gutkin, T.B. (1986). Consultees' perceptions of variables relating to the outcomes of school-based consultation interactions. *School Psychology Review, 15,* 375–382.

Gutkin, T.B., & Curtis, M.J. (1982). School-based consultation: Theory and techniques. In C.R. Reynolds & T.B. Gutkin (Eds.), *The handbook of school psychology* (pp. 796–828). New York: John Wiley & Sons.

Gutkin, T.B., & Curtis, M.J. (1990). School-based consultation: Theory, techniques, and research. In T.B. Gutkin & C.R. Reynolds (Eds.), *The handbook of school psychology* (2nd ed.) (pp. 577–611). New York: John Wiley & Sons.

Gutkin, T.B., & Hickman, J.A. (1988). Teachers' perceptions of control over presenting problems and resulting preferences for consultation versus referral services. *Journal of School Psychology, 26,* 395–398.

Henning-Stout, M., & Conoley, J.C. (1988). Influencing program change at the district level. In J.L. Graden, J.E. Zins, & M.J. Curtis (Eds.), *Alternative educational delivery systems: Enhancing instructional options for all students* (pp. 471–490). Washington, DC: National Association of School Psychologists.

Idol, L., Paolucci-Whitcomb, P., & Nevin, A. (1986). *Collaborative consultation.* Rockville, MD: Aspen Systems.

Idol-Maestas, L. (1983). *Special educators' consultation handbook.* Rockville, MD: Aspen Systems.

Johnson, D.W., & Johnson, R.T. (1989). Cooperative learning and mainstreaming. In R. Gaylord-Ross (Ed.), *Integration strategies for students with handicaps* (pp. 233–248). Baltimore: Paul H. Brookes Publishing Co.

Martens, B.K., Peterson, R.L., Witt, J.C., & Cirone, S. (1986). Teacher perceptions of school-based interventions. *Exceptional Children, 53,* 213–223.

Medway, F.J., & Updyke, J.F. (1985). Meta-analysis of consultation outcome studies. *American Journal of Community Psychology, 13,* 489–504.

Paine, S.C., Radicchi, J., Rosellini, L.C., Deutchman, L., & Darch, C.B. (1983). *Structuring your classroom for academic success.* Champaign, IL: Research Press.

Phillips, V., & McCullough, L. (1990). Consultation-based programming: Instituting the collaborative ethic in schools. *Exceptional Children, 56,* 291–304.

Pinnell, G.S., & Galloway, C.M. (1987). Human development, language, and communication: Then and now. [Special Issue]. *Theory into Practice, 26,* 353–357.

Pugach, M.C., & Johnson, L.J. (1989a). Prereferral interventions: Progress, problems, and challenges. *Exceptional Children, 56,* 217–226.

Pugach, M.C., & Johnson, L.J. (1989b). The challenge of implementing collaboration between general and special education. *Exceptional Children, 56,* 232–235.

Reynolds, B., Martin-Reynolds, J., & Mark, F. (1982). Elementary teachers' attitudes towards mainstreaming educable mentally retarded students. *Education and Training of the Mentally Retarded, 17,* 171–176.

Rosenfield, S.A. (1987). *Instructional consultation.* Hillsdale, NJ: Lawrence Erlbaum.

Saxe, L., Cross, T., & Silverman, N. (1988). Children's mental health: The gap between what we know and what we do. *American Psychologist, 43,* 800–807.

Shapiro, E.S. (1989). *Academic skills problems: Direct assessment and intervention.* New York: Guilford Press.

Shea, T.M., & Bauer, A.M. (1987). *Teaching children and youth with behavioral disorders* (2nd ed.). Englewood Cliffs, NJ: Prentice-Hall.

Stainback, S., Stainback, W., & Forest, M. (Eds). (1989). *Educating all students in the mainstream of regular education.* Baltimore: Paul H. Brookes Publishing Co.

Stainback, S., Stainback, W., & Slavin, R. (1989). Classroom organization for diversity among students. In S. Stainback, W. Stainback, & M. Forest (Eds.), *Educating all students in the mainstream of regular education* (pp. 131–142). Baltimore: Paul H. Brookes Publishing Co.

Stainback, W., & Stainback, S. (Eds.). (1990). *Support networks for inclusive schools: Interdependent integrated education.* Baltimore: Paul H. Brookes Publishing Co.

Thousand, J.S., & Villa, R.A. (1989). Enhancing success in heterogeneous schools. In S. Stainback, W. Stainback, & M. Forest (Eds.), *Educating all students in the mainstream of regular education* (pp. 89–104). Baltimore: Paul H. Brookes Publishing Co.

Tombari, M.L., & Bergan, J.R. (1978). Consultant cues and teacher verbalizations, judgments, and expectancies concerning children's adjustment problems. *Journal of School Psychology, 16,* 212–219.

Villa, R.A., & Thousand, J.S. (1988). Enhancing success in heterogeneous classrooms and schools: The powers of partnership. *Teacher Education and Special Education, 11,* 144–153.

Wang, M.C. (1989). Accommodating student diversity through adaptive instruction. In S. Stainback, W. Stainback, & M. Forest (Eds.), *Educating all students in the mainstream of regular education* (pp. 183–198). Baltimore: Paul H. Brookes Publishing Co.

Wang, M.C., Reynolds, M.C., & Schwartz, L.L. (1988). Adaptive instruction: An alternative educational approach for students with special needs. In J.L. Graden, J.E. Zins, & M.J. Curtis (Eds.), *Alternative educational delivery systems: Enhancing instructional options for all students* (pp. 199–220). Washington, DC: National Association of School Psychologists.

Ysseldyke, J.E., & Christenson, S.L. (1987). *The Instructional Environment Scale*. Austin, TX: PRO-ED.

Zins, J.E., Curtis, M.J., Graden, J.L., & Ponti, C.R. (1988). *Helping students succeed in the regular classroom*. San Francisco: Jossey-Bass.

6

Integrating Support Personnel in the Inclusive Classroom

Jennifer York, Michael F. Giangreco, Terri Vandercook, and Cathy Macdonald

ALTHOUGH CLASSROOM TEACHERS have a range of curricular and instructional skills, educating some students in inclusive classrooms requires contributions from professionals representing a variety of disciplines. The need for the services of support personnel in inclusive classrooms is not a negative reflection on the adequacy of classroom teachers. Instead, it reminds us that no single individual, no matter what her or his discipline or experience, has the ability to meet the range of diverse student needs that may be present in a heterogeneous classroom.

One of the most significant contributions any educational team member can make is to identify and build on an individual student's strengths and gifts to form a basis for future success in personal, academic, and vocational pursuits. When given a choice, people rarely

Development of this chapter was supported, in part, by Grant No. 496125-11924 to the University of Minnesota, Institute on Community Integration from the Minnesota Department of Education; Grant No. H086D00014 to the University of Minnesota, Institute on Community Integration from the United States Office of Special Education and Rehabilitative Services; and Grant No. H086H80017 to the University of Vermont, Center for Developmental Disabilities from the United States Office of Special Education and Rehabilitative Services. The opinions expressed herein do not necessarily reflect the position or policy of the Minnesota Department of Education or the United States Department of Education and no official endorsement should be inferred.

spend a majority of their days engaged in activities that focus on their weaknesses. One of the great ironies of education is that even though most professionals presumably have selected their careers based on personal interests and strengths, many educators attempt to teach students by focusing on what is perceived to be their deficits. This does not mean that remediation of or accommodation for student challenges are inappropriate educational pursuits. Rather, approaches that emphasize individual strengths are more likely to result in student success, positive self-esteem, and interest in being a lifelong learner.

Increasingly, students with even the most severe disabilities are receiving educational and related services in general education classrooms (Ford & Davern, 1989; Forest & Lusthaus, 1990; Giangreco & Meyer, 1988; Giangreco & Putnam, 1991; Sapon-Shevin, 1990; Stainback & Stainback, 1990; Thousand et al., 1986; Williams, Villa, Thousand, & Fox, 1989; York & Vandercook, 1990; York, Vandercook, Macdonald, Heise-Neff, & Caughey, in press; York, Vandercook, Macdonald, & Wolff, 1989). Progressive inclusion and relocation of students with disabilities from special education classes and schools to general education classes has not automatically resulted in appropriate education or effective teamwork among those hired to support students. Ineffective collaboration and lack of programmatic integration among professionals results in a large part from: 1) differing values, orientations, and experiences of various disciplines (Giangreco, 1990a); 2) lack of preservice preparation in knowledge of other disciplines and of collaborative teamwork (Askamit & Alcorn, 1988; Rainforth, 1985; Sapon-Shevin, 1988; Stainback & Stainback, 1987); 3) confusion about the types of support personnel available to inclusive classrooms and their supportive knowledge; and 4) logistical and pragmatic barriers.

The purposes of this chapter are to: 1) discuss the characteristics and types of support offered in inclusive classrooms, 2) outline considerations for selecting needed supports and helpful personnel, 3) present several myths about various disciplines, and 4) provide general guidelines for providing support in inclusive classrooms.

CHARACTERISTICS OF SUPPORT

Providing support to the inclusive classroom requires more than having specific disciplinary expertise and being physically present in the classroom. In this section a definition of support and a description of four types of support are provided. In addition, questions regarding who decides the type and amount of support needed are addressed.

What Is Support?

support . . . 1. to carry or bear the weight of; keep from falling, slipping, or sinking; hold up or to give courage or bear (a specified weight, strain, pressure, etc.)   2. to give courage, faith, or confidence to; help or comfort   3. to give approval to or be in favor of; subscribe to; uphold   4. to maintain or provide for (a person or institution, etc.) with money or subsistence   5. to show or tend to show to be true; help prove, vindicate, or corroborate [evidence to support the claim]   6. to bear, endure; submit to; tolerate   7. to keep up, maintain; sustain; specific to maintain (the price of a specified commodity) as by purchases or by making loans 8. Theater to act a subordinate role in the same play as (a specified star) . . . (Webster's New World Dictionary of the American Language, 1986, p. 1431)

This dictionary definition of *support* refers to various forms of help. Shel Silverstein's (1974) poem *Helping* reminds us that ". . . some kind of help is the kind of help that helping is all about, and some kind of help is the kind of help we all can do without" (p. 101). While well intended, efforts to help students, families, and teachers often lead to the assignment of support personnel; merely labeling someone as a support does not ensure that he or she will be perceived as helpful by those receiving the intended support.

The provision of real (as opposed to intended) support is contingent, in part, upon a mutual understanding of the outcomes sought as a result of the support. In the case of an inclusive classroom, there are at least two major desired outcomes: 1) that all students are successful in their educational and social endeavors, and 2) that the classroom teacher feels genuinely supported in his or her efforts to promote student success and positive interdependence in the classroom.

Real support exists when: 1) the recipient of support perceives that he or she has been helped; 2) the responsibility for achieving desired student outcomes is shared among team members (i.e., positive interdependence among team members develops); 3) the goal of meeting diverse educational needs of students is better accomplished; 4) the effort required for collaboration is worth the outcomes; and 5) priority outcomes for students at school, at home, and in the community are achieved.

Whether or not real support is achieved depends on how the actions of one person affect another. Support personnel can engage in a variety of behaviors, but unless those behaviors result in supportive effects for the recipient, support has not been provided. Quasi-support occurs when a mismatch exists between the content, type, or intensity of support desired and the support provided. Table 1 provides examples of practices that would likely fit this description of support and those that would not.

Table 1.   Examples of what support means and what support does not mean

Support means:

helping students and families realize their own vision of a good life

listening to and acting on the support needs identified by students, families, and other team members

reallocating resources so that students can be included in regular school life, and teams can learn and work together

remembering that the students are the "stars" and that the educational team members are the supporting actors

acknowledging the efforts of fellow team members

designing curricular and instructional methods that assist the student to be an active learner

designing curricular and instructional methods that assist the classroom teacher to effectively include the student

designing curricular and instructional methods that promote positive interdependence among students in the class

providing constructive feedback to fellow team members that results in more effective team member interactions and ultimately improved student learning

providing enough information, but not too much

being around and available, but not too much

Support does *not* mean:

conducting a classroom observation and then writing and depositing notes on the teacher's desk with no opportunity for follow-up discussion

giving your opinions, advice, and recommendations and then leaving before a discussion can ensue

requesting to meet with the classroom teacher during instructional time without making prior arrangements

presenting the classroom teacher with a list of skills or activities to be integrated into the classroom day

telling the teacher or family what to do

giving the classroom teacher a file folder of resources when she asked for problem-solving support

hovering near students with disabilities in the classroom

doing "therapy" in the back of the room

suggesting interventions that interfere with the classroom routine

providing more support than is needed

What Are the Types of Support?

Support for inclusive classrooms can be classified into four types—resource, moral, technical, and evaluation. The type and/or the intensity of support provided in an inclusive classroom will vary depending on needs at different points in time.

Resource Support   Resource support consists of providing a consumer with tangible material (e.g., lab equipment, adapted computer keyboard), financial resources (e.g., funds for community experiences), informational resources (e.g., professional literature), or human resources (e.g., instructional assistant, peer tutor). However, resources alone do not ensure quality of support. More money or people do not necessarily meet the support needs of an inclusive classroom. Likewise, a paucity of resources does not necessarily preclude the availability of needed support for a classroom. For example, in some resource-scarce schools, teams are forced to find creative and often more positive and interdependent ways to address challenges. Some of the best examples of inclusion-oriented classes are in economically disadvantaged, rural areas.

Moral Support   Moral support refers to person-to-person interactions that validate the worth of people as individuals and as knowledgeable colleagues. It includes active listening characterized by nonjudgmental acceptance of ideas and feelings. The person providing moral support does not always agree with the speaker, but adequate trust exists so that perspectives can be shared without fear of putdowns, criticism, or breeches in confidentiality.

Technical Support   Technical support refers to offering concrete strategies, methods, approaches, or ideas. Providing a teacher with a journal article on instructional methods is a form of resource support (informational), not technical support. Technical support can be provided through inservice training, staff development activities, on-site collaborative consultation, peer coaching, or other methods. It provides the recipient with skills that can then be implemented, adjusted, and reimplemented in a cyclical fashion to meet student needs. Technical assistance is a dynamic process that is individualized and requires interpersonal interactions.

Evaluation Support   Evaluation support refers to assistance in collecting information that allows support to be monitored and adjusted. It also refers to assistance in determining the impact of support on students, families, and professionals. The scope of evaluation should extend beyond acquisition of specific targeted skills by students to include outcomes of educational experiences on the lifestyle or quality of life of the students and their families (Horner, 1991; Meyer & Janney, 1989; Schalock, 1990).

Who Decides the Type of Support?

Collaboration is required to identify and agree on the type of support needed. The intended recipients of support know their situations best and therefore have a primary role in identifying supports. This means that support personnel are not "in charge" of making support decisions. Decisions about the type of support needed in any particular situation belong to everyone involved. Furthermore, all members of the team have the capacity to provide and receive support. This seemingly benign concept may be a challenge to actualize since many professionals are socialized and accustomed to retaining authority over decisions related to their discipline (Giangreco, 1990a). At the same time, the knowledge and broad-based experience of many support personnel provide them with perspectives that may assist consumers in making decisions about support needs. Additionally, support personnel may be knowledgeable about whether they can provide the kind of support being requested or whether others could offer thát support more effectively. Recently developed strategies such as the Vermont Interdependent Services Team Approach (VISTA) are designed to assist teams in reaching consensus regarding support needs (Giangreco, 1990c).

Who Decides How Much Support?

Sometimes well-intentioned recommendations to provide support services on behalf of a student or teacher can backfire. More is not necessarily better. In fact, providing more services than necessary can have negative ramifications, such as: 1) decreasing the time available for the student's interaction and participation with peers in school activities, 2) causing disruption for students and teachers in carrying out their normal classroom activities, 3) causing inequities in the distribution of scarce resources when other students or educators in need of supports remain unserved or underserved, 4) overwhelming consumer families with an unnecessarily high number of professionals, or 5) unnecessarily complicating communication and coordination among all involved persons. An alternative is to provide supports that are "only as special as necessary" (Biklen, 1987; Giangreco & Eichinger, 1990). In such cases, needed services are provided and caution is exercised to avoid the inherent problems of well-intentioned, yet often undesirable, overservice.

CONSIDERATIONS FOR SELECTING SUPPORT PERSONNEL

Support may be needed by some students and teachers to make school inclusion successful. Supports may be needed to overcome or circumvent difficulties experienced as a result of a student's ability or disability, environmental influences, or a combination of both. Characteristics of students that may influence support selection include skills acquired, experiences, and/or aspects of their intellectual, communication, social, physical, sensory, or health functioning. The knowledge, skills, and previous experiences of teachers as well as the class members can also have an impact on the type and degree of support needed. In addition, environmental influences including school, home, and community factors can have a dramatic effect on the success of students and teachers in inclusive classrooms and schools.

In a recent book, *The Challenge of Complex School Problems*, Norby, Thurlow, Christenson, and Ysseldyke (1990) present a model of interaction among community, home, school, and student factors that affect student performance in school. Twenty-two case studies dramatically illustrate the complex interaction of variables affecting school performance. Too often, educational team members focus exclusively on challenges related to a child's disability (e.g., physical difficulty, mental retardation) without sufficient knowledge of contributing external factors (e.g., nutrition, expectations at home, peer pressure), or they attribute student challenges to presumed disabilities when, in fact, challenges may be the result of school, home, or community variables external to the child.

The support model that has developed in education is designed to match certain disciplines to specific student or teacher challenges. For example, a student who exhibits difficulty or a teacher who is unsure of how to facilitate skills among some class members, such as getting from place to place in the school or manipulating books and other educational materials, can be assisted by professionals trained in physical therapy, occupational therapy, or adapted physical education. If classroom challenges involve how to communicate, a speech and language therapist or an educator with experience in augmentative and alternative communication might be of assistance. Some students have diverse health care needs that require support for eating, physical activity, and other routines and activities that are part of the school day. School nurses can assist in developing ways to address these special health care needs. Finally, it should be stressed that support personnel need to focus more now than in the past on environmental adjustments and improvements (e.g., better cues and assistance in getting from place to place; more accommodating communication environments, such as learning symbols on a communication board) rather than just focusing on what a particular student can do to better fit into the existing environment.

After everyone involved agrees on which educational supports are needed to modify the environment or accommodate an individual student or teacher, appropriate support personnel can be identified. As shown in Table 2, there are several disciplines that could provide support for any particular type of situation. In addition to professionals, the direct experiences of family members and classmates make them invaluable as support for meeting various challenges. In

Table 2.   Support personnel to assist in meeting specific student challenges

Student challenge	Potential support personnel
Cognitive/learning processes	
Curricular/instructional adaptations or alternatives	Educator, speech-language pathologist, occupational therapist, psychologist, vision or hearing specialist, classmate, support facilitator
Organizing assignments, schedules	Educator, occupational therapist, speech-language pathologist, support facilitator
Communication/interactions	
Nonverbal communication	Speech-language pathologist, teacher, family members
Socialization with classmates	Speech-language pathologist, teacher, psychologist, classmates
Behaving in adaptive ways	Educator, psychologist, speech-language pathologist, classmates
Physical/motor	
Functional use of hands	Occupational therapist, physical therapist, family member, classmate
Mobility and transitions	Physical therapist, occupational therapist, orientation and mobility specialist, educator, family member, classmates
Posture (body alignment)	Physical therapist, occupational therapist
Fitness and physical activity	Physical therapist, physical educator, nurse
Sensory	
Vision	Vision specialist, occupational therapist, orientation and mobility specialist
Hearing	Audiologist, hearing specialist, speech-language pathologist
Health	
Eating difficulty	Occupational therapist, speech-language pathologist, physical therapist, nurse, educator
Medications	Nurse
Other health needs	Nurse
Current and future living	
Career and vocational pursuits	Vocational educator, counselor, educator
Leisure pursuits	Educator, occupational therapist, community recreation personnel
Support from home and community	Social worker, counselor, educator

deciding who can be supportive of specific student challenges, the range of school, home, and community supports should be considered. Final decisions about support personnel and the type and amount of support needed are reached by team consensus. Consensus decision making reduces the risks of overlap, gaps, and contradictions in service provision (Giangreco, 1990c; Giangreco, Dennis, & Edelman, in press).

DISCIPLINE MYTHS

There are a sufficient number of myths that exist about the roles and responsibilities of the various disciplines. The authors present these *discipline myths* here as they frequently represent a source of team conflict, sometimes without those people involved recognizing their influence.

First, it is a myth that a person's expertise is the primary prerequisite for carrying out the role of a support person. Of equal importance to an individual's disciplinary expertise is his or her ability to work collaboratively. This includes: 1) letting go of strong disciplinary beliefs when they get in the way of a holistic view of the child, 2) solving problems even if the problems are not considered in the arena of an individual's expertise, and 3) providing support to improve interactions within the inclusive classroom and school community. An individual with outstanding disciplinary skills will be hampered in his or her support efforts if he or she has inadequate collaboration skills.

Second, strictly defined boundaries among disciplines is a myth. There is, in fact, tremendous overlap among many disciplines. Case management, for example, is a responsibility now claimed by at least six different disciplines that support students and teachers in schools (e.g., social workers, parents, teachers, counselors, psychologists, nurses). When working with children, there is considerable overlap in the knowledge and skills of physical and occupational therapists. In the area of daily living skills, occupational therapists and teachers have overlapping competencies. In the area of reading difficulty, any number of licensed reading teachers have overlapping expertise.

In a time of curricular and economic crisis in the public schools and increasing decentralization of students with common characteristics and needs, educators are encouraged to employ service provision models that use support resources efficiently. Instead of fighting over "turf," professionals could acknowledge overlap and divide up work accordingly. For example, if a physical therapist and an occupational therapist have overlapping areas of knowledge and skill needed to support a particular student, the persons involved (including the families) could designate one of the therapists as the primary specialist for the student (Rainforth, York, & Macdonald, 1992). The result is fewer children on each therapist's roster and more time to spend with each student. This can facilitate increased continuity in a student's educational program and decreased logistical constraints due to having fewer people to coordinate. When using a primary specialist model, it is appropriate to provide opportunities for specialists to work together occasionally with regard to an individual student.

A third myth is that each individual trained in a particular discipline has the same competencies. Most professional fields of practice or disciplines have diverse arenas of practice. Physical therapists, for example, can work in sports medicine, obstetrics, neonatal intensive care, nursing homes, orthopedics, pediatrics, and developmental disabilities. Individual professionals within a discipline tend to be more or less interested and skilled in selected areas of practice. The key to determining appropriate support personnel is to focus on the competencies of the individual, not his or her specialty label.

The final myth is that individuals with a specific discipline label own an area of expertise. In other words, only an individual trained in a particular discipline can execute the skills commonly associated with it. As mentioned previously, there is considerable overlap among specific disciplines (Giangreco & Eichenger, 1990). Furthermore, all professionals have a responsibility to learn as much as they can to assist students be successful learners. If one person learned to correctly implement a given procedure, it is very likely that other people can do so as well with appropriate training and support. The knowledge and skills that need to be transferred from one team member to another are identified based on the needs of an individual student in his or her educational program. There is a core group of people (e.g., family members, classroom teachers, paraprofessionals, classmates, friends) who surround and support students and teachers all day, every day. These individuals know the student and teacher best and are most accessible for assisting them to be successful in the classroom and school. For example, if a student uses alternative forms of communication or mobility, the core people in that student's life can and must learn effective means of facilitating these forms. To do this they need support, recommendations, and training from various disciplines. This is not to say that individuals trained in various disciplines need to pass all of their skills on to other people. It would be inefficient, for example, to teach everyone involved with a particular student specific disciplinary, diagnostic, and evaluation competencies.

The specific methods of support vary tremendously. Any number of creative variations are possible to more effectively meet the needs of students and teachers (Skrtic, 1987). The most important issue is deciding who has or could develop the competence to support a student—not who has the correct label. After the priorities of an individual in an educational setting have been identified, the specific person(s) who is able to assist in meeting the needs can be determined.

STRUCTURES FOR PROVIDING SUPPORT

Traditional approaches used by the numerous and diverse professionals providing support to an individual student consist of spending individual or small group time with the student to focus on a specific challenge. For example, a physical therapist might have worked with a student on improving walking skills using parallel bars in a separate therapy room. Or, a speech and language therapist may have spent individual time increasing a child's response to greetings by practicing in the therapy room. Greater inclusion of students with diverse needs into general education classes and other integrated environments has created the need for support personnel to modify their traditional methods of service provision. Specifically, structures that allow support personnel to observe and work with students and their teachers and peers in the context of their educational programs is essential to ensure the educational relevance of their support. This requires two major logistical changes: 1) flexible scheduling so that support personnel can spend time in general education classes and other integrated environments, and 2) scheduling opportunities for the people involved to collaborate.

Scheduling Time in Integrated Environments

An alternative to traditional scheduling of specialist time (i.e., back-to-back direct sessions of 30–45 minutes in a separate environment) is the use of *block scheduling* (Rainforth, York, & Macdonald, 1992; Rainforth & York, 1987; York, Rainforth, & Wiemann, 1988). Block scheduling refers to allocating longer periods of time (e.g., a half or full day) for a specialist to move flexibly to each environment where students and teachers may require assistance, input, and/or support. For example, a speech-language therapist might spend one full day every other week in an elementary school where four students and/or teachers require the therapist's expertise. Prior to block scheduling, the therapist would meet briefly (10–15 minutes) with classroom teachers (primary level) or case managers (secondary level) to: 1) identify priorities that need to be addressed, and 2) determine where the therapist needs to be and at what times in order to attend to the priorities.

There are countless ways to implement a block scheduling

model. The specific strategies will vary given the array of demographic, student, district, and scheduling variables. Perhaps the only two guidelines to follow are: 1) allow adequate flexibility for meeting the differing needs of those individuals requiring assistance and for changing needs over time, and 2) be certain that scheduling is communicated among everyone involved to maximize preparation and efficiency. Typically, a block scheduling model results in less frequent direct service provision to students, but provides the flexibility needed to ensure educational relevance. (See Rainforth, York, & Macdonald, 1992, for more detailed information about scheduling support personnel in inclusive classrooms.)

Scheduling Time To Collaborate

Collaboration opportunities occur informally during block scheduling times as well as during regularly scheduled team meeting times, special purpose meetings (e.g., IEP meetings), and staff development and/or training meetings. When support personnel working with other involved persons (e.g., teachers, family members, students) are just starting to design and implement individualized education programs (IEPs) in inclusive classrooms, more collaboration time is required. As those involved learn to collaborate more efficiently and as the program of support is worked out, less time is needed for collaboration. Initially, the authors suggest scheduling regular meeting times and classroom times for support personnel—but only those support personnel who are recognized as necessary for the student's and/or teacher's initial priorities. For a small number of students who have very intensive support needs, weekly team meetings may be necessary in the beginning.

To maximize meeting efficiency, the following parameters are offered:

1. Begin and end the meetings on time.
2. Identify a facilitator and recorder for each meeting and rotate these roles among all members of the group (additional roles might be assigned, such as timekeeper or "jargon buster" [term coined by staff of the Addison-Northeast Supervisory Union in Bristol, Vermont] depending on individual team needs).
3. Generate an agenda prior to the meeting.
4. Review and prioritize items at the beginning of the meeting if necessary.
5. Identify follow-up activities and assign responsibility for each.
6. Copy and disseminate minutes to each person present within 2 days following the meetings.

Classroom and meeting times both provide a forum for all types of support (e.g., resource, moral, technical, evaluation). In an effort to be efficient, teams may focus all their attention on resource, technical, and evaluation support and forget what can be the most important and easiest support to provide—moral support. Although moral support can be demonstrated by the manner used to address other support needs (e.g., active listening to the resource concerns of an involved person), specific strategies for validating individual and team efforts are important as well. For example, adding a "celebrate success" item to the meeting agenda would be one way of attending to the provision of moral support.

CONCLUSION

As the student population in inclusive classrooms becomes more heterogeneous, models of providing support will evolve to meet increasingly diverse learning and social needs. In fact, recent education reform initiatives aimed at developing capacity at the school building level (e.g., site-based management, teacher empowerment, adhocratic school organization) reflect a shift to empower the people closest to students, as well as the students themselves. The safeguard against any one individual not acting in a student's best interest is the collaborative support group structure. Empowerment of direct service personnel is a departure from traditional school organizational models in which support has been part of a unidirectional hierarchy; that is, support and direction from higher up in the organization or from external resources (e.g., "expert" consultants). The evolving interdependent models of support create opportunities for multidirectional, more immediate, and possibly more relevant support. In addition, to gain even more relevant support, there may eventually be a group structure that involves fewer members. However, more intensive involvement by these members is preferred over a structure that involves a large number of disciplines that have very little time to spend in each situation or to provide ongoing problem-solving support.

Regardless of the specific disciplines that will be involved as support personnel, it is likely that the two most important areas of "expertise" for assisting students to become valued and contributing members of schools and larger communities are: 1) expertise specific to the student and teacher (i.e., knowing student and teacher well and having a stake in their success), and 2) community-building expertise (i.e., knowing local resources and working collaboratively with others to achieve the needed support).

Although much of the focus in this chapter has been on support personnel with ascribed professional discipline labels, schools are increasingly drawing upon educators, parents and families, students, community members, and others to provide support within the inclusive school community. Members of collaborative educational teams provide support to one another. Those traditionally considered recipients of support (e.g., classroom teachers, students, family members) are assuming more active and collaborative roles in planning, problem solving, and implementation (Giangreco, 1990b; Giangreco, Cloninger, & Iverson, 1990; Vandercook, York, & Forest, 1989).

Several summary guidelines are offered to assist educational teams in making decisions about the support personnel needed and the nature of that support. First, priority educational needs and other learning outcomes are identified through consensus decision making by a group consisting of students, family members, the classroom teacher, and others identified as essential in this process. Second, goals and objectives related to accomplishing the priority needs are determined. Third, support personnel who have the knowledge and skills, regardless of their discipline label, to address the needs are identified. This, too, is accomplished through consensus decision making in order to decrease overlap, gaps, and contradictions in service provision. Fourth, an organizational structure that allows the support personnel to be involved in natural, ongoing educational contexts and to collaborate with other persons involved is developed. Finally, as educational priorities and needs change, the provision of support is reexamined and altered as necessary.

REFERENCES

Askamit, D., & Alcorn, D. (1988). A preservice mainstream curriculum infusion model: Student teachers' perceptions of program effectiveness. *Teacher Education and Special Education, 11,* 52–58.

Biklen, D. (1987, October). *Excellence in education: Can we have it without integration?* Keynote address at the annual conference of the Finger Lakes Association for Persons with Severe Handicaps, Syracuse, NY.

Ford, A., & Davern, L. (1989). Moving forward with school integration: Strategies for involving students with severe handicaps in the life of the school. In R. Gaylord-Ross (Ed.), *Integration strategies for students with handicaps* (pp. 11–32). Baltimore: Paul H. Brookes Publishing Co.

Forest, M., & Lusthaus, E. (1990). Everyone belongs with MAPS action planning system. *Teaching Exceptional Children, 22,* 32–35.

Giangreco, M.F. (1990a). Making related service decisions for students with severe disabilities: Roles, criteria, and authority. *Journal of The Association for Persons with Severe Handicaps, 15*(1), 22–31.

Giangreco, M.F. (1990b). *Using creative problem-solving methods to include students with severe disabilities in general education classroom activities.* Manuscript submitted for publication.

Giangreco, M.F. (1990c). *Vermont interdependent services team approach (V.I.S.T.A.): Pilot evaluation of effects on team decision-making.* Manuscript submitted for publication.

Giangreco, M.F., Cloninger, C.J., & Iverson, V.S. (1990). *Cayuga-Onondaga assessment for children with handicaps—Version 6.0.* Stillwater: National Clearinghouse of Rehabilitation Training Materials at Oklahoma State University.

Giangreco, M.F., Dennis, R., & Edelman, A. (in press). Common professional practices that interfere with the integrated delivery of related services. *Remedial and Special Education.*

Giangreco, M.F., & Eichinger, J. (1990). Related services and the transdisciplinary approach. In M. Anketell, E.J. Bailey, J. Houghton, A. O'Dea, B. Utley, & D. Wickham (Eds.), *A series of training modules for educating children and youth with dual sensory impairments.* Monmouth, OR: Teaching Research Publications.

Giangreco, M., & Meyer, L.H. (1988).Expanding service delivery options in regular schools and classrooms for students with severe disabilities. In J. Graden, J. Zins, & M. Curtis (Eds.), *Alternative educational delivery systems: Enhancing instructional options for all students* (pp 241–267). Washington, DC: National Association for School Psychologists.

Giangreco, M., & Putnam, J.W. (1991). Supporting the education of students with severe disabilities in regular education environments. In L.H. Meyer, C.A. Peck, & L. Brown (Eds.), *Critical issues in the lives of people with severe disabilities* (pp. 245–270). Baltimore: Paul H. Brookes Publishing Co.

Gurlanik, D.B. (Ed.). (1986). *Webster new world dictionary of the American language.* New York: Simon & Schuster.

Horner, R.H. (1991). The future of applied behavior analysis for people with severe disabilities: Commentary I. In L.H. Meyer, C.A. Peck, & L. Brown (Eds.), *Critical issues in the lives of people with severe disabilities* (pp. 607–611). Baltimore: Paul H. Brookes Publishing Co.

Meyer, L.H., & Janney, R. (1989). User-friendly measures of meaningful outcomes: Evaluating behavioral interventions. *Journal of The Association for Persons with Severe Handicaps, 14*(4), 263–270.

Norby, J.M., Thurlow, M.L., Christenson, S.L., & Ysseldyke, J.E. (1990). *The challenge of complex school problems.* Austin, TX: PRO-ED.

Rainforth, B. (1985). *Collaborative efforts in the preparation of physical therapists and teachers of students with severe handicaps.* Unpublished doctoral dissertation, University of Illinois.

Rainforth, B., & York, J. (1987). Integrating related services in community instruction. *Journal of The Association for Persons with Severe Handicaps, 12*(3), 193–198.

Rainforth, B., York, J., & Macdonald C. (1992). *Collaborative teams serving students with severe disabilities: Integrated therapy in educational programs.* Baltimore: Paul H. Brookes Publishing Co.

Sapon-Shevin, M. (1988). Working toward merger together: Seeing beyond the distrust and fear. *Teacher Education and Special Education, 11,* 103–110.

Sapon-Shevin, M. (1990). Schools as communities of love and care. *Holistic Education Review, 3,* 22–24.

Schalock, R.L. (1990). *Quality of life: Perspectives and issues.* Washington, DC: American Association on Mental Retardation.

Silverstein, S. (1974). *Where the sidewalk ends.* New York: Harper & Row.

Skrtic, T. (1987). An organizational analysis of special education reform. *Counterpoint, 8*(2), 15–19.

Stainback, S., & Stainback, W. (1987). Facilitating merger through personnel preparation. *Teacher Education and Special Education, 10*, 185–190.

Stainback, W., & Stainback, S. (Eds.). (1990). *Support networks for inclusive schooling: Interdependent integrated education.* Baltimore: Paul H. Brookes Publishing Co.

Thousand, J.S., Fox, T.J., Reid, R., Godek, J., Williams, W., & Fox, W.L. (1986). *The homecoming model: Educating students who present intensive educational challenges within regular education environments.* Burlington: University of Vermont, Center for Developmental Disabilities.

Vandercook, T., York, J., & Forest, M. (1989). MAPS: A strategy for building the vision. *Journal of The Association for Persons with Severe Handicaps, 14*(3), 205–215.

Williams, W., Villa, R., Thousand, J., & Fox, W.L. (1989). Is regular class placement really the issue?: A response to Brown, Long, Udvari-Solner, Schwarz, VanDeventer, Ahlgren, Johnson, Gruenewald, & Jorgensen. *Journal of The Association for Persons with Severe Handicaps, 14*, 333–334.

York, J., Rainforth, B., & Wiemann, G. (1988). An integrated approach to therapy for school aged learners with developmental disabilities. *Totline, 14*(3), 36–40.

York, J., & Vandercook, T. (1990). Strategies for achieving an integrated education for middle school students with severe disabilities. *Remedial and Special Education, 11*(5), 6–15.

York, J., Vandercook, T., Macdonald, C., Heise-Neff, C., & Caughey, E. (in press). Feedback from teachers and classmates about integrating middle school learners with severe disabilities in regular classes. *Exceptional Children.*

York, J., Vandercook, T., Macdonald, C., & Wolff, S. (Eds.). (1989). *Strategies for full inclusion.* Minneapolis: University of Minnesota, Institute on Community Integration.

7

Student Collaboration

An Essential for Curriculum Delivery in the 21st Century

Richard A. Villa and Jacqueline S. Thousand

"MANY OF OUR most critical problems are not in the world of things, but in the world of people. Our greatest failure as human beings has been the inability to secure cooperation and understanding with others" (Hersey & Blanchard, 1977, p. 1).

The history of collaboration among educators in North American schools in the development, delivery, and modification of curriculum and instruction has been relatively short. Emerging in the 1960s in the form of team teaching arrangements (Bair & Woodward, 1964; Beggs, 1964) and evolving and expanding in the 1970s and 1980s to consultation and special education prereferral approaches, such as child study teams (Graden, Casey, & Christenson, 1985), teacher assistant teams (Chalfant, Pysch, & Moultrie, 1979), consulting teacher

The authors gratefully acknowledge the contributions of the following Vermont students and educators for providing examples of effective student collaboration strategies: Chandra Duba, Gary Ellenboden, Michael Giangreco, John Gempka, Joanne Godek, Moriah Gosselin, Tracy Harris, Sharon James, Nancy Keller, Laurie LaPlant, Lisa Ledwith, Karen Lewis, Linda Libuda, Jason Messick, Bill Niquette, Mary Jane Peters, Don Schneider, Laurie Soutiere, Michelle Steady, and Nadine Zane. Their actions give us hope for the 21st century.

The authors dedicate this work to the memory of Bob Cota, whose soul dwells in the house of tomorrow. In his short lifetime, Bob taught many the value of diversity and mutually beneficial collaborative relationships.

systems (Knight, Myers, Paolucci-Whitcomb, Hasazi, & Nevin, 1981), and collaborative consultation approaches (Idol, Paolucci-Whitcomb, & Nevin, 1986; Nevin, Thousand, Paolucci-Whitcomb, & Villa, 1990; Pugach & Johnson, 1989; Tharp, 1975), collaboration has become a "buzzword" in futurists' conceptualizations of the effective 21st century school (Benjamin, 1989).

Although collaboration is not yet the norm in North American schools (Timar, 1989), it is generally thought of as adults (professional educators) sharing planning, teaching, and/or evaluation responsibilities for students. The purpose of this chapter is to examine forms of school collaboration that tap the resources of children in determining and delivering the school community's agreed-upon curriculum. Recently, there have been calls for the inclusion and empowerment of students in decision-making processes regarding discipline (Curwin & Mendler, 1988) and the delivery of instruction and social support to peers (Glasser, 1986; Johnson, Johnson, Holubec, & Roy, 1984; Villa & Thousand, 1988). The recognized benefits and rationale for greater involvement of students in the determination of the form and content of their own education include enhanced motivation (Glasser, 1986; Johnson & Johnson, 1987a) and achievement (Bloom, 1976; Johnson, Maruyama, Johnson, Nelson, & Skon, 1981).

The most powerful arguments for enhanced student collaboration, however, are concerned less with traditional notions of (tested) performance and motivation and more with the development of the information-seeking and problem-solving citizen who is able to thrive in a more complex, diverse, information-rich, and technologically driven 21st century. Benjamin (1989), in an analysis of futurist literature, and Wiggins (1989), in a prescription for a "modern" curriculum, forecast interdependent, international societal trends that will make it difficult for school curricula to keep pace with the exponential growth of information and technological and scientific information discoveries. "There is simply too much for any one of us to know, never mind teach to dozens of students in a crowded day. Such a tragic fact leads to a liberating realization: wisdom matters more than knowledge" (Wiggins, 1989, p. 58).

Wisdom, in the futurist's eye, includes "habits of mind," (Wiggins, 1989, p. 48) such as the ability to suspend disbelief, knowing how to listen to someone who knows something "new," questioning to clarify an idea's meaning or value, openness to new and strange ideas, and the inclination to question confusing or "pat" statements (Wiggins, 1989). Wisdom involves having strategies for coping with diversity and continuing to be a lifelong learner; wisdom means social competence to communicate and interact with others, including people in international, democratic workplaces (Benjamin, 1989).

How, then, do futurists see schools operating in the 21st century so that graduates acquire wisdom?

In the educational futurist literature, the most frequently occurring recommendation for 21st century schools is to increase active learning on the part of the student (Benjamin, 1989). Active learning involves students participating in all aspects of the learning process. Active learning also means empowering students to determine what and how they will learn. Given the projected information explosion of the next century, futurists also recommend that schools concentrate on students learning how to be lifelong learners, rather than only learners of facts. Additionally, futurists consider the school responsible for helping students to extend their concerns beyond themselves and gain a community service ethic through real-life service experiences and in-school analyses of the experiences.

The future world suggests "a new collaborative role for teachers and students in which students accept an active senior partnership role in the learning enterprise" (Benjamin, 1989, p. 9). Therefore, teachers in 21st century schools must become familiar with existing methods and be encouraged to experiment with strategies for actively engaging students in their own and others' acquisition of humanistic, public service ethics; communication, information-seeking, and problem-solving skills; and core curriculum deemed essential by the school and greater community.

This chapter describes a number of collaborative arrangements and strategies that engage students in instructional and advocacy roles with their peers and in decision-making roles to determine the school's curriculum, organization, and governance. However, before examining these strategies the reader should reflect upon personal experiences as a student in 20th century schools and assess the extent to which these experiences exemplified or incorporated a collaborative spirit by responding to the questions in the Student Collaboration Quiz presented in Figure 1.

First, after reading the remainder of this chapter, the reader should envision himself or herself as a student enrolled in a school that utilizes the recommended peer empowerment strategies and, upon readministration of the quiz, find dramatic positive shifts in collaboration scores. Second, this chapter should empower readers to further explore and implement some of the discussed student collaboration strategies in community schools so that, before this century's end, graduates of schools who take this same quiz not only give themselves and their schools high scores, but are able to articulate what life would be like in the 21st century and how their schooling has prepared them for this life.

The authors have grouped the "peer power" (Villa & Thousand,

1. Did you, as a student, observe or experience your teachers modeling collaboration in instruction (e.g., team teaching), planning, or evaluation?

    Never   Rarely   Sometimes   Often   Very Often

2. Were you, as a student, given the opportunity and training to serve as an instructor for a peer?

    Never   Rarely   Sometimes   Often   Very Often

3. Were you, as a student, given the opportunity to receive instruction from a trained peer?

    Never   Rarely   Sometimes   Often   Very Often

4. How often was the instruction you received structured in such a way as to encourage the use of higher level reasoning skills (e.g., analysis, synthesis, evaluation, creative problem solving, meta-cognition)?

    Never   Rarely   Sometimes   Often   Very Often

5. How often were you expected to support the academic learning of other students as well as be accountable for your own learning?

    Never   Rarely   Sometimes   Often   Very Often

6. How often were you expected to support other students' acquisition and performance of interpersonal skills as well as your own social behavior?

    Never   Rarely   Sometimes   Often   Very Often

7. How often were you asked to evaluate your own learning?

    Never   Rarely   Sometimes   Often   Very Often

8. How often were you given the opportunity to assist in determining the educational outcomes for you and your classmates?

    Never   Rarely   Sometimes   Often   Very Often

9. How often were you given the opportunity to advocate for the educational interests of a classmate?

    Never   Rarely   Sometimes   Often   Very Often

10. How often were you, as a student, encouraged to bring a support person to a "difficult" meeting in order to provide you with moral support?

    Never   Rarely   Sometimes   Often   Very Often

11. How often were you, as a student, asked to assist in determining modifications and accommodations to curriculum or instruction so that a peer who was having difficulty learning could more meaningfully participate in a lesson?

    Never   Rarely   Sometimes   Often   Very Often

12. How often were you involved in a discussion of the teaching act with an instructor?

    Never   Rarely   Sometimes   Often   Very Often

(continued)

Figure 1. Student collaboration quiz.

Figure 1. *(continued)*

13. How often were you asked to provide your teachers with feedback as to the effectiveness and appropriateness of their instruction and classroom management?

Never   Rarely   Sometimes   Often   Very Often

14. How often did you participate as an equal with teachers, administrators, and community members on school committees (e.g., curriculum committee, discipline committee, school board)?

Never   Rarely   Sometimes   Often   Very Often

15. How often did you, as a student, feel that the school "belonged" to you—that school experiences were structured primarily with student interests in mind?

Never   Rarely   Sometimes   Often   Very Often

1988, p. 145) or student collaboration strategies discussed in this chapter into three categories: 1) students as members of the instructional team, 2) students as peer advocates, and 3) students as decision makers. The category of students as members of the instructional team describes and provides specific examples of students in partner learning or peer tutoring relationships, cooperative group learning systems, teacher–student team teaching arrangements, determining curricular and instructional accommodations for classmates, and training in effective instruction elements as a method of monitoring instructional effectiveness. The category of peer advocacy offers examples of students developing and implementing transition plans for peers with intensive needs who are new to the school, students serving as a support or as a peer's voice in individualized education program (IEP) and transition planning meetings, and students developing a variety of social support networks for peers. The third category of students as decision makers deals with student accountability, teacher and administrator accountability, and student representation on school committees and the school board.

STUDENTS AS MEMBERS OF THE INSTRUCTIONAL TEAM

"Teaching teams" (Thousand & Villa, 1990, p. 151) are a promising instructional arrangement for providing intensive services to students based on the assumption that all students can be educated effectively within the same school and classroom structures.

> A teaching team is an organizational and instructional arrangement of two or more members of the school and greater community who distribute among themselves planning, instructional, and evaluation responsibilities for the same students on a regular basis for an extended period of time. Teams can vary in size from two to six or seven people.

They can vary in composition as well, involving any possible combination of classroom teachers, specialized personnel (e.g., special educators, speech and language pathologists, guidance counsellors, health professionals, employment specialists), instructional assistants, student teachers, community volunteers (e.g., parents, members of the local "foster grandparent" program), and students, themselves. (Thousand & Villa, 1990, pp. 152-153)

Teaching teams allow any student to receive intensive instructional support within the classroom, thereby eliminating the need for a special educational "second system" (Wang, Reynolds, & Walberg, 1988, p. 248) and a referral process for gaining access to that system. Teaching teams take advantage of the diverse knowledge and instructional approaches of the team members (Bauwens, Hourcade, & Friend, 1989) as well as a higher instructor:learner ratio, which allows for more immediate and accurate diagnosis of student needs and more active student learning.

Partner Learning or Peer Tutor Systems

Same-age and cross-age partner learning systems can be established within a single classroom, across more than one classroom, or across an entire school. The benefits to students receiving instruction from peers are well documented (Pierce et al., 1989) and include significant academic gains, the development of positive social interaction skills with another student, and heightened self-esteem. Tutors also benefit from this instructional relationship; they receive training and coaching in the effective communication skills they are to use in tutorial sessions (e.g., giving praise and corrective feedback) (Pierce, Stahlbrand, & Armstrong, 1989). By assuming the higher status of teacher, the tutors' self-esteem may be enhanced (Gartner, Kohler, & Riessman, 1971). Also, the preparation for effective teaching requires the use of higher level thinking skills (e.g., synthesis, task or concept analysis) and promotes more indepth understanding of the curricular content being taught (Johnson et al., 1984).

Teachers who are most effective in collaborating with students in peer tutoring arrangements have well-organized strategies for recruiting, training, supervising, and evaluating the effectiveness of the peer tutors. (Readers may refer to Cooke, Heron, & Howard [1983], Good & Brophy [1987], and Pierce et al., [1989] for models and suggestions for organizing same-age and cross-age tutor systems that add instructional resources to the classroom without additional adult personnel.)

Example #1: The Evolution of a Peer Tutoring System in an Elementary School Formalized schoolwide peer tutoring systems cannot be organized overnight. Teachers unaccustomed to or skeptical of tutoring arrangements need to become familiar with the research and strategies for establishing such systems, see firsthand examples of successful partner learning relationships, and have access to technical assistance in initiating and supervising peer tutor programs.

The John F. Kennedy Elementary School in Winooski, Vermont, completed a 3-year evolutionary process in its peer tutoring program. It started as the informal use of a handful of tutors in three classes and evolved into a formalized training and supervision program that involves more than 60% of the student body as tutors and tutees in 15 out of 21 classrooms.

During the 1987–1988 school year, the establishment of peer power strategies such as peer tutor systems and cooperative learning groups was made a priority. This was done in an effort to strengthen an in-class model for delivering specialized service and collaboration among general and special education personnel. In this first year, classroom teachers were prompted by guidance and other support personnel to request peer tutor services. Three teachers took advantage of cross-age peer tutors who were recruited from the junior high school and trained and supervised by the classroom teachers.

The cross-age peer tutoring arrangement continued throughout the 1988–1989 school year. In addition, a fourth grade teacher and one of her collaborating support staff members established a peer tutoring system within the class that involved all of the students as tutors and/or tutees. Within a few months, a first grade teacher requested that the fourth grade tutors become cross-age tutors in her classroom. Aware of the potential benefits to her students (e.g., enhanced self-esteem, practice using higher level thinking skills, content mastery), the fourth grade teacher arranged for seven tutors to provide math review to the first graders for 30 minutes every other Friday. Each tutor worked with three or four first graders, allowing all students in the class to receive tutorial instruction. The specialized support person, who worked in both classes, trained and monitored the tutors in the delivery of instruction and correction procedures. This support was phased out over a 2-month period, and supervisory responsibilities were shifted to the first grade teacher, although the support person continued to conduct brief pre- and postinstructional conferences with tutors, tutees, and the teacher. Tutors eventually became responsible for creating their own instructional materials.

At the end of the school year, a number of the fourth grade tutors approached their assigned fifth grade teachers, requesting reassurance that they would be able to continue in tutoring roles. Furthermore, one tutor presented the benefits of the tutoring experiences at a summer leadership course that focused on integration strategies and included 10 of the elementary school staff. Finally, job descriptions for all teachers were changed to include shared responsibility for training, supervising, and evaluating peer tutors.

It was decided for the following year that the established same-age and cross-age tutoring programs would continue. In addition, a system was formalized for negotiating a formal contract with each tutor and for gaining permission from and sharing information about tutoring with the tutor's parents. Over 60% of the students at John F. Kennedy Elementary School are involved in this tutoring program, with 47 contracted fourth and fifth grade tutors providing services in first, second, and third grade classrooms every other week. On the alternate weeks they are engaged in an intensive training session with a collaborating teacher—the professional label now used to refer to any specialized support person in the Winooski School System. In the biweekly sessions, specific instructional procedures and behavior management and communication skills are modeled and coached.

An important feature of this program is that many of the students who serve as tutors have "special" needs of their own that teachers believe will be helped through the tutoring experience (e.g., high achieving students in need of experiences that require creative problem solving; students eligible for special education; students identified as withdrawn, shy, or having low self-esteem; students needing incentives and contingencies, such as the opportunity to teach, to motivate work completion). Tutors, for example, who have their own academic deficit areas may provide instruction to younger students in those same academic areas. This enables these tutors to serve and experience success in the esteemed teacher role, while simultaneously addressing IEP objectives or practicing basic skills in non-strength areas.

A second important feature is that classroom teachers may be periodically relieved by tutors so that they may observe their students performing in other contexts. It is considered particularly important for teachers to see students who pose academic or behavioral challenges in their own classrooms performing successfully and exhibiting responsible and appropriate social behavior elsewhere.

Example #2: Peer Tutoring Roles for Learners with Intensive Behavioral Challenges   Serving as tutors has had a powerful, positive impact on learners in the Winooski School System identified as seriously emotionally disturbed (SED). One sixth grader serves as a cross-age tutor the last 45 minutes of the school day when an individual aide is not assigned to be available to intervene with disruptions. His tutoring is contingent upon appropriate behavior as outlined in his behavior contract. Although this young man still presents intensive behavior challenges to his own teachers and peers, he is described as a model of appropriate behavior and a valuable instructional asset by the second grade teacher who has major responsibility for his training and supervision as a tutor in her classroom (M. Steady, personal communication, January 2, 1990). A Christmas story illuminates the importance of this collaborative relationship to this student. The week before the Christmas holiday break, the sixth grader chose to forego his own class party to attend the second grade class celebration; he presented gifts to the entire class—a large, stuffed teddy bear for the teacher and individual presents for each of the students.

For a fourth grade student identified as SED, the tutoring role has served to help her identify and moderate her own antisocial behavior. Following each of her tutoring sessions with second grade students, she is "debriefed" and asked to analyze the effectiveness of the instructional and behavior management strategies she employed. Emphasis is placed upon the discussion of the behaviors exhibited by her tutees that interfere with learning and management techniques. Analogues are drawn with regard to the tutor's own behaviors, her effects upon learning, and strategies for effectively moderating the behaviors.

Cooperative Group Learning Systems

Cooperative group learning systems are the most researched of the instructional strategies that allow for and promote heterogeneous student grouping (Glatthorn, 1987; Johnson & Johnson, 1987a; Slavin, 1984, 1989). In this learning structure, students are responsible not only for their own learning, but the learning of the other members of their group. They are also responsible for exhibiting certain prosocial behaviors with their peers. The role of the teacher who structures cooperative groups shifts from a presenter of information to a facilitator of learning. The five major jobs of the teacher in this student–teacher collaborative arrangement are to: 1) clearly specify the objectives of the lesson, 2) make decisions about placing students in learning groups to ensure heterogeneity, 3) clearly explain what learning activities are expected of the students and how positive interdependence will be demonstrated, 4) monitor the effectiveness of collaborative interactions and intervene to provide task assistance (e.g., answer questions or teach task-related skills) or to increase students' interpersonal and group skills, and 5) evaluate students' achievement and group effectiveness (Johnson et al., 1984, p. 26).

Teachers new to cooperative learning often ask how to meaningfully and actively include a student with intensive educational needs into heterogeneous cooperative learning groups. Several strategies have proven to be effective (Johnson & Johnson, 1987b). The teacher may pretrain the student in select collaborative or task-related skills so that the student can bring unique expertise to the group. The student may be assigned a specific collaborative role within the group (e.g., praising members for their contributions, checking that all members are able to explain the group's answer), which promotes the student's participation while minimizing potential anxiety about working with more capable peers.

A major responsibility for the teacher in structuring cooperative groups is to adapt lesson requirements for individual students. This can be accomplished in numerous ways. Each group member may have different success criteria; the amount of material each group member is to learn may be adjusted; or group members may rehearse different math problems, spelling or vocabulary lists, or reading materials. If a test is given, all group members may receive a common grade based upon the degree to which members exceeded their individualized success criteria.

Example #1: A Cooperative Group Lesson Adapted for a Young Learner with Multiple Disabilities   A lesson that included John, an 8-year-old boy with multiple disabilities, illustrates effective adaptation strategies. When this lesson occurred, John had only been in his local school for 1 month and was integrated into the combined first and second grade. Although John occasionally vocalized loudly, he did not use his vocal behavior to communicate. A major educational goal in developing an augmentative communication system was to assess and develop John's use of various switches on communication devices such as tape recorders. Other behavioral goals were for John to remain with a group throughout an activity, refrain from grabbing others' materials, and refrain from making loud vocalizations when in a group.

In this lesson, students were assigned to groups of five. All of the group members, including John, were expected to sit in a circle, remain with the group throughout the activity, and keep their voices at a conversational level. Groups were first assigned the task of listening to a "talking book" while following along with the illustrations from the original story text. Members of each group were assigned specific jobs or roles to perform during the lesson. One job was to turn the pages of the story book in coordination with the tape recording; another was to turn the tape recorder on and off. John was assigned the latter role for his group. The role was adapted so that John operated the tape recorder by pushing on a panel switch that needed to be pressed down continuously in order for the tape to play. John received hand-over-hand assistance to activate the switch, as needed, from one of the two teachers.

This assignment not only gave John a valuable and needed role in his group, but also addressed two of his IEP goals. First, it introduced him to a new switching mechanism and created an opportunity to assess the switch's potential for use in a meaningful real-life situation. Second, it inhibited John's grabbing behavior by requiring him to perform, with at least one of his hands, the incompatible response of pushing a switch to activate the tape recorder. It should be noted that a tape recorder is a popular educational and leisure device among children and adults and would be appropriate for John to eventually learn to use independently.

When each group finished listening to the story, members generated and agreed upon answers to a set of related questions. They then formed a large group and shared their responses. John's objectives for this portion of the lesson continued to be behavioral in nature—to stay with the group and to refrain from making loud noises or grabbing others' materials.

Example #2: A Cooperative Group Lesson Adapted for an Adolescent with Multiple Disabilities   Bob, a young man with multiple disabilities who attended his local junior high school, is the focus of an example of a cooperative group lesson adapted for an adolescent with multiple disabilities. At the time of this lesson, Bob was 13 years old and in the seventh grade. The lesson occurred in Bob's biology class where the teacher had been trained in cooperative group learning and used a cooperative learning structure in the class.

Students were clustered in groups of three or four and were engaged in dissecting a frog to identify body parts. While all of the other groups used the lab tables to do their dissection work, Bob's group used the lap tray attached to his wheelchair as their work space. Bob's objectives for this lesson were different from those of the other class members. He was engaged in one of his formal communication programs, a two-choice discrimination task with real objects. This was a relatively simple program to deliver and one that his peers easily implemented along with their dissection activities. The choice materials for this program were periodically presented to Bob on either side of his tray.

Another of Bob's objectives was to increase his frequency of vocalizations. A powerful motivator for vocalization was the conversation and verbal reinforcement of peers, which occurred naturally during this activity. Bob's group members had received instruction to conduct the discrimination and vocalization programs by the classroom teacher and her collaborating teacher. No adult was directly involved in guiding the peers' interactions with Bob during the activity, although a teacher assistant sat to the side of Bob's group, collecting data regarding Bob's two structured programs.

A Teacher–Student Team Teaching Arrangement

"It is pretty neat when you can help out students who are having trouble learning, challenge a gifted student at the same time, and it doesn't cost the school district a dime" (B. Niquette, personal communication, December 29, 1989).

Bill Niquette is a high school senior who exhausted the school's mathematics curriculum offerings after his sophomore year and has attended university mathematics courses since that time. In September 1989, Bill arranged for an independent study course in mathematics to team teach the most advanced math class offered within the high school during the fifth period of each day. Bill decided to initiate this arrangement to refine his instructional skills. He now tutors students in mathematics after school and plans to continue his tutoring in college.

In the first week of this team teaching arrangement, Bill observed the classroom teacher. At the end of the second week, he began teaching the last 10–15 minutes of the class. His responsibility during that time was to introduce the new math concept or operation to be addressed in the next day's lesson. The classroom teacher and Bill met daily so that the teacher could review and approve his instructional plan for these "mini-lessons." After a month in the classroom, Bill taught his first full class period. He continued to teach one full period lesson approximately once a week for the remainder of the semester.

When Bill was not instructing the group as a whole, he worked individually with students who had missed work because of absences or who had difficulty with a concept. He continued to observe the teacher's instructional methods and conferred with the teacher on a daily basis to receive feedback on his instruction. He also solicited regular feedback from the class members.

Bill was available to any of the class members for after school help or tutoring; students occasionally called him at home for assistance. In Bill's words, "They don't mind calling me, because I am just another kid" (B. Niquette, personal communication, December 29, 1989).

Good and Brophy (1987) have suggested that peer instructors may be more effective than adults in teaching certain concepts, such as mathematics (Cohen & Stover, 1981). They speculate that their superior effectiveness is attributable to their tendency to be more directive than adults, their use of more age-appropriate language and examples, and their recent familiarity and awareness of their peers' potential frustration with the content. These speculations are validated by the comments made by one of the students in the advanced class who commented that "Bill is easier to understand and uses better examples. He knows what we're going through" (L. Soutiere, personal communication, December 5, 1989).

Bill's membership on this mathematics team has had several positive effects. Bill reported, "I feel I am furthering my math education and learning about people at the same time" (B. Niquette, personal communication, December 29, 1989). He noted that his self-confidence grew as a result of this experience. Also, having been a student in the class just 2 years before, he empathized with the students' struggles with the material and believed the students recognized and appreciated this empathy. The classroom teacher was impressed with the professional and serious manner with which he conducted himself, the positive response of students to his presence, and his growth in the use of effective instructional strategies (S. James, personal communication, December 11, 1989).

Students Determining Accommodations for Classmates with Intensive Educational Needs

One of the challenges that teachers face in a heterogeneous classroom is determining meaningful curricular adaptations and instructional modifications to enable students with intensive educational needs to be active members of the daily classroom routine. One effective and simple strategy for meeting this challenge is employed by a number of Vermont teachers who have students identified as dual sensory impaired (i.e., deaf and blind) who are regular members of the general education classroom (M. Giangreco, personal communication, December 18, 1989). These teachers ask, as a part of the routine introduction of lessons, "How could we make [student's name] a meaningful part of this activity?" Teachers report that their students are creative problem solvers who generate many realistic modification strategies from which to choose.

In the elementary school of Swanton, Vermont, the planning team for a sixth grade girl with multiple disabilities includes two peers from her regular sixth grade classroom (L. LaPlant, personal communication, January 6, 1990). Joining the two peer members on the planning team are the student's parents, the classroom teacher, the principal, the school nurse, a paraprofessional, and two collaborating teachers. The team meets biweekly during school hours to generate and agree upon strategies for actively and meaningfully including the student with multiple needs in planned activities. During "homeroom" the following day, the members report the decisions made by the team to the class. On occasion, they have been assigned the responsibility of calling and informing the parent of the outcomes of meetings the parents could not attend. Finally, when modifications are made to formal instructional programs delivered by classmates, changes are presented and rehearsed with the peer team members during the team meeting. The peers then present the changes to the student's peer tutors.

Student Involvement To Improve Instructional Effectiveness

Schools throughout North America have been actively engaged in a school improvement movement and have dedicated a great deal of in-service training effort to establishing "a common conceptual framework, language and set of technical skills in order to communicate about and implement practices which research and theory suggest will enable them to better respond to a diverse student body" (Villa, 1989, p. 173). Although school districts make different choices of instructional models (Block & Anderson, 1975; Hunter, 1982; Wang & Gennari, 1983), all have a common need for a comprehensive inservice training agenda that moves teachers from acquisition to mastery of the selected model.

Recently, the Winooski, Vermont, school community collaborated in the generation of a school restructuring proposal for creating a "community of high performers" (Villa, Peters, Zane, Ellenboden, & Soutiere, 1989). A writing committee with community, student, teacher, and administrative representation identified desired future outcomes and strategies for achieving them. One of the more unconventional recommendations of the committee was to initiate a student training program that would complement the instructional strategies (Cummings, Nelson, & Shaw, 1983; Hunter, 1982) already being delivered to the district's teaching staff.

Students in the training program would be introduced to the same elements of effective instruction that teachers practice. An expected benefit of the training would be empowerment; students experiencing difficulty in a lesson would be more comfortable asking the teacher to review or provide an alternative representation of the concept being discussed. Additionally, students could provide teachers with immediate feedback regarding their instructional effectiveness and engage with the teacher in active problem solving to identify ways to change the task, change the standard, or provide supports to enhance the likelihood of success. Finally, teachers could use students' feedback as diagnostic information for setting professional growth goals.

STUDENTS AS PEER ADVOCATES

Students may act as advocates for their peers by participating in team teaching situations with teachers and by being involved in determining accommodations for their classmates.

Peers on Transition Planning Teams

Peers have proven to be valuable in assisting with the transition of students with intensive needs from one educational setting to the next. The transition of Bob into and out of the Winooski School District illustrates this point. Bob, a student with multiple disabilities, was 13 years old when he moved to Winooski from a segregated residential facility. The student body of the small junior high school met with school staff in small groups to plan Bob's transition. Their participation in the planning helped develop a genuine sense of "ownership" and responsibility for Bob's success among his future classmates. The advice they gave faculty members greatly facilitated his immediate acceptance; suggestions ranged from providing an augmentative communication device they thought would help Bob communicate to what kind of notebook, backpack, and musical tapes he should have to "fit in" (Scagliotti, 1987).

After almost 2 years at Winooski, Bob's family moved to a neighboring community. His classmates offered to talk with teachers and students in the new community to ease his adjustment and acceptance. Three students were invited to speak to Bob's new peers. A letter of thanks from the teacher responsible for Bob's program in the new community clearly summarized the importance and impact of peers in successful transitions.

> Moriah Gosselin and Jason Messick spoke to Bob's afternoon classes. They spoke articulately and with humor and covered many important aspects of Bob's integration at your school. Most important was the regard and fondness for Bob evident in their presentations. They were excellent.
>
> Chardra Duba, who came to school at 7 A.M. to speak with Bob's morning classes, discussed not only Winooski's experiences with Bob but also her own experiences with handicapped siblings.
>
> Although Bob was the focus of their work, the impact of these young people went far beyond Bob. The attitudes and behaviors they modeled were lessons for us all about friendship and mutual respect. What they taught made the way easier for many handicapped students [here]. (K. Lewis, personal communication, November 20, 1989)

Winooski also has a formalized transition process for linking high school students with postsecondary work, living, and social support services. The core team that designed and oversees the implementation of the process includes community agency personnel, a parent, a school counselor, a collaborating teacher, an administrator, and a student representative. In designing the transition process, student input was considered important for bringing their perspective to the group. Students and their representative from the core team serve as advocates for their Winooski classmates requesting support as they make the transition from school to postsecondary options.

Peer Advocacy on Individualized Education Program Teams

In Vermont, many schools now include students on their own IEP planning teams. Peers serve a number of functions on the team— they can be a voice for students who are not able to speak for themselves (e.g, a nonverbal student with severe disabilities); or they can offer other students "moral support" and assistance in self-advocacy, particularly when students differ with parents or professional educators in terms of the focus of their education or the content of their IEPs.

A structured process that has become increasingly popular in North America for determining the day-to-day program of students in integrated general education environments is the McGill Action Planning System (MAPS) (Lusthaus & Forest, 1987; Vandercook, York, & Forest, 1989). Critical to the MAPS process is the inclusion of two to five peers on a problem-solving team with the focus student, family members, and school personnel. Peer involvement is viewed as beneficial not only to the focus student, but to the peers who, through this intensive experience, have the opportunity to learn acceptance and to value diversity (Vandercook et al., 1989). In the MAPS process, team members collaborate in responding to seven questions that help them "creatively dream, scheme, plan, and produce results" (Vandercook et al., 1989) relative to the design of an integrated school day. (See Forest & Lusthaus [1989] and Vandercook et al. [1989] for specific examples of the effective use of MAPS.)

Peer Support Networks

Historically, students with intensive needs have been excluded not only from academic but also cocurricular and nonacademic aspects of school life (e.g., school clubs, school dances, athletic events). Peer support networks have been established in some schools to rectify this situation. The purpose of peer support networks was clearly articulated by a student who helped organize one in her school.

Peer support is a bunch of kids working together to break down the barriers that society has built into the public's idea of what the norm is. Teachers and peers need to be trained; they need to understand that the goal of peer support is not competitive academics. The goal is to belong, to meet new people, to learn to break down the barriers. (Budelmann, Farrel, Kovack, & Paige, 1987, not paginated)

Peer Buddy Systems   One type of peer support network is a peer buddy system comprised of volunteer students who serve as "peer buddies." Students have stressed the importance of recruiting a diverse group of students who are active in a variety of cocurricular and community activities to be peer buddies. These networks are effective because peer buddies are active and have a rich social network into which another student can be introduced.

The range of social support that buddies can provide other students is unlimited. For example, a buddy might assist a student with physical limitations to use school lockers, get on and off the school bus, "hang out" in the halls before and after classes, or attend school sporting events or dances. Peer buddies can assist with a student's transition by talking with other students, teachers, or community members about the unique characteristics and daily challenges of their friend.

In some schools, peer buddies meet periodically with a faculty facilitator or a veteran peer buddy to receive important information about individual students (e.g., how to respond to a student's hyperactive choke reflex; how to implement a behavior management procedure in the community); to receive instruction on the social skills for seeking, developing, and maintaining friendships; or to discuss their experiences as buddies. Some schools, viewing a buddy relationship as an opportunity to teach responsibility, require new peer buddies to write contracts that outline their minimum commitments to another student. For example, if a peer buddy is responsible for an important regular activity, such as assisting a student off the morning bus, a contract would include a "back up" substitute system when the buddy is absent.

Circles of Friends   Snow and Forest (1987) have described a process for building a "circle of friends" around a new student with intensive needs. In the process, potential peer buddies draw four concentric circles that become progressively larger around a central stick figure. Each participant includes his or her closest relationships in the first circle (e.g., family members, best friend). Additional people are placed in the second and third circles, based upon their degree of closeness to the student. In the fourth circle are the people who are paid to be in the students' lives (e.g., doctors, teachers). The task is repeated for the new student. The objective of the "circles of friends" process is to sensitize peers to a new student's friendship needs through a visual representation of the imbalance between the number of people within their own friendship circles and the number within the new student's circles. Forest and Lusthaus (1989) emphasize that the outcome of the process is not to engage peers in a special, short-term helping relationship, but to create "a network that allows for the genuine involvement of children in a friendship, caring, and support role with their peers" (p. 47).

Collaborative Enterprises Among Peers   Peer support, in its various forms, can quickly become the norm within a school. Recently, in a school where peer support systems have been functioning for 2 years, over 25% of the junior high school body volunteered to be buddies for a new seventh grader whose primary school experiences had been in segregated special classes. In this same school, collaborative enterprises have emerged that are more multidirectional than unidirectional in nature. These enterprises are concerned with mutually beneficial collaboration among students (including one or more students with special needs) rather than social support of a focus person. An example of such an enterprise is Cota's Cool Cookies—chocolate chip cookies made by a company that operates out of the school. The company derives its name from the last name of a student with multiple disabilities who was the company founder and the cool mint chocolates that are used in the product (Hemingway, 1989). Three students and their families formed the business with each student having a specific job. The student with multiple disabilities was responsible for mixing the cookie batter through the use of a panel switch and the assistance of another student business partner. Other student partners were responsible for the jobs of baking, packaging, and delivering the product to sell at several school and community sites. The broader school community also became involved in the business— art students competed for the "best" label for the product and one of the business classes developed the company's contract. Within the first few months the company turned a profit.

A second collaborative enterprise within the school is the Job Club that meets daily as a course option within the high school. The club is designed for students who are seeking employment or who are currently working. In the club, students work on developing skills important in a workplace (e.g., punctuality, accepting criticism). They discuss issues from their individual work places and use the group to problem solve regarding these issues. They also developed a plan to operate the school store. In preparation, they disseminated a "marketing" survey to determine student interest in potential store items and created agendas for and role-played meetings with school staff to negotiate their control of the store.

Futuristic Assumptions and Peer Support   William Stainback (Stainback & Stainback, 1990, p. 54) has suggested that within each classroom there should be a peer support committee with a rotating membership and a goal of determining ways class members could be more supportive of one another—be a more caring community. This recommendation as well as the other peer support approaches presented are based upon at least three futuristic propositions. School is a place where children: 1) actively determine the curriculum and participate in their education, 2) problem solve regarding real-life situations, and 3) practice being caring members of a community. Whatever approach a school employs to empower students to support one another "the assumption underlying the students' involvement is that it is a valid and vital educational experience for students to participate in planning their own lives and also in helping others" (Forest & Lusthaus, 1989, p. 46).

STUDENTS AS DECISION MAKERS

Equity and parity among students and adults in educational decision making is more likely to promote active student participation and problem solving, a community spirit, and a climate of mutual respect than situations in which most or all decisions are made by adults. Students may join in decision making in areas that are no different from those generally controlled by the adults of the school. The following sections offer ideas for student–teacher decision-making partnerships in the management of student behavior, the improvement of teacher and administrator job performance, and the determination of curriculum, inservice training, and overall school governance.

Student Accountability

Student accountability involves, at a minimum, behaving within the limits of agreed behavioral and social norms established for the school community. Curwin and Mendler (1988, p. iii) begin their book, *Discipline with Dignity*, with a poem that asks, "Whose school is this, anyway?" They conclude that schools are for children, that children learn about adulthood through their interactions with the adults who teach and discipline them, and that discipline methods and the values underlying them greatly influence students' "development of self-concept; the ability to take responsibility for one's actions, the way children learn to communicate with others, and how they learn to work cooperatively with others" (p. 241).

Curwin and Mendler (1988), Glasser (1965, 1986) and others concerned with student discipline and empowerment recommend procedures for determining classroom rules, schoolwide norms, and consequences for rule violation that are jointly determined by students and their teachers. Discipline strategies suggested by these authors deal more with student responsibility than obedience. This involves students being able to determine and negotiate "natural" and logical consequences for their unacceptable actions, and being willing and able to formulate a plan of action or social contract for more appropriate future behavior.

Among the many ideas advanced by Curwin and Mendler for student involvement are ones that engage students in determining, with the teacher, the rules and consequences of the classroom. Curwin and Mendler (1988, pp. 52–53) recommend that students develop rules for their teachers (e.g., homework is handed back to students within 3 days; the teacher can't drink coffee in class if students can't eat) as well as negotiate rules for themselves. They also present the following recommendations for student empowerment formulated by a suburban middle school:

1. A student council of "poor achievers" and "in-trouble students" (different labels were used) to help set school policy and to help modify rules and consequences.
2. Students who served detention were given the job of commenting on how school climate could be improved.
3. Students took the job of running the school for a day once a year with the teachers and administrators taking student roles.
4. Each class was required to have at least two student rules for the teacher. (Curwin & Mendler, 1988, pp. 17–18)

It seems that graduates of schools that have empowered students to actively problem solve regarding their own behavior will be better prepared for the complex life forecasted for the 21st century. Specifically, they will have had opportunities to use creative problem-solving skills to deal with the behaviors of others—a skill needed for their future work environment. They will have had opportunities to recognize that some solutions are more successful than others and that it is acceptable to have a second approach when the first fails. They will have observed teachers and peers modeling with one another appropriate ways for coping with stress and adversity and for responding when caught breaking a rule. In short, they will have had multiple opportunities to develop a healthy appreciation for the complexity and diversity of human behavior.

Teacher and Administrator Accountability

Clearly, students are not the only "performers" within a school. Teachers and administrators have designated roles as managers and facilitators of the learning environment (Glasser, 1986) and as instructional leaders. Students can play a very positive and active role in improving instruction in a number of ways. For example, students trained in the elements of effective instruction might use this knowledge to provide teachers with prompts and constructive feedback that promote more effective teaching and learning. Students can also provide teachers with feedback about their consistency in enforcing classroom rules, delivering consequences, and modeling a teaching versus emotional response to students' challenging behavior and stress.

Students are best able to notice and report to administrators information regarding: 1) school climate, 2) the visibility of school leadership personnel and their availability to listen actively to student concerns, and 3) the degree they are involved in learning and in determining schoolwide policies and procedures.

Student Representation on School Committees and the School Board

For student–adult collaboration to extend beyond the classroom, students will need to be welcomed in forums where more global decisions are made regarding the school's mission, curriculum, inservice training, hiring of personnel, procedures for evaluating instruction, incentives and rewards for teachers, and the restructuring of the school organization. To welcome students as decision makers on school committees—even the school board—is a radical step in school organizational restructuring that actualizes the advice of futurists to create "a new collaborative role for teachers and students in which students accept an active senior partnership role in the learning enterprise" (Benjamin, 1989, p. 9).

The Winooski, Vermont, community collaborated to generate a school restructuring proposal. The proposal's four goals expressly targeted the expansion of student responsibilities in "school governance, goal setting, curriculum, assessment, performance, climate/discipline, and role clarification" (Villa et al., 1989). Specific objectives called for student representation on the school board; curriculum, discipline, and inservice training committees; and a proposed creativity committee that would have the ongoing responsibility of determining future organizational, curricular, and instructional change needs.

CONCLUSION

The role of the public school in North America has always been to prepare children for their roles in society. This has seen dramatic change during the 20th century. In the early 1900s, a major function of the public schools was to induct the waves of immigrants into the culture, language, and democratic processes of the United States and Canada (Stainback, Stainback, & Bunch, 1989, p. 5) and to prepare the "masses" for work in the factories of the new industrial age. The public school was hallowed as the "great equalizer" because of the common knowledge and skills it imparted to school children.

As an organizational structure, however, the school came to mirror the standardized and bureaucratic model of the factories (Skrtic, 1987). Like the factory, the school was structured to create a standard product; all students experienced and were expected to master the same curriculum, at the same rate, through the same instructional methodologies (e.g., large group). There was little tolerance of or appreciation for the natural differences among children in culture, learning style, interests, and values. Students were not to question the content or method of instruction or the teacher's authority. This was a time when left-handed children were routinely forced to learn to write with their right hand, as right handedness was the standard. Students who did not do well in the standard program were allowed or encouraged to drop out. Segregation of segments of the school population also occurred. Native Americans and African-Americans were educated separately; students identified as disabled were largely excluded from the public school; and tracking became popular, with poor and disadvantaged youth assigned to the lowest tracks (Stainback et al., 1989, p. 5).

Society at the end of the 20th century is much more complex, global, interdependent, information rich, technological, and inclusionary in its values than at its beginning. There has been a shift in values and a steady trend to include all students in the mainstream of general education (Reynolds & Birch, 1982), making the schools more diverse and more reflective of the 21st century society that its graduates will enter. Wisdom at the end of the 20th century involves having strategies for coping with diversity. Entering the 21st century, "the world of work will require the abilities to manage information and to work with people. Workers will need high-level thinking skills as well as the ability to adapt" (Benjamin, 1989, p. 8). "The world's store of knowledge has doubled and doubled again during the 20th century" (Cornish, 1986, p. 14) and the amount of knowledge will continue to increase geometrically in the next century, so that no one will be able to keep pace with it (Kirschenbaum & Simon, 1974). As a result of the short "half-life" (Alley, 1985) of knowledge, our children will need to learn to be inquiring, lifelong learners.

Given these changes in society, what changes are needed in public education? Organizationally, there is a need for schools to model collaboration among school personnel, community members, and students (Benjamin, 1989; Nevin et al., 1990; Thousand & Villa, 1989,

1990; Villa & Thousand, 1990), and for educators to share their power and decision-making responsibilities with their students in a climate of mutual respect. The curriculum must expand to include the development of students' values, attitudes, and "character" (Brandt, 1989, p. 37). Instructionally, there is a need for "responsive and fluid instructional options rather than pigeonholing [of] students into one of several standing, standard programs (Skrtic, 1987)" (Thousand & Villa, 1989, p. 89). Finally, educational assumptions and practices must be examined regularly in order to ferret out and eliminate those that impede students' opportunities to actively determine and be involved in their education, to practice being contributing members of society through real life experiences (e.g., peer tutoring, peer advocacy, creative problem solving to manage the behavior of a disruptive peer, community service), and to experience and cope with diversity. Teacher-dominated instruction, the emphasis upon student competition over collaboration, a focus on academic performance over the development of social competence, segregated schooling, and tracking are all examples of educational practices that will come to be viewed as archaic in the 21st century as was the early 20th century practice of tying down a student's left hand to ensure a society of right-handed writers.

Benjamin forecasts that "the future will arrive ahead of schedule" (1989, p. 12). Therefore, it is imperative for us to demonstrate wisdom and courage by acting to change schools now so that students may be more actively engaged in their own and others' acquisition of humanistic ethics; communication, information-seeking, and problem-solving skills; and core curriculum deemed essential by their community. Starting points for change include the implementation of student collaboration strategies presented in this chapter. Hopefully, by the 21st century, students taking the Student Collaboration Quiz (see Figure 1) will be able to give themselves and their schools higher ratings than graduates of 20th century schooling—a result of the multiple opportunities to participate in collaborative arrangements in learning, advocacy, and leadership.

School belongs to the children (Curwin & Mendler, 1988), and so does the future. "Your children are not your children. They are the sons and daughters of Life's longing for itself . . . . [T]heir souls dwell in the house of tomorrow, which you cannot visit, even in your fondest dreams" (Gibran, 1923, p. 18).

REFERENCES

Alley, J. (1985, April-May). *Future research data and general education reform.* Paper presented at the annual forum of the Association for Institutional Research, Portland, OR. (ERIC Document Reproduction Service No. ED 259 674)

Bair, M., & Woodward, R.G. (1964). *Team teaching in action.* Boston: Houghton Mifflin.

Bauwens, J., Hourcade, J.J., & Friend, M. (1989). Cooperative teaching: A model for general and special education integration. *Remedial and Special Education, 10*(2), 17–22.

Beggs, D.W., III. (1964). *Team teaching: Bold new venture.* Indianapolis: Unified College Press.

Benjamin, S. (1989). An ideascape for education: What futurists recommend. *Educational Leadership, 47*(1), 8–14.

Block, J., & Anderson, L. (1975). *Mastery learning in classroom instruction.* New York: Macmillan.

Bloom, B.S. (1976). *Human characteristics and school learning.* New York: McGraw-Hill.

Brandt, R. (1989). On liberal education for tomorrow's world: A conversation with Douglas Heath. *Educational Leadership, 47*(1), 37–40.

Budelmann, L., Farrel, S., Kovack, C., & Paige, K. (1987, October). *Student perspective: Planning and achieving social integration.* Paper presented at Vermont's Least Restrictive Environment Conference, Burlington.

Chalfant, J., Pysch, M., & Moultrie, R. (1979). Teacher assistance teams: A model for within building problem solving. *Learning Disabilities Quarterly, 2,* 85–96.

Cohen, S.A., & Stover, G. (1981). Effects of teaching sixth-grade students to modify format variable of math work problems. *Reading Research Quarterly, 16,* 175–200.

Cooke, N.L., Heron, T.E., & Howard, W.L. (1983). *Peer tutoring: Implementing classwide programs in the primary grades.* Columbus, OH: Special Press.

Cornish, E. (1986). Educating children for the 21st century. *Curriculum Review, 25*(4), 12–17.

Cummings, C., Nelson, C., & Shaw, D. (1983). *Teaching makes a difference.* Edmonds, WA: TEACHING.

Curwin, R., & Mendler, A. (1988). *Discipline with dignity.* Alexandria, VA: Association for Supervision and Curriculum Development.

Forest, M., & Lusthaus, E. (1989). Promoting educational equality for all students: Circles and maps. In S. Stainback, W. Stainback, & M. Forest (Eds.), *Educating all students in the mainstream of regular education* (pp. 43–57). Baltimore: Paul H. Brookes Publishing Co.

Gartner, A., Kohler, M., & Riessman, F. (1971). *Children teach children: Learning by teaching.* New York: Harper & Row.

Gibran, K. (1923). *The prophet.* New York: Alfred A. Knopf.

Glasser, W. (1965). *Reality therapy.* New York: Harper & Row.

Glasser, W. (1986). *Control theory in the classroom.* New York: Harper & Row.

Glatthorn, A. (1987). How do you adapt the curriculum to respond to individual differences? In A. Glatthorn (Ed.), *Curriculum renewal* (pp. 99–109). Alexandria, VA: Association for Supervision and Curriculum Development.

Good, T.L., & Brophy, J.E. (1987). *Looking into classrooms* (4th ed.). New York: Harper & Row.

Graden, J., Casey, A., & Christenson, S. (1985). Implementing a prereferral intervention system. *Exceptional Children, 51,* 377–384.

Hemingway, S. (1989, November 10). High school feels loss of Bob Cota. *Burlington Free Press*, Section B, p. 1.

Hersey, P., & Blanchard, K.H. (1977). *Management of organizational behavior: Utilizing human resources*. Englewood Cliffs, NJ: Prentice-Hall.

Hunter, M. (1982). *Mastery teaching*. El Segundo, CA: TIP Publications.

Idol, L., Paolucci-Whitcomb, P., & Nevin, A. (1986). *Collaborative consultation*. Austin, TX: PRO-ED.

Johnson, D.W., & Johnson, R.T. (1987a). *A meta-analysis of cooperative, competitive and individualistic goal structures*. Hillsdale, NJ: Lawrence Erlbaum Associates.

Johnson, D.W., & Johnson, R.T. (1987b). *Learning together and alone: Cooperation, competition, and individualization* (2nd ed.). Englewood Cliffs, NJ: Prentice-Hall.

Johnson, D.W., Johnson, R.T., Holubec, E., & Roy, P. (1984). *Circles of learning*. Arlington, VA: Association for Supervision and Curriculum Development.

Johnson, D.W., Maruyama, G., Johnson, R.T., Nelson, D., & Skon, L. (1981). Effects of cooperative, competitive and individualistic goal structures on achievement: A meta-analysis. *Psychological Bulletin, 89*, 47–62.

Kirschenbaum, H., & Simon, S. (1974). Values and the futures movement in education. In H. Kirschenbaum & S. Simon (Eds.), *Learning for tomorrow: The role of the future in education* (pp. 257–271). New York: Random House.

Knight, M.F., Meyers, H.W., Paolucci-Whitcomb, P., Hasazi, S.E., & Nevin, A. (1981). A four year evaluation of consulting teacher services. *Behavior Disorders, 6*(2), 92–100.

Lusthaus, E., & Forest, M. (1987). The kaleidoscope: A challenge to the cascade. In M. Forest (Ed.), *More education integration* (pp. 1–17). Downsview, Ontario: G. Allan Roeher Institute.

Nevin, A., Thousand, J., Paolucci-Whitcomb, P., & Villa, R. (1990). Collaborative consultation: Empowering public school personnel to provide heterogeneous schooling for all. *Journal of Educational and Psychological Consultation, 1*(1), 41–67.

Pierce, M., Stahlbrand, K., & Armstrong, S. (1989). *Increasing student productivity through peer tutoring programs*. (Monograph No. 9–1). Burlington: University of Vermont, Center for Developmental Disabilities.

Pugach, M.C., & Johnson, L.J. (1989). Prereferral interventions: Progress, problems, and challenges. *Exceptional Children, 56*, 217–226.

Reynolds, M., & Birch, J. (1982). *Teaching exceptional children in all America's schools* (2nd ed.). Reston, VA: Council for Exceptional Children.

Scagliotti, L. (1987). Helping hands: School works to overcome student's handicap. *Burlington Free Press*, Section B, pp. 1, 10.

Skrtic, T. (1987). An organizational analysis of special education reform. *Counterpoint, 8*(2), 15–19.

Slavin, R.E. (1984). Review of cooperative learning research. *Review of Educational Research, 50*, 315–342.

Slavin, R.E. (1989). Research on cooperative learning: Consensus and controversy. *Educational Leadership, 47*(4), 52–54.

Snow, J., & Forest, M. (1987). Circles. In M. Forest (Ed.), *More education integration* (pp. 169–176). Downsview, Ontario: G. Allan Roeher Institute.

Stainback, W., & Stainback, S. (1990). Facilitating peer supports and friendships. In W. Stainback & S. Stainback (Eds.), *Support networks for inclu-*

sive schooling: Interdependent integrated education (pp. 51–63). Baltimore: Paul H. Brookes Publishing Co.

Stainback, W., Stainback, S., & Bunch, G. (1989). Introduction and historical background. In S. Stainback, W. Stainback, & M. Forest (Eds.), *Educating all students in the mainstream of regular education* (pp. 3–14). Baltimore: Paul H. Brookes Publishing Co.

Tharp, R.G. (1975). The triadic model of consultation: Current considerations. In C.A. Parker (Ed.), *Psychological consultation: Helping teachers meet special needs* (pp. 133–151). Reston, VA: Council for Exceptional Children.

Thousand, J., & Villa, R. (1989). Enhancing success in heterogeneous schools. In S. Stainback, W. Stainback, & M. Forest (Eds.), *Educating all students in the mainstream of regular education* (pp. 89–103). Baltimore: Paul H. Brookes Publishing Co.

Thousand, J., & Villa, R. (1990). Sharing expertise and responsibilities through teaching teams. In W. Stainback & S. Stainback (Eds.), *Support networks for inclusive schooling: Interdependent integrated education* (pp. 151–166). Baltimore: Paul H. Brookes Publishing Co.

Timar, T. (1989). The politics of school restructuring. *Phi Delta Kappan, 71,* 265–275.

Vandercook, T., York, J., & Forest, M. (1989). The McGill action planning system (MAPS): A strategy for building the vision. *Journal of The Association for Persons with Severe Handicaps, 14,* 205–215.

Villa, R. (1989). Model public school inservice programs: Do they exist? *Teacher Education and Special Education, 12,* 173–176.

Villa, R., Peters, M.J., Zane, N., Ellenboden, G., & Soutiere, L. (1989). *Reinventing Vermont schools for very high performance—Winooski challenge grant proposal.* (Available from Richard Villa, Winooski School District, Normand St., Winooski, VT 05404)

Villa, R., & Thousand, J. (1988). Enhancing success in heterogeneous classrooms and schools: The powers of partnership. *Teacher Education and Special Education, 11,* 144–154.

Villa, R., & Thousand, J. (1990). Administrative supports to promote inclusive schooling. In W. Stainback & S. Stainback (Eds.), *Support networks for inclusive schooling: Interdependent integrated education* (pp. 201–218). Baltimore: Paul H. Brookes Publishing Co.

Wang, M.C., & Gennari, P. (1983). Analysis of the design, implementation, and effects of a data-based staff development program. *Teacher Education and Special Education, 6,* 211–216.

Wang, M.C., Reynolds, M.C., & Walberg, H.J. (1988). Integrating children of the second system. *Phi Delta Kappan, 70,* 248–251.

Wiggins, G. (1989). The futility of trying to teach everything of importance. *Educational Leadership, 1*(3), 44–59.

8

Support and
Positive Teaching Strategies

Wade Hitzing

It isn't only that integration is good for people with handicaps but also that it is necessary for all people. Normalization is not only for people with handicaps. By definition it can't be only for people with handicaps. It must be imbedded in each of us—in each of you, in me. Working with people who have disabilities is important not only for them, not only for those that do the work, but if it is to mean anything it will be important to everyone. The question always comes back to, How do we maximize variance? How can our lives be enlarged by living, by working, by associating with people of all colors, all backgrounds, all ages, all interests? (Blatt, 1985, p. viii)

BLATT MIGHT ALSO have added "behavior" to his list of personal differences we must learn to understand, appreciate, and respect. While significant progress has been made toward the inclusion of minority groups in public school programs, including students with severe mental and physical disabilities, educators have a long history of expelling and excluding students because of their disruptive, dan-

This work was supported in part by a series of grants awarded to the Society for Community Support by the Ohio Developmental Disabilities Planning Council. The material in this chapter does not necessarily reflect the position or policy of the Ohio Developmental Disabilites Planning Council.

Appreciation is expressed to the following persons whose work in the Society's projects contributed substantially to the production of this chapter: Larry Douglass, Deborah Luciano, Kathy Hulgin, and Layne Dillon.

gerous, or otherwise challenging behavior[1] (Gliedman & Roth, 1980;
Wooden, 1976).

UNDERSTANDING AND
DEALING WITH CHALLENGING BEHAVIOR

This chapter focuses on understanding the causes for challenging behavior and applying this understanding to the design of a school curriculum that is more supportive of the full inclusion of all students,
including those with challenging behavior.

Traditional Behavior Management Approach

Before making decisions about how best to deal with a student who
exhibits challenging behavior it is important to look carefully at how
educators think and talk about challenging behavior. This is important because the way they view a student's behavior will determine
how they: 1) "frame" or define the problem, 2) select goals, 3) decide
on appropriate "intervention" procedures, and 4) define success.

Framing the Problem A typical approach to behavior management is to label or categorize a student's challenging behavior as inappropriate or a "problem"—behavior that must be decreased or
eliminated. In fact, the case is often made that until a student's challenging behavior is decreased or eliminated nothing "positive" can be
achieved. Although there may be some acknowledgment that inadequate instructional practices may contribute to the problem behavior, there is a strong presumption that the problem is the student's
behavior and that the student must change.

Goal Selection The teaching or behavior plans that are developed
focus on the elimination of the student's disruptive or dangerous behavior (Bailey & Bostow, 1969; Foxx, 1982). Alternative, appropriate
behaviors may also be identified and teaching procedures developed
to strengthen them, but the real focus of the teacher's energy and
time is on attempts to decrease the problem behavior (Rose, 1979).

Intervention Procedures Most "intervention" procedures or behavior plans that are developed to deal with problem behavior focus
on altering the contingencies of reinforcement and punishment in
the school setting. The typical behavior plan usually calls for school
staff to change their reaction to inappropriate behavior by ignoring,
not rewarding, or in some cases punishing the student when the "tar-

---

[1]As this chapter was being finalized in the fall of 1990, the Columbus, Ohio, Public
School system opened a special, segregated high school that will serve only students
labeled as having "severe behavior handicaps."

get" behavior occurs. The plan may also call for the staff to "catch the student being good" and provide a schedule of positive reinforcement for the teaching staff to follow.

Defining Success   Success is defined as meeting the goals for reduction or elimination of the target behavior. The process is justified since: 1) a seriously disruptive and possibly even dangerous behavior has been eliminated or at least decreased, and 2) the decrease in problem behavior now allows staff to move on to accomplishing more positive teaching goals.

Use of Supports and Positive Teaching Strategies

A fundamentally different way to look at challenging behavior is to view the disruptive and sometimes dangerous behavior of the student as communication/feedback about his or her needs and wishes or the quality or appropriateness of instructional strategies, at least as perceived by the student (Carr & Durand, 1985a; Donnellan, Mirenda, Mesaros, & Fassbender, 1984; Prizant & Wetherby, 1987). Some students learn to communicate needs such as "Leave me alone," "Pay attention to me," "Give me that," "I don't want to do this," "I don't understand this—I need help" by engaging in disruptive and sometimes even dangerous behavior. The following learning cycle provides a brief description of how such learning takes place and Figure 1 illustrates the procedure.

1. Antecedents or factors that precede the behavior may affect the person. There are many factors that can make a person feel happy, bored, confused, interested, angry, sad, satisfied, or mad. The student may be given tasks that are too difficult, changes in schedules may be confusing, or he or she may have little if any choice about school assignments.
2. People react, in part, based on how they feel. When people feel confused, frightened, angry, or in pain, they often behave in ways that are disruptive and even dangerous. When people are bored or confused their behavior often becomes more erratic and less predictable.
3. The person learns that disruptive and/or even aggressive behavior often "works." People learn from experience and tend to repeat actions that *work.* Behaviors that work are strengthened (rewarded or reinforced); those that aren't rewarded or result in pain or discomfort are weakened and eventually eliminated. The consequences or results of behavior are very important in determining future actions.

4. Even though the disruptive behavior often "works," at least on a short-term basis, in the long run more problems such as alienation, exclusion, and isolation are created. These problems usually increase the discomfort and confusion in the student's life, which results in even more disruptive behavior. This "vicious" cycle is clearly evident in the lives of many students with challenging behavior.

Framing the Problem   Many behavior "problems" are learned in the same way as sign language. For example, a student may be presented with a task he or she finds confusing and frustrating, and if the student does not have effective vocal or standard sign language skills it may be hard for the teacher to understand that the student is confused and that a more appropriate task should be substituted. Or, as is more often the case, the teacher does understand, by listening to the student or observing body language or other relevant signs, but proceeds with the task because of a focus on behavioral compliance or task completion. In fact, many behavior programs call for the teacher to ignore all "inappropriate" requests to stop or take a break. The teacher is advised to act as if he or she cannot "hear" the student if the student is behaving inappropriately. However, few if any, teachers can continue to ignore a punch in the stomach, a slap in the face, or loud yelling and screaming. If the teacher waits until the student's behavior escalates to the point of disruption or danger before allowing the student to stop the task, the student is taught, in effect, to engage in disruptive behavior to escape from the task or situation (Carr, Newsom, & Binkoff, 1980; Weeks & Gaylord-Ross, 1981). The formal behavior plan may call for the teacher to ignore or not reward disruptive or dangerous attempts at communication, but in the classroom

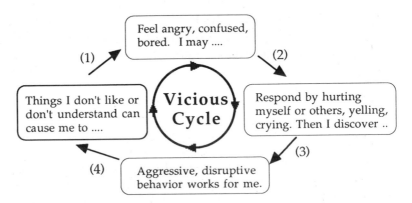

Figure 1.   Learning cycle describing the acquisition of challenging behaviors.

the most disruptive, especially dangerous behavior, is in fact listened to and rewarded.

To gain a better understanding of the cause(s) of the student's behavior it is usually necessary to complete a functional analysis that results in a comprehensive description of the school environment. Special attention should be paid to the settings, events, and actions (antecedents) that are present or typically precede occurrences of the disruptive behavior and its consequences, especially the reactions of fellow students and teaching staff (Durand & Crimmins, 1988; LaVigna & Donnellan, 1986). This analysis can lead to an understanding that the student's disruptive and dangerous acts are not simply target behaviors to be eliminated and allows the issue to be framed in a way that recognizes the functional, adaptive role of the behavior and the staff's role in contributing to its development.

Goal Selection Recognizing disruptive, even dangerous, acts as communication does not mean the behavior is acceptable and that the student should not learn to make better choices. However, it should result in a better understanding of the adaptive and functional role it plays in the person's life. Donnellan et al. (1984) pointed out that:

> There is a growing awareness among educators that the long-term successful functioning of persons with severe handicaps depends on expanding their limited response repertoires rather than simply limiting their inappropriate behaviors. Interventions designed to teach functionally related behaviors in place of aberrant responses make good educational sense in this regard. Further, such an approach explicitly acknowledges the functional legitimacy of even aberrant behavior and, in so doing, communicates a respectful attitude concerning the individual exhibiting the behavior. (p. 209)

Recognizing that much of the student's disruptive and dangerous behavior serves a communicative function, the major goal of any intervention or behavior change plan should focus on helping the student learn to communicate in ways that are equally effective and adaptive, but are not disruptive or dangerous.

It is important to note, however, that there may be goals that are even more fundamental or basic that must first be addressed, especially for students with long histories of dangerous and disruptive behavior. The following story provides a good example of how important it is to be clear in defining a student's educational goals and to select goals that are consistent with the needs of the student.

> Betty works as an aide in a third grade classroom. Although she helps the teacher in many different ways, her main responsibility is to provide special assistance for Robbie, the only student in the classroom with a severe disability—severe mental and physical

handicaps and a reputation for hurting himself and others. Recently, Betty and the teacher met with the school psychologist in an attempt to develop a more effective way of working with Robbie. They explained that if either of them sits by Robbie and attempts to engage him in a task, he tries to escape by rolling his wheelchair away from the table. If Betty prevents his escape by holding his wheelchair, he then begins to yell and refuses to cooperate in the task. If she tries to manually guide him through the task, he bites and scratches. Betty indicated that she usually attempts to "work through" these episodes by ignoring, as much as possible, his aggressive behavior and redirecting him to the task. Both agreed that if Robbie appears to be really upset they leave him alone for a while and introduce the task again later. Betty's major concern was that this strategy was not working; in fact, the frequency and severity of Robbie's disruptive behavior seemed to be increasing.

Betty did not have a clear answer when the psychologist asked her what she was trying to accomplish with Robbie. She tended to think more in terms of what she was supposed to *do*, rather than what she was trying to *accomplish*. However, as the discussion progressed, the teacher showed the psychologist an example of one of the goals from Robbie's IEP that Betty was trying to help him achieve. The task criterion was described as: "The student will sort 20 objects, of four different colors, within 10 minutes with at least 90% accuracy, with the teacher providing only verbal prompts." The goal was for Robbie to achieve this criterion 3 days in a row and then move on to the next goal in the teaching sequence. Neither the classroom teacher nor Betty had considered whether one of the factors contributing to Robbie's problem behavior was a poor "match" between the instructional goals the team had selected and Robbie's current needs. The goals in Robbie's education program, like those for most students, focused primarily on skill acquisition (mainly self-help, academic, and social skills) and decreasing or eliminating behaviors that were seen as inappropriate. Teaching color sorting skills might seem to be a reasonable goal until it is realized that: 1) if the teacher or aide sits by Robbie to work with him he attempts to escape; 2) if the staff do not let him escape he yells and refuses to cooperate; and 3) if they attempt to assist him in completing the task he tries to bite, hit, and scratch them.

Given Robbie's long history of severely disturbing behavior it would probably be more appropriate to help him first learn that: 1) the classroom is a safe place and that he can trust his teachers; and 2) it will be interesting, fun, engaging, and worthwhile if he does cooperate and work with the teaching staff. His current behavior in the classroom suggests that from his point of view there is little reason to cooperate and he is willing to "work" (yell, hit, bite) very hard to escape the situation. It is difficult to believe that the most effective way to help Robbie learn to trust his teachers and that cooperation might somehow "pay off" is to attempt to teach him to complete a task he may not understand, clearly sees no reward for doing, and is almost certain to lead to negative interactions with his teachers. While this seems obvious, the above situation can be observed many times each day in classrooms across the country. School staff attempt to make significant changes in a student's behavior before first achieving a reasonable working relationship by establishing a sense of safety, trust, and cooperation.

Adopting this approach to goal setting does not imply a lack of commitment to helping the student make major changes in behavior (i.e., enhancing competence and decreasing challenging behavior). In fact, for many students with long histories of challenging behavior it may be the only effective way of *beginning* to make important, major changes in behavior. Far too often the imposition of predetermined curriculum packages and disciplinary rules that apply to "all" students result in such a high rate of disruptive behavior that the student is expelled or excluded from the school or classroom. This is all seen as necessary because the assumption is that the student "must" have certain objectives in his or her IEP and that all students must obey general rules of behavior. Educators must not be misled by the fact that a lack of individualization in curriculum design and teaching strategies does not result in severe behavior challenges for most students. Many students are just as dissatisfied as Robbie, but they have given up "telling" about it or have not yet learned that yelling, property destruction, aggression, and self-injury are examples of sign language that work well at school.

Guidelines for Establishing a Sense of Safety, Trust, and Cooperation   At first it may seem bizarre to think in terms of developing formal teaching strategies to help the student learn that it is safe to be in the classroom and that the teacher can be trusted. Educators never try to teach the student that the classroom is a place to be feared or that teachers cannot be trusted. However, some teachers may have been involved in the implementation of behavior plans that contributed to such feelings and beliefs on the part of the student. Many behavior plans call for rewarding or reinforcing behavior that is seen as appropriate and punishing behavior that is disruptive or dangerous. Students are rewarded with M&Ms, tokens, and praise for on-task behavior and cooperation, and punished with restraint, time outs, or spankings for their inappropriate behavior. There is ample research and common experience to prove that such a combination of rewards and punishment can result in a decrease in disruptive or dangerous behavior. However, there can be other, unintended negative effects of these procedures, such as "What is the teacher going to do next? First, he patted me on the shoulder and said 'good job,' but 2 minutes later he squirted hot sauce in my mouth while I was biting my hand—it tasted awful." Even if the student has no experience with such practices in a particular classroom, teachers may still have to deal with her or his past school experiences. The student may view the teacher as a clone of past instructors, responding as if he or she is "one of them," until proven otherwise.

Teachers can think in terms of a hierarchy[2] of goals, such as, I want to help the student learn that:

Level 1.   It is safe to be with me and I can be trusted.

Level 2.   It will be fun, interesting, engaging, or somehow "pay off" to cooperate and work with me.

Level 3.   He or she can make a change in behavior—learn a new skill, gain competence, or decrease problem behavior.

There are a variety of different strategies that can be used to achieve the first two goals, both of which can usually be addressed at the same time. First, and most important, teachers must maintain a clear focus on trying first to achieve these two goals. Most teachers have been trained to emphasize behavior change and skill acquisition and it is often difficult, almost impossible, to set these goals aside for the moment and focus on safety, trust, cooperation, and building a strong positive working relationship. For example, a teacher who had a young man recently join her class said that she wanted to "sit with Joe and share a glass of juice" (P. Hulgin, personal communication, October 22, 1990). They both had a rough day; Joe had hit himself in the head many times. She wanted to spend a few minutes with him that were as calm and pleasant as possible. She began by pouring them both a small glass of juice. He drank only a little and then spilled the rest of it. She did not make a big deal about the spilling, but did attempt to show him how to handle the glass more carefully. He resisted her efforts and refused to cooperate. She poured the juice herself and then offered it to him. He refused to drink the juice, even when she held it to his mouth, eventually knocking the glass from her hand. (It was clear that the teacher was gradually, but significantly making a major change in her goals for the interaction.) Again, she did not overreact, she simply picked up the glass and attempted to assist him in pouring more juice. When he refused to cooperate, she poured the juice and held it up for him to drink. At this point, anyone

[2]The author understands that the selection of this specific hierarchy is arbitrary and that there are a number of different ways to describe this analysis. The intent is simply to emphasize the sequence of goal selection.

observing their interaction would have concluded that no matter what the teacher might have said or intended, she was in fact trying to get the student to comply with a drinking program. The focus and energy of the teacher had clearly shifted to promoting behavior change—the situation was neither calm nor pleasant.

If the teacher had kept to her original goal, she would not have cared whether Joe spilled the juice or whether he cooperated in pouring. In this case, as soon as she realized that she had probably made a mistake in selecting this particular situation as the way to relax and share a few pleasant moments, she could have said, "I'm sorry, I thought you would like some juice. What else could we do?" She would not have taken this as an opportunity to teach him how to pour juice or to work on compliance training. The focus of her efforts would have been on attempting to engage the student in something that he might find interesting and rewarding and that would allow them both to experience time together with little, if any, demands on either of them.

While it is usually possible and appropriate to address goals at the first two levels simultaneously, it is important to keep the distinction between the two levels in mind. For example, it is likely that a sense of safety and trust has already been established, but the student may not have been provided with the kind of classroom experiences that result in interest, engagement, and cooperation. The student may trust the teacher and feel safe in the classroom, but he or she may have no reason, from his or her point of view, to cooperate or work with the teacher—especially on *school* work. There are, of course, students who enter the class willingly. They cause very few problems until the teacher says, "Time for work, let's all sit down and begin our work." The school day seems to cycle between: 1) disruption and problems when attempts are made to engage the student in school work, and 2) relative quiet when the student is allowed to do preferred tasks and few instructions or demands are made by the staff.

Such students will require a great deal of the teacher's energy and creativity. In the beginning there may not be a variety of activities available that will interest the student, especially traditional educational activities. At this stage, the primary objective is for the teacher and the student to "survive" the school day. Too often rigid behavioral criteria are imposed and strict, intensive behavior management procedures are instituted to increase on-task performance and decrease problem behavior. Usually, because school staff are bigger and stronger, they win such power struggles. However, when these behavior management procedures don't succeed, it is the student who suffers the most. Exposed to the standard instructional curriculum and held accountable to general standards of behavior, the student "fails" and is then moved to a more restrictive/segregated school program, put on home instruction, or expelled. Instead, teachers could use a "survive first" strategy to implement a curriculum and use traditional teaching strategies that have the best chance of interesting or engaging the student—whether or not these activities can be justified as "educationally appropriate." After establishing a history of interest and success in the classroom, it is possible to gradually negotiate with the student and to gradually phase in more activities that focus on building competencies and strengthening deficits.

Intervention Procedures   Recognizing the student's disruptive and dangerous behavior as communication also has a significant impact on the selection of intervention strategies that might be developed to improve the situation. Four alternatives that can be chosen individually or in combination are discussed on the following pages.

Implement Support Strategies   Support strategies should be implemented first because they: 1) contribute to the development of a positive working relationship between teacher and student; and 2) make it easier for the student to learn less destructive, alternative forms of communication by removing at least some of the sources of frustration and confusion.

The typical educational planning process does not lend itself well to the development of comprehensive support plans. Too often a number of important environmental influences, such as the student's curriculum, class size and composition, and staffing arrangements, are taken as "givens" and are not adaptable to meet the student's needs. For many students with long histories of severe behavior challenges, especially those students whose needs are not being met by the existing educational strategies (i.e., more of the same is probably not the solution), a more comprehensive "student driven" planning approach, such as Personal Futures Planning, may be necessary (Mount & Zwernik, 1988; O'Brien, 1987).

It would be consistent with the goal hierarchy described earlier in this chapter to first focus on removing as many of the negative aspects (judged from the student's point of view) in the instructional environment as possible. There are a number of studies that show that decreasing the difficulty of school tasks and changing the freuency and form of instructional directives can have a significant impact in decreasing disruptive behavior (i.e., the student has less to complain about) (Carr et al., 1980; Gaylord-Ross, Weeks, & Lipner, 1980).

Prior to designing a curriculum that is more supportive and facilitates the student's learning that cooperation in the classroom might be fun, interesting, or in some way "profitable," the teacher might ask the following questions:

Would the student ever choose to do this task?
Will the acquired skill be functional in ways that have meaning to the student or directly benefit him or her?
Would the student be willing to pay for help in achieving this instructional objective?
If we delete this goal will the student miss it and ask for it to be re-included?

It is not likely that the teacher will be able to develop a curriculum that could elicit a "yes" answer to all of the above questions despite their benefits. For example, most people benefited from learning multiplication tables, but it was hard to see the advantages or be interested in the process at the time. Similarly, teachers are likely to have to include some instructional objectives that the student would not choose. However, this is not an excuse for implementing an educational plan that contains few or no activities that the student finds interesting, engaging, or would choose if given a choice. The ratio often seems to be reversed—the *more* difficulties that exist in teaching the student, the *less* likely it is that he or she will have preferred goals. Their plans seem to become a collection of compliance training activities.

Developing effective support plans is difficult. Perhaps as a result of training that focuses on student behavior, most educators are more skilled at and comfortable with teaching students to handle frustration than they are at devising strategies to remove it from the student's school program.

Teach Alternative Ways To Communicate   For a variety of reasons, a student may have never learned standard ways to communicate or may even, as a result of physical or cognitive disabilities, be unable to communicate effectively in a typical (vocal) manner. This becomes especially significant since researchers have reported an inverse relationship between the ability to effectively use some form of sign or verbal communication system and the presence of behavior challenges (Cantwell, Baker, & Mattison, 1981; Carr, 1979; Durand, 1987). Therefore, it is not surprising that teaching the student to substitute a less destructive, yet still effective, form of communication can result in a significant decrease in challenging behavior (Carr & Durand, 1985a, 1985b; Carr et al., 1980; Eason, White, & Newsome, 1982).

Help the Student Learn To Tolerate School Conditions   Helping a student learn how to tolerate certain school conditions is a strategy that should only be used to assist the student when conditions definitely cannot or should not be changed (i.e., it is clearly in the best interest of the student to learn to adapt to, or tolerate, the condition). Strategies can range from formal desensitization or relaxation procedures to help the student overcome phobias and fears (Morris & Kratochwill, 1983; Workman & Williams, 1980) to simply empathizing with the student and letting him or her know that the teacher is there to help.

Teach the Student To Be Quiet and Stop Communicating   Intensive efforts to understand the cause(s) for a student's disruptive and dangerous behavior will almost always result in information that can be used to implement support and positive teaching strategies based on the above three alternatives. However, there may be rare times when even the best analysis efforts do not give the information required to make changes or when changes needed in setting, staff, or curriculum are not possible. Under these circumstances (i.e., in the absence of a better idea), the teacher may have to implement behavior *management* procedures to directly decrease the student's challenging behavior, especially if it is highly disruptive or dangerous. When forced to make this sort of compromise, it is important to use the least intrusive, least aversive teaching procedures possible. It may be sufficient to simply take steps to ensure that the disruptive communication behavior is not rewarded. However, if that is not effective the teacher may have to also reward the student for not engaging in the disruptive behavior. There should never be a need to implement more than mild disciplinary procedures, such as restrictions on rewarding activities. There is nothing inherently abusive or stigmatizing in teaching a student that one of the consequences of his or her aggressive and dangerous behavior on the playground is being told to return to the classroom. However, it would always be preferable to deal with such a situation by first trying to understand the conditions that seem to lead to anger and aggression and also to help the student learn that there are other equally effective ways of dealing with the situation. Various positive programming strategies are well described in a number of books (Donnellan, LaVigna, Negri-Shoultz, & Fassbender, 1988; Evans & Meyer, 1985; LaVigna & Donnellan, 1986; Meyer & Evans, 1989).

Some positive teaching strategies have unpleasant components, at least from the student's point of view. For example, students do not enjoy being put "on extinction" or ignored; most students who are refusing to do a school task would prefer to be left alone, rather than be redirected. They would rather have free access to rewarding activities than have to earn access by *not* behaving disruptively. However, there can *never* be justification for the use of pain, either emotional or physical, to control student behavior.

Defining Success   Most of a student's disruptive and dangerous behavior is valuable feedback about what he or she is thinking and feeling, especially about the quality of our educational strategies. This feedback makes it clear that educators should not settle for teaching students to simply stop communicating or "shut up." The following story shows how important it is to define goals in terms of how the student views success:

> Cathy, who was labeled profoundly mentally retarded, had a lot of difficulty adjusting to her new school program. During the first few months she would often cry and try to run out of the room. Her teacher handled these situations by ignoring her crying as much as possible and redirecting her back to her desk if she attempted to run from the classroom. These procedures worked to reduce Cathy's crying and running away; however, her teacher became concerned about a new behavior that presented even more serious problems—Cathy began to vomit while at school. At first it occurred infrequently, but gradually increased until she was throwing up in the classroom every day.
>
> A behavior specialist was called in to consult with the teacher. The specialist asked what typically happened when Cathy vomited at school. Cathy's teacher said that almost everytime she vomited she had to be sent home and that often she did not return to school until the next day. Based on this evidence, a behavior plan was developed to eliminate the vomiting. The plan was a simple one—the teacher was instructed to ignore Cathy's vomiting behavior, clean her up if necessary, but otherwise act as if nothing had happened. She was to praise Cathy and reward her if she went short periods of time without vomiting.
>
> At first it did not seem as though the plan would work. Cathy threw up repeatedly during the first few days. In fact, on the third day she threw up, or at least tried to throw up, 23 times. However, after the third day things began to improve. The frequency of the vomiting steadily decreased over the next 27 days and by the 30th day of the new procedure she went the entire day without vomiting. She never threw up in class again.

The teacher and the behavior specialist had clearly accomplished their objective. Cathy's vomiting behavior was completely eliminated. However, it is questionable whether this is really a success story. It is important to look at the "success" of the behavior plan from the point of view of *all* the people concerned. The teacher and the behavior specialist certainly judged their efforts as a success. The other students in the class probably appreciated the change in Cathy's behavior. Yet, would Cathy agree that the plan was a success? If she had been interviewed on the 30th day of the new behavior plan, the first time she went the whole day without throwing up, what would she have said? "I just love it here ! My school work is very interesting and I am learning a lot." Or she may have said, "I still don't like it here. I'd rather leave. I just don't tell anyone about it anymore . . ."

Cathy was not very likely to consider the results of her behavior plan a success because nothing was done to help her with *her* "problem." A reasonable functional analysis would probably have shown that her "problem" was that either: 1) she disliked or was afraid of the classroom setting, or 2) nothing at school was more interesting or engaging than being at home. Her behavior plan did not help or improve these concerns. The behavior plan was just that—a *behavior* plan. It was successful in making an improvement in Cathy's behavior, but it did not help the basic reasons for the problem behavior.

CONCLUSION

The major message of this chapter was clearly portrayed in a comic strip that featured the famous cat, Garfield. The cartoon shows Garfield sitting in a tree, saying to himself:

> Why do I climb up trees when I can't climb down? The neighborhood always turns out to see me. Then the fire department comes to get me. Then my picture ends up in the newspaper. [Garfield reflects on this and concludes] I just answered my own question. (Garfield, 1984. Reprinted by permission of UFS, Inc.)

By his own admission it is clear that Garfield engages in behavior that is dangerous, at least to him and those who walk beneath the tree. In this situation, most people were taught to define "tree climbing" as a target behavior that needs to be eliminated. A subsequent functional analysis of the situation would probably show that Garfield was right—he gets attention, a lot of it, when he climbs the tree. Based on this information a behavior plan could be developed, which, if implemented appropriately, would result in fire trucks staying in the station, no pictures in the paper, and signs on the lawn instructing people not to look up if Garfield is in the tree. A really comprehensive plan would probably also call for Garfield to receive tokens that he could exchange for a variety of rewards—if he did *not* climb the tree. There is little doubt that if the plan were rigorously carried out by everyone in the community, the tree climbing behavior could be eliminated.

However, as discussed in the beginning of this chapter, a more important issue should be addressed—Why does Garfield think he has to climb a tree to get our attention? Why is Garfield's life so boring or unengaging that he finds the attention he gains when he climbs the tree to be more rewarding than his life on the ground? Stating the issue this way makes it clear that this is a problem for teachers, too, not just Garfield. There are students who figuratively "climb the tree" rather than participate and cooperate in their school program. They "cut" class, rock in their chairs, or run around the room causing disruption because they find this behavior more rewarding than cooperating and completing their school work. Problems should not be described as: "She does nothing all day but sit and rock, what can I do to stop the rocking?" These problems should be addressed by saying, "She prefers to sit and rock all day, rather than work at her school tasks. How can I make school more interesting and engaging?" Viewing the issue this way also makes it clear that the responsibility is really on teachers to change, to listen to the critical feedback provided by students, and to adapt their instructional practices to meet students' needs.

REFERENCES

Bailey, J.S., & Bostow, D.E. (1969). Modification of severe disruptive and aggressive behavior using brief time out and reinforcement procedures. *Journal of Applied Behavior Analysis, 2,* 31–37.

Blatt, B. (1985). Foreword. In D. Biklen (Ed.), *Achieving the complete school.* New York: Teacher's College Press.

Cantwell, D. P., Baker, L., & Mattison, R.E. (1981). Prevalence, type and correlates of psychiatric diagnoses in 200 children with communication disorders. *Developmental and Behavioral Pediatrics, 2,* 131–136.

Carr, E.G. (1979). Teaching autistic children to use sign language: Some research issues. *Journal of Autism and Developmental Disorders, 9,* 345–359.

Carr, E.G., & Durand, V.M. (1985a). Reducing behavior problems through functional communication training. *Journal of Applied Behavior Analysis, 18,* 111–126.

Carr, E.G., & Durand, V.M. (1985b). The social-communicative basis of severe behavior problems in children. In S. Reiss & R. Bootzin (Eds.), *Theoretical issues in behavior therapy* (pp. 219–254). New York: Academic Press.

Carr, E.G., Newsom, C.D., & Binkoff, J.A. (1980). Escape as a factor in the behavior of two retarded children. *Journal of Applied Behavior Analysis, 13,* 113–129.

Donnelan, A.M., LaVigna, G.W., Negri-Shoultz, N., & Fassbender, L.L. (1988). *Progress without punishment.* New York: Teacher's College Press.

Donnelan, A.M., Mirenda, P.L., Mesaros, R.A., & Fassbender, L.L. (1984). Analyzing the communicative functions of aberrant behavior. *Journal of The Association for Persons with Severe Handicaps, 9,* 201–212.

Durand, V.M. (1987) Assessment and treatment of psychotic speech in an autistic child. *Journal of Autism and Developmental Disorders, 17,* 17–28.

Durand, V.M., & Crimmins, D.M. (1988). Identifying the variables maintaining self-injurious behavior. *Journal of Autism and Developmental Disorders, 18*(1), 99–117.

Eason, L.J., White, M.J., & Newsom, C. (1982). Generalized reduction of self-stimulatory behavior: An effect of teaching appropriate play to autistic children. *Analysis and Intervention in Developmental Disabilities, 2,* 157–169.

Evans, I.M., & Meyer, L.H. (1985). *An educative approach to behavior problems: A practical decision model for interventions with severely handicapped learners.* Baltimore: Paul H. Brookes Publishing Co.

Foxx, R.M. (1982). *Decreasing behaviors of severely retarded and autistic persons.* Champaign, IL: Research Press.

Garfield. (1984, August 8). New York: United Media; UFS, Inc.

Gaylord-Ross, R.J., Weeks, M., & Lipner, C. (1980). Analysis of antecedent, response and consequence events in the treatment of self-injurious behavior. *Education and Training of the Mentally Retarded, 15,* 35–42.

Gliedman, J., & Roth W. (1980) *The unexpected minority: Handicapped children in America.* San Diego: Harcourt Brace Jovanovitch.

LaVigna, G.W., & Donnellan, A.M. (1986). *Alternatives to punishment: Solving behavior problems with non-aversive strategies.* New York: Irvington.

Meyer, L.H., & Evans, I.M. (1989). *Nonaversive intervention for behavior problems: A manual for home and community.* Baltimore: Paul H. Brookes Publishing Co.

Morris, R.J., & Kratochwill, T.R. (1983) *Treating children's fears and phobias: A behavioral approach.* Elmsford, NY: Pergamon.

Mount, B., & Zwernik, K. (1988). *It's never too early, it's never too late,* St. Paul, MN: Metropolitan Council.

O'Brien, J. (1987). A guide to life-style planning: Using *The Activities Catalog* to integrate services and natural support systems. In B. Wilcox & G.T. Bellamy, *A comprehensive guide to The Activities Catalog: An alternative curriculum for youth and adults with severe disabilities.* Baltimore: Paul H. Brookes Publishing Co.

Prizant, B.M., & Wetherby, A.M. (1987). Communicative intent: A framework for understanding social-communicative behavior in autism. *Journal of the American Academy of Child and Adolescent Psychiatry, 26,* 472–479.

Rose, T.L. (1979). Reducing self-injurious behavior by differentially reinforcing other behaviors. *The American Association for the Education of the Severely/Profoundly Handicapped, 4,* 179–186.

Weeks, M., & Gaylord-Ross, R. (1981). Task difficulty and aberrant behavior in severely handicapped students. *Journal of Applied Behavior Analysis, 14,* 449–463.

Wooden, K. (1976). *Weeping in the playtime of others: America's incarcerated children.* New York: McGraw-Hill.

Workman, E.A., & Williams, R. L. (1980). Self-cued relaxation in the control of an adolescent's violent arguments and debilitating somatic complaints. *Education and Treatment of Children, 3,* 315–322.

9

It's Not a Matter of Method

Thinking About How To Implement Curricular Decisions

*Dianne L. Ferguson
and Lysa A. Jeanchild*

AS DISCUSSED IN other chapters in this book, deciding *what* to teach is rarely straightforward or easy. Deciding *how* to teach is equally complex. Teachers have a variety of choices depending on the student. They can: 1) use a variety of learning materials, 2) teach in unique places, 3) organize diverse groups of students, or 4) plan lessons in ways that achieve varied learning experiences for each student. Teachers can even orchestrate learning "from a distance" by allowing students to teach each other or by using computers in an instructional role. Depending on how teachers begin to think about implementing curricular decisions, they can create a host of options that all have value for each student.

This chapter first discusses how teaching or "implementing curriculum" is the same for all students, even those who are very able or very disabled. Following is a discussion about how teaching must be different for students with varied abilities to make sure that they achieve a common schooling outcome. Finally, some "rules and tricks" for accomplishing heterogeneous group instruction are offered. We include this last topic because reforms throughout education, including integration, cooperative learning, and cross-age teaching all seem to rest upon teachers having more heterogeneous groups of learners (Giangreco & Putnam, 1991).

The range of options available for teaching is listed in Table 1. This list includes: 1) materials (what is used to teach), 2) lesson design (how teaching is organized), 3) locations (where teaching takes place), and 4) learning interactions (what actually happens in teaching). Deciding when and how to effectively choose among the range of options presented in Table 1 is a real challenge. This chapter includes some guidelines and strategies for making these choices and accommodating the widest possible range of students without overwhelming the teacher. Teaching is difficult enough without making teachers risk their own mental and physical health or diminish their professional enjoyment and satisfaction. We believe that teachers *can* effectively teach every different kind of student and enjoy doing it.

BUT FIRST, WHAT DO YOU MEAN BY *ALL* STUDENTS?

All of the chapters in this book are grounded in the notion that children and youth should receive compulsory public education in the schools closest to where they live. This is a fairly recent idea. During most of the history of public schooling in America, educators have believed that students who were thought to be "different" in any way should receive *their* compulsory public schooling in some other place and manner. As a consequence, many school professionals have come to think of most students as "different" in some way (Ferguson, 1987). Some students learn too quickly and too much, leaving their peers behind. Others learn awkwardly, or need more time to comprehend and use certain kinds of information. Still others possess a variety of physical, sensory, emotional, or cognitive impairments that render them able to learn only some of what their peers learn through the simple processes of daily routines.

In this chapter, a reference to *all students* means any student who lives in the neighborhood of the school, regardless of his or her abilities or disabilities. Readers should think about how the information presented here applies to the "smartest," most able student they have ever encountered, as well as the most disabled student they may know or can imagine, and, of course, all those in between.

HOW CAN TEACHING REALLY BE THE SAME?

It is difficult for teachers to imagine how teaching groups of students that are each very different can be the same. We suggest two ways: schooling outcomes and teaching process.

Schooling Outcomes

It is easy to become confused about what schooling is supposed to accomplish for students. Too much of what teachers do is caught up

Table 1.   Options for implementing curriculum

MATERIALS: What is used to teach

Standard curriculum texts: Books and workbooks selected and purchased by the district

Library books: Supplemental text materials available in school and public libraries, including art books, biographies, poetry, fiction, histories, and reference books

Public print media: Books, magazines, and newspapers, including comic books, news and household magazines, romance novels, how-to and self-help books

Educational videos and filmstrips: Supplemental visual materials produced for schools and purchased by the district for a range of curriculum areas

Television/movies/videos: Popular visual media commonly available in homes, including programs produced for adults and children with or without a specific educational focus

Other visual media: General public information available through commercials, posters, billboards, public art, and signs

Family print and visual media: Materials available within families including photo albums, art work, recipe files, correspondence, shopping and task lists, business and financial papers

Learning objects: Educational manipulative materials purchased by the district as part of or for use with standard curriculum, including math manipulatives, puzzles, learning games, art supplies, sports equipment, and lab materials

Daily life objects: The materials commonly used in homes and community settings including personal items (e.g., wallets, purses, jewelry, make-up, clothing, accessories); household items (e.g., dishes, food, radios and tapes, clocks, cameras, bikes, skateboards); and community materials (e.g., bus/subway tokens and transfers, church/concert programs, menus, shopping carts and bags, tickets)

LESSON DESIGN: How to organize what is taught

Lecture/illustrate/practice: The traditional teaching paradigm

Activity simulations: Short learning activities designed either to elaborate content or emulate use of content, including solving puzzles, playing learning games, taking apart or assembling things, drama, book reports, and role play

Real activities: Teaching a variety of specific learning content, either directly or indirectly, in the context of an activity students typically engage in at school, home, or in the community (e.g., checking out books at the library, purchasing things at the school store, working in the office, being a teacher's helper, cleaning the lunch tables or blackboards, delivering attendance, being a library helper or sports equipment monitor)

Real expanded activities: Teaching a variety of specific learning content in the context of a chain of activities that might extend over several days, such as planning a lunch menu, creating the shopping list, purchasing the ingredients, using recipes to prepare food, serving and eating, and cleaning up

Themes: Teaching individual lessons, simulated activities, real activities, and real expanded activities that are organized into daily, weekly, or longer content themes (e.g., doing a unit on Central America that includes content across all curriculum areas designed in a variety of ways)

(continued)

Table 1. *(continued)*

LOCATION: Where teaching takes place

Homeroom: Centralized classroom with the same group of students over an extended period of time, including classes organized by a single grade or multiple grades

Classes within the school: Classrooms for varying content areas, including math, foreign languages, shop, physical education, computer, science, home economics, or art

In school: Areas within the school, including the library, cafeteria, office, playground, student lounge, hallways, bathrooms, or nurse's office

Routine community sites: Common places in the community that students regularly frequent, including public library, grocery stores, offices, shopping malls, post office, coffee shops, churches, restaurants, and banks

Nonroutine community sites: Places in the community students visit less frequently, including recreation areas, parks, ball parks, concert halls, or hospitals; and all the places students might go infrequently for education or recreation, such as zoos, jails, modeling agencies, dairy farms, fire/police stations, and museums

Transit sites: Locations that involve transition or transportation, such as trains, buses, subways and their stations; streets, hallways, bike paths, and parking lots

LEARNING INTERACTIONS: What actually happens in teaching

Individual instruction: One student interacts with a teacher or other adult, including individual tutors, related service staff, counselors, or volunteers.

Small or large homogeneous group instruction: Teacher or other adult instructs a group of students who are learning more or less the same content at more or less the same learning rate.

Small or large heterogeneous group instruction: Teacher or other adult instructs a group of students who may be learning the same content in different ways at different learning rates or learning different things at different rates.

Small peer group instruction: Either homogeneous or heterogeneous groups of peers work together competitively or cooperatively to generate a product or outcome usually identified by a teacher or other adult.

Cross-age peer teaching: Older students, either individually or in groups, teach younger students lessons that were already introduced in some other format.

Computer drill and practice: Individual students use a variety of educational software, word processing, or computer games for practicing learning concepts or skills.

Computer enrichment: Individual students use a variety of educational and programming software, computer games, and databases to expand and extend learning.

in rules, tests, regulations, scores, and grades. While these have their importance and roles, they often serve to obfuscate their mission. Despite the details of schooling and teaching that need attention, the real accomplishment of schooling for all students is quite simple— whatever students learn should allow them to be active participants in their communities so that others care enough about what happens to them to look out for them. Schools should help all students become socially embedded, active participants in the life of the community.

Obviously, each student will achieve this outcome in different ways. Regardless of the details, however, this way of thinking about what schooling should accomplish can be helpful in two important ways. First, it helps remind us that whatever it is that students actually *do* in school must be applicable in their daily lives. School is only where a student "practices" being a socially embedded, actively participating community member. Each student's learning must apply to something outside of school both now and in the future. Second, students' learning must occur in ways that enhance their social images. Sometimes students learn important content in a manner that actually encourages others to think of them as different. For example, one student in a math class might be learning how to write numerals and compute single digit addition facts while the other students in the class are working on subtracting fractions—at slightly different degrees of understanding and competence. Although number writing and addition might be important for the one student to learn, the differences in learning content may damage more than enhance his social image. Other students are at risk of viewing this student as a "special" and "different" member of the math class for whom different rules of learning and evaluation apply. If this student practiced this same learning in the context of a science class where he wrote down and added up the measures of compounds in different experimental groups, the image produced could be different. In the first situation, he is a student doing "easy" math; in the second, he is a student helping to accomplish the shared goals of a science experiment.

Teaching Process

Regardless of what students are learning, the process of teaching and learning is the same. Learning is not only about the right answer or doing something the "right" way. Sometimes students can give their teachers "right" answers and behaviors without knowing why or how they are right. Learning for all students involves determining what the learning means and how it fits into their understanding and experience. Students must be able to make sense of what is being taught if they are going to learn it well enough to be able to use it without the assistance of a teacher.

There are many factors that can affect how students learn. Table 2 describes the instructional components that teachers must manage for any student to achieve complete and usable learning.

Table 2.   The range of instructional components critical to teaching all students

Natural cues: Teachers must determine how to make sure that students will learn to apply their learning in natural contexts. Instead of depending upon teachers to tell them when and how to use what they have learned, students need teachers to help them learn how to use their abilities fluently and naturally when teachers are not around.

Set up the learning environment: Teachers need to plan instruction *before* it happens so the environment encourages and supports student success. Ways to do this include having needed materials, prosthetic devices, or other adaptive equipment handy, and being thoughtful about the arrangement of the students and the teachers, as well as the furniture.

Individual assistance: Teachers need to determine the appropriate type and amount of assistance needed to support students' acquisition of learning content. This will vary not just from student to student, but for each student depending on the demands and familiarity of the task. Decisions about individual assistance constantly change.

Student motivation: Teachers need to make it worth students' time to learn by identifying the incentives that are most valuable for each student, to use those rewards conditionally, and to vary the type and amount of reward provided as students' acquisition of learning material changes.

Maintain positive learning environment: Teachers need to structure a positive learning environment that supports students' acquisition of cooperative social behaviors, by maintaining a positive ratio of reward to correction and supporting students' choice and initiation within learning activities.

Individual assessment and ongoing adjustments: Teachers need to determine how students are understanding learning content and the meaning of their mistakes so that they can help students learn to correct those mistakes. Teachers need to intervene in students' problem solving with just enough assistance to help students understand, while at the same time providing further opportunities for students to apply their learning in both familiar and novel contexts.

HOW MUST TEACHING BE DIFFERENT?

Even though the fundamental teaching process is the same for all students, it must be constructed differently for each student. Some students will require more time to observe or practice new skills. Others learn more efficiently by reading first, and then watching someone else. Still others may always require certain kinds of reminders or assistance to begin a task, but can complete it alone.

Of course, it is not just a matter of discovering each student's individual learning style. Students' needs change over time and according to the task, so teachers must constantly match their interpretation of the critical instructional components in different ways, at different times, and for different students.

The second important way teaching must be different for all students concerns how much of the school's standard curriculum the student acquires. We believe that any student will master the district's (or school's) standard curriculum in one of three ways. Many students will acquire almost all of the information and skills contained in the designated curriculum. These students are very forgiving of teachers' weaknesses. They also excite teachers' strengths because, in most cases, they seem to be "tuned in" to what teachers are doing and trying to teach them, often learning more than anticipated.

Other students, perhaps a smaller number, will only acquire the information and skills of the official curriculum if teachers are very attentive and skillful. Teachers will have to make many adaptations in the curriculum to achieve the schooling outcomes of participation and social inclusion. These students will challenge teachers' abilities and patience. Some of them take a lot of time to figure things out; others need different kinds of assistance. What often makes these students challenging for teachers is that they struggle to learn. Learning is more work than play, labor than pleasure. Students become easily discouraged, impatient with themselves, and sometimes angry with their teachers. Their learning difficulties are less tolerant of teachers' weaknesses than more able students—a situation that can make both the student and the teacher want to give up on each other.

Teachers will also encounter a few students whose abilities and lack of abilities simply make it impossible for them to learn even some of the community's selected curriculum. Instead, teachers will have to depend upon the guidance of the schooling outcomes we described earlier to bring these students' learning needs into closer correspondence with the standard required curriculum. They will learn to look for ways the curriculum can serve students' needs to become more active participants in life inside and outside of school. Teachers' creativity will be stretched to determine how 20th century American history can aid a student's community participation. Many teachers will find, however, that current events can greatly improve a student's social conversation repertoire. In the process they will also find these students to be the most humbling of any of the others in their class because they will learn exactly what is taught to them—nothing more. However, these more instructionally challenging students can also help teachers hone their teaching skills for *all students.*

"RULES AND TRICKS" FOR HETEROGENEOUS GROUP INSTRUCTION

When teachers start to make decisions about what and how to teach, they should begin by choosing from the same list of materials, lesson designs, teaching locations, and instructional components for all of their students.

Next, they should assume heterogeneity, and actually seek to structure differences among students. Sometimes, when teaching specific skills or procedures, teachers will find that homogeneous grouping is the best way to quickly teach new sets of facts to some students. However, when teaching basic concepts, problem solving, conceptual applications, or learning that is embedded within real activities, careful structuring of heterogeneous group instruction will usually be more effective.

The rest of this section describes three "rules" that can help implement curriculum using more heterogeneous group instruction. For each of these rules, we offer several "tricks" to assist in using the rule more effectively. Teachers experimenting with these ideas will undoubtedly discover and use their own tricks.

Rule 1: Maximize Variation Across Student Characteristics

Simply grouping students who have very different characteristics together will neither enhance each student's learning, nor build positive relationships among them. In fact, if teachers are not careful, the opposite may happen. Physical proximity is a necessary, but not sufficient, condition. How teachers organize groups of students and then plan their learning experiences are the two critical factors that will determine the success or failure of heterogeneous group instruction.

The first task is to decide which students can be grouped together. The first rule related to this task encourages teachers to begin by creating groups that include students who have the most different characteristics. Teachers should purposefully seek to mix students according to a range of characteristics, including gender, ethnicity, high–medium–low task performance abilities, and high–medium–low communication and social interaction abilities. The following are a few "tricks" that will help to determine which students can be grouped together:

1. Group students whose communication abilities vary. Include at least one student who has strong interpersonal and group engagement skills and, at most, one student who requires extensive assistance with these skills. Groups should be balanced with students who are quite verbal, or even noisy, and students who are very quiet.
2. Group students who vary in ability along task demand dimensions. Balance students who require extensive assistance to complete the task objectives with students who are more able. In

some situations there may also need to be a balance among the kinds of assistance students require. For example, it would be too difficult to group together three or four students who all require a great deal of physical assistance and support from the teacher.

3. Do not isolate any student. Try setting up groups by asking each student to choose three other students with whom he or she wants to learn. Everyone should be in a group with at least one student he or she chose. Students who are not chosen should be surrounded by able and supportive students who might develop enough interest to pursue a relationship.

4. Start small. There are many ways to think about optimal group size. Different people have different general rules. We recommend that teachers set up groups that have two to six members, varying the size according to students' individual needs, objectives of the lesson, and the teacher's instructional energy. Until teachers discover their own preferences and limits, starting small will be more likely to result in good experiences.

5. Have students work with everyone in the class at different times during the semester or year. As with group size, there are many different recommendations for how long groups should stay together. Teachers will discover their own rules about this as well. Whatever decisions are made about group duration, teachers should at least arrange for students to work with everyone in the class at some point during the year.

Rule 2: Maximize Positive Interdependence

There are two key reasons for heterogeneous group instruction. One is for students to learn the material and accomplish the learning task by working together. The other is for students to build reciprocal relationships, generate a sense of shared experience, appreciate human diversity, and develop skills of collaboration and cooperation. After teachers make a decision about group composition, the next critical rule for successful heterogeneous group instruction is to carefully orchestrate students' learning experiences in ways that contribute to their abilities to learn the material, to work together, and to build relationships with each other. How students perceive each other, and how readily they learn the material, depends upon how teachers structure their learning experience.

The second rule encourages teachers to organize the group's learning experiences so that, in as many ways as possible, students learn to depend upon each other, to accomplish shared goals, and to help each other. Teachers will discover many ways to create this positive interdependence. The following are a few "tricks" to assist teachers:

1. Arrange the environment so that students within each group can see each other, share materials, and help each other. Arrangements will vary depending upon the number of groups. Teachers should keep in mind that they will need easy access to each group as well as to individual group members who may need extra assistance. Surround students with the most severe disabilities with particularly helpful students who might be more able to ensure their full involvement in the group by physically helping them and by interpreting their sometimes idiosyncratic communication.

2. Arrange materials and information to encourage students to depend upon each other and to work toward shared goals. There are several ways that this can be accomplished. For example, only one copy of materials could be used so that group members must share; or each student could be given only one part of the materials or information needed to complete the task.

3. Design instruction so the efforts of all members are perceived as needed by the group. Arrange for students who are less able, or perhaps who are less well liked because of various annoying behaviors, to have some expertise that the group needs in order to accomplish its task. For example, arrangements could be made for students who have significant disabilities to have essential materials or information, or to distribute or collect needed materials.

4. Maximize student to student interactions throughout the activity. Assign roles that are essential to the group's process—helper, reader, checker, data collector, encourager, or reporter. These roles can be rotated among the students. In some situations teachers can orchestrate group learning by making one student's learning "trial" another student's antecedent. For example, someone who is practicing how to grasp and use objects might pass other students their materials, which in turn prompts them to begin working.

5. Balance interactions. Teach students to work with all group members and to learn about themselves as they learn about other students. For example, one way to teach collaborative skills to a student who has trouble listening or who sometimes disrupts the group is to have that student observe and collect data on other students' turn-taking behaviors. Another strategy would be to have the student assume the role of "encourager" with the assignment of praising others' listening and cooperative behaviors.

6. Balance instruction across the day and week rather than the

lesson. Making instructional groups heterogeneous allows the opportunity to focus attention and support on different students at different times. Some learners will naturally need less instructional support and teacher attention because they either learn well on their own or they are already skilled at the task. While one student may be just beginning to learn the material, another student may be using the lesson for drill and practice. Therefore, in any one group there may be "low intensity" learners as well as "high intensity" learners. It is helpful to use a weekly schedule, or some other form of weekly instructional summary, to help ensure that students' learning opportunities are balanced across the week. A quick glance should reassure teachers that all students have a balance of high and low intensity instructional learning opportunities.

7. Reward the group for developing strategies for helping each other, involving everyone in the group, and solving any interpersonal difficulties. Groups can report these support and problem-solving experiences to the teacher as one way of helping the teacher keep track of them.

8. Establish a clear beginning and end to each group. The group should know that helping, cooperating, and finding ways to include each other in the group is part of the group objective. Each group could begin with a review of the group objectives, and end with self-evaluation of each member's efforts and progress. Bracketing the group's activity with this kind of organization can help teachers and students make a smooth transition between groups and activities.

9. Collect information on students' interpersonal and cooperative behaviors and inform and adapt teaching strategies. Collect data unintrusively, and try to include students in the gathering of information. Most importantly, information should be collected routinely to guide teaching decisions.

Rule 3: Maximize Individual Accomplishments

The overall purpose of heterogeneous group instruction is to use students' differences to enhance the learning of each student in the group. The first two rules focused on setting up heterogeneous groups and designing the group learning experience to encourage students' development of cooperative skills and reciprocal relationships. The third rule focuses on enabling students to master the instructional content.

School is not just about social interactions and building friendships. Although social embeddedness is an important schooling outcome, schools must also help students learn things that will allow them to actively participate in life outside of school. In order to be an active participant, students need to acquire competence along numerous dimensions. A few "tricks" are offered below:

1. Minimize variation across task characteristics. When teachers design group instruction, they should combine activities or tasks that are related and have similar time demands in the same location or in close proximity. This helps the teacher with the logistics of group instructional demands and helps students understand the meaning and importance of the lesson.

2. Vary the amount of learning each student is expected to master. Criterion-referenced instruction should be used to decide critical learning outcomes for each student, including specification of desired behaviors. Students can work on different parts of a joint instructional activity or give different assignments (lists, words, problems, tasks) to students within the group.

3. Focus on cooperation rather than competition. In addition to academic or performance objectives, each student should be learning about him- or herself and others. Less able students suffer the most from the social perceptions generated by competitive learning situations. Teachers should use individual improvement scores, average group scores, individual learning objectives, or some combination to evaluate learning success. Teachers should keep in mind that one student's learning task may be a support or antecedent to another student's learning experience. This will help teachers' creativity.

4. Note and reward individual academic achievements. The academic task and criterion for success needs to be explained so students understand the objectives of the lesson. Students must understand that the objectives of the lesson are both to attain their own academic objectives and to make sure everyone in the group achieves their objectives. This sharing of learning responsibility will help to build peer cooperation regardless of student ability.

5. Reward individual and group achievements. Praise correct responses and bring individual achievements to the attention of other group members. Teachers should encourage students' support of each other and monitor students' perceptions of each other; making sure that every group member views his or her colleagues as competent and contributory to the group's activities. Try to avoid excessive or different praise of students who have disabilities—it may encourage others in the group to think of them as different or less competent.

6. Provide assistance to ensure individual success, especially with regard to mistakes. Identify why students are making mistakes and give them the assistance that will help them to correctly perform the task without making mistakes. Learning from mistakes and confusion only occurs when teachers help students understand why the incident happened.
7. Systematically assess and monitor each student's performance. Teachers can randomly select students' work to correct or score, choosing alternating students to observe and collect information on their performance, or randomly choosing one member's work to represent the group as a whole. Data should be collected on varying days and only if it is used to make instructional decisions and changes.
8. Teach students to evaluate their learning. Use a criterion-referenced system to evaluate students' achievements and a product (report, single set of answers) by all members who contributed or the number of group members who reached a specific criterion. Include students in discussions of their achievements and how they might try something different the next day.

CONCLUSION

Traditionally, it has been the assumption in the field of teaching that in order to meet the needs of students who have different abilities, schools and teaching must be organized for them in different ways, using separate means, located in separate places, and having different outcomes (Ferguson, 1989). Consequently, students with different abilities have been educated along a continuum of separateness (Laski, 1991; Lipsky & Gartner, 1989). Most of us are familiar with the result—students with fewer abilities are isolated and stigmatized, while more able students miss the opportunity to develop relationships with peers who are different.

In this chapter we discussed two ways of thinking about schooling and teaching that support the inclusion of *all students*, regardless of their differences. The first involves understanding the purpose of schooling as being identical for all students. Schools need to enable all students to be socially embedded, active participants in their communities both inside and outside of school. The second involves viewing the teaching process as equivalent for all students. The instructional components that are critical to teaching are the same for all students, although they may be used in various ways to accommodate different learning needs and styles. The decisions teachers make about instructional materials, lesson design, location of instruction, and what actually happens within learning interactions, will all help the student "figure out" what is being taught and how it applies to their lives outside of school.

We also described three ways that students are different from each other that still allow teachers to structure schooling so that all students are included and benefit. Some students may require adaptations to help them acquire the same learning as other students. A few students require significant accommodations to bring their learning needs into closer correspondence with the standard curriculum.

The final section outlined some "rules and tricks" for heterogeneous group instruction. We offered some general conceptual theory, as well as some practical assistance to help teachers determine how to design instruction that supports all three types of students to achieve the same schooling outcomes.

We believe it is not only possible to use students' differences as a strength, but that these differences are necessary for schools and teachers who seek to make a positive impact on students' lives. The issue is not that schools can include all students *in spite of* their different abilities or disabilities, but that schools can enhance the learning of each student *because of* their differences.

If educators begin with the assumption that schooling outcomes and essential learning processes are identical for all students, it follows that assisting schools to include all students is not a matter of method. Deciding what and how to teach, although not easy decisions, are also not different decisions for students with different abilities.

REFERENCES

Ferguson, D.L. (1987). *Curriculum decision-making for students with severe handicaps: Policy and practice.* New York: Teachers College Press.

Ferguson, D.L. (1989). Severity of need and educational excellence: Public school reform and students with disabilities. In D.P. Biklen, D.L. Ferguson, & A. Ford (Eds.), *Schooling and disability* (pp. 25–58). Chicago: National Society for the Study of Education.

Giangreco, M.F., & Putnam, J.W. (1991). Supporting the education of students with severe disabilities in regular education environments. In L.H. Meyer, C.A. Peck, & L. Brown (Eds.), *Critical issues in the lives of people with severe disabilities* (pp. 409–421). Baltimore: Paul H. Brookes Publishing Co.

Lipsky, D.K., & Gartner, A. (Eds.). (1989). Beyond separate education: Quality education for all. Baltimore: Paul H. Brookes Publishing Co.

SUGGESTED READINGS

The following readings provide further information on some of the ideas addressed in this chapter. There are, of course, many other books and articles that are also useful. Readers are encouraged to share other related references with their colleagues and the authors of this chapter.

Ferguson, D.L., & Wilcox, B. (1987). *The elementary/secondary system: Supportive education for students with severe handicaps. Module 1: The activity-based IEP.* Eugene: Specialized Training Program, University of Oregon.

Procedures are described for completing family-referenced educational assessments; coordinating the contribution of various disciplines; identifying, selecting, and analyzing locally relevant activities for instruction; and making critical decisions about curricular focus. It includes blank forms, examples of completed forms, and a series of exercises to assist readers in applying and practicing key concepts and procedures.

Forest, M., & O'Brien, J., with Snow, J., & Hasbury, D. (1989). *Action for inclusion: How to improve schools by welcoming children with special needs into regular classrooms.* Toronto, Ontario: Frontier College Press.

The authors discuss fundamental assumptions about the value and purposes of schooling and learning. Practical lessons are included that outline ways to address the demands and challenges presented by building neighborhood schools that include all students.

Jeanchild, L., & Ferguson, D.L (1990). *The elementary/secondary system: Supportive education for students with severe handicaps. Module 2B: Programming and instruction.* Eugene: Specialized Training Program, University of Oregon.

This module for teachers describes assumptions about good instruction, planning effective activity and skill programs, designing and implementing quality instruction, collecting information, and communicating instruction to others. It includes descriptions of specific instructional support strategies to use with students who have a range of abilities and disabilities. It also includes examples, forms, and exercises to assist readers to apply concepts and strategies.

Johnson, D.W., & Johnson, R.T. (1986). Mainstreaming and cooperative learning strategies. *Exceptional Children, 52,* 553–561.

The elements of cooperative learning and specific actions teachers need to take to implement them are presented in this article. The authors say that positive relationships between handicapped and nonhandicapped students result from effective implementation of cooperative learning strategies.

Johnson, D.W., Johnson, R.T., & Holubec, E. (Eds.). (1986). *Circles of learning: Cooperation in the classroom* (rev. ed.). Edina, MN: Interaction Book Company.

This book offers a comprehensive overview of the differences between competitive, individualistic, and cooperative learning research validating the effectiveness of cooperative learning, components of cooperative learning, and strategies for implementation.

Kameenui, E.J., & Simmons, D.C. (1990). *Designing instructional strategies: The prevention of academic learning problems.* Columbus, OH: Charles E. Merrill.

Although this book concentrates on designing instruction for homogeneous groups of learners, most of whom require adaptations in standard curriculum, the text offers an excellent overview of the theory of instruction, as well as several specific strategies for teaching a range of academic skills. Also included are discussions of a set of assumptions about teachers and learners, the relationship between the beliefs a teacher brings to the instructional context and student outcomes, and ways of thinking about classroom management that readers may find provocative and instructive.

Todd, A., Benz, M., & Ferguson, D.L. (1988). *The elementary/secondary system: Supportive education for students with severe handicaps. Module 2A: Integrated group instruction.* Eugene: Specialized Training Program, University of Oregon.

This module for teachers describes grouping strategies and instructional procedures for heterogeneous group instruction. It gives suggestions for constructing groups of learners, planning and implementing group instruction, and evaluating student performance. It includes blank forms, examples of completed forms, and instructions for their use.

10

Measuring and Reporting Student Progress

Brian Cullen and Theresa Pratt

ALBERT SHANKER (1988) argues that education has "never worked well for more than 20% of our children" (p. 8). Serving the rest, as education must do, will require fundamental changes in curriculum, pedagogy, and management (Neill & Medina, 1989).

Creating or redefining a school system that truly includes all children and adults in the learning process is certainly a current educational issue. Volumes of recent research and observations of educational practice indicate a strong and growing trend toward inclusive education. There is a movement in North America today that recognizes the heterogeneity among students. Although today's educators have the opportunity to create school systems, schools, and classrooms that value human diversity, the challenge for inclusive schools should also include parameters that ensure quality education for all students and evaluation of education in terms of current educational thought and classroom practice.

This chapter explores various forms of past and current practices relative to measuring student progress and the communication practices associated with student evaluation. The need to employ more humane, effective, and efficient means of student evaluation is paramount. In discussing the various subissues in this chapter, it is important to note that while academic research on the topic must be considered, it is equally important to listen to the daily practitioners in the classroom. Indeed, much of this chapter is based on findings from verbal and written interviews of current classroom teachers, support personnel, and school and district administrators.

Learning involves taking risks, being unsuccessful a number of times, having a lot of practice before success, and then gradually getting closer to the desired end result. Motivation to learn involves anticipating a measure of success and being aware of making progress even when the desired result is not near. If students are only working for marks and teacher approval, there is a serious flaw in the system. If reading, writing, and mathematics have no purpose other than to gain a score or grade, there are no intrinsic rewards in learning. It seems that students cannot learn anything unless they can judge their own progress.

Educators need to ask themselves, "What do students learn by taking a test?" It is the authors' belief that for evaluation to be of any use to the learner, it must be an integral part of the learning experience. Students need to know how they are doing while they are doing it—there is no better way to learn. When learning something new, the student needs someone to understand what he or she is trying to do and to help him or her do it better, then get out of the way so the learner can practice on his or her own. Students do not need a critic, they need a coach. Teachers need to help their students view ongoing evaluation as part of the process of doing a task and understand that the purpose is to help the student be successful at it. This is more likely to support learning and to tell the teacher more about the students' learning processes than an after-the-fact assessment of how well they did. Assessment must be perceived as assistance and not a hindrance to the student. Evaluation must do more than support teaching—it must be an indistinguishable part of any learning experience. It also must facilitate the student in learning how to evaluate his or her own learning.

In the Waterloo Region Catholic School Board, as in many school districts, educators are no longer satisfied with merely admitting students with any form of disability into regular education, but have clearly begun to review programs and services to ensure that quality education is being delivered. Intricately involved with quality education for students is how student progress (learning) is measured and how this information is communicated to everyone associated with the individual student.

WHAT IS STUDENT EVALUATION?

The word "evaluation" is often used narrowly as a synonym for "testing." More appropriately, the term includes all available methods of obtaining information regarding a student's education and a teacher's effectiveness (Board of Education for the City of Etobicoke, 1987). Historically, in the educational context, evaluation has been seen as the final thing educators do to or for the student. Educators have, in many instances, attempted to evaluate students in the same way products on a production line are evaluated.

Raw material + Processing = Final product
(Student)   (Teaching)   (Adult for work force)

Essentially there are various quality control mechanisms associated with an industrial model throughout the processing phase. The question that should be asked is "Do we want schools to be like machine bureaucracies or do we want schools to provide quality education based on the needs of the learner?" The key point here is the need of the learner (student) as opposed to the arbitrary needs of teachers, administrators, and/or educational bureaucrats.

Therefore, evaluation should be seen as a process that begins with the start of school life and continues throughout a given school day, week, month, and career. "It is not a casual unplanned, unstructured endeavour; it is a process in which teachers and students learn about their respective achievements and about the possible need for change if growth is to take place" (Board of Education for City of Etobicoke, 1987, p. 4). It is essential that not only should student evaluation be part of a continuous process, but that the process needs to have clearly defined objectives. The evaluation process obviously needs to be understood by teachers, students, and parents within the context of the objectives identified for a particular student.

WHY STUDENTS ARE EVALUATED

As long as traditional evaluative methods remain in vogue, evaluation strictly for the purpose of grades, marks, and comments will continue. However, there are several other aspects of evaluation that suggest a much broader and more purposeful use of evaluation. The evaluation of students should:

1. Determine if objectives were achieved.
2. Assist in the development and implementation of an educational plan that meets student needs.
3. Assist the teacher to determine the direction of the future.
4. Provide information on the quality of the learning environment for specific kinds of learning.

5. Determine how effective the teaching process or methodology has been.
6. Provide a basis for extra help where needed.

If learners are to grow, they must receive feedback on what they do and thus become aware of their strengths and needs. The primary goal of evaluation is diagnosis. If the learner is to show a true indication of his or her competence, then the expectations of a given task or assignment must be clear to the learner and the teacher. Therefore, when evaluation strategies are being developed, objectives and outcomes must be specified. Program objectives and evaluation strategies must be equal partners in the teaching–learning process.

PRINCIPLES OF EVALUATION

Evaluating student progress is one of the most important aspects of the educational process. Evaluation and interpretation of what a student has learned should not be an activity conducted outside and apart from instruction, but an integral part of it. Evaluation should go well beyond simple measurement of students' academic achievement. The following are principles of evaluation that can assist in ensuring that evaluation is an inherent part of instruction:

1. Continuous evaluation of student achievement as an integral part of the teaching–learning process should identify concerns and difficulties quickly and provide a basis for immediate action.
2. The form of evaluation should be appropriate to the task, the kind of learning, and the stage of learning.
3. The effect of evaluation must be constructive. Evaluation techniques must increase, not diminish, a student's feeling of personal worth and of what is important in his or her learning.
4. A variety of evaluation techniques must be used in order to obtain information on the different aspects of student learning, thus providing a reliable foundation of judgment and decisions.
5. Evaluation must go beyond the cognitive and psychomotor areas to the affective domain including an exploration of interests, values, and attitudes.
6. In order for evaluation to be effective, there must be communication in many directions: student–student, student–teacher, teacher–student, teacher–parents, and teacher–colleagues. There must be effective communication of goals, expectations, criteria, and performance. Students need to understand the immediate purpose and expectations of their studies and how they can demonstrate their learning to themselves and others.

7. The evaluation process should help students learn how to evaluate their own learning.

THE ROLE OF NORM-REFERENCED STANDARDIZED TESTING IN EVALUATION

One of the earliest methods of attempting to evaluate student learning included a heavy reliance on norm-referenced assessment. The misuse of norm-referenced testing has been chronicled extensively in recent times (Biklen, 1985; Lipsky & Gartner, 1989; Stainback, Stainback, & Forest, 1989; Stainback & Stainback, 1990); yet, the use of norm-referenced testing remains in some form in all school districts. Arguably, norm-referenced testing programs can produce positive outcomes for students. The inherent danger in the use of these tests, however, is that some school districts, schools, or classrooms rely extensively or exclusively on data from these tests to determine student progress.

Schools have started to become centers that value diversity and uniqueness. To meet the diverse student needs in regular classes, adaptations of evaluative methods are required to maintain consistency. As classrooms become more diverse, so too must evaluative practices; this is what is meant by "consistency in diversity." This need for consistency also means that curriculum must become more attuned to the needs of students; that is, it must become more diverse.

Conflict can emerge when a district or school encourages child-centered, needs-based educational programs and services and then advocates norm-referenced testing as an exclusive or primary tool of student evaluation.

A Rationale for Change

It seems that concerns and complaints about formal, standardized, norm-referenced tests have increased in both volume and intensity. In the journal article "Searching for Alternatives to Standardized Tests: Whys, Whats and Whethers" (Neill & Medina, 1989), the authors summarize these recurring criticisms into four categories. They suggest that standardized tests: 1) give false information about the status of learning; 2) are unfair to (or biased against) some kinds of students (e.g., minority students, those with limited proficiency in English, females, and students from low-income families); 3) tend to corrupt the processes of teaching and learning, often reducing teaching to mere preparation for testing; and 4) focus time, energy, and attention on simple skills that are easily tested and ignore more advanced thinking skills and creative endeavors.

The injustice is not only seen in the negative effects on students, but also in the labels they receive in terms of local, state, and national averages. Lipsky and Gartner (1989) point out that such norm-referenced assessments can result in lack of motivation and even negative attitudes toward learning and achievement. It should be noted that norm-referenced testing means that some students always have to be in the bottom half.

The authors' experiences as well as input from other educators acknowledge that standardized assessment tools can provide benchmarks in terms of the student's ability, however, too often such tests do not have direct impact on the student's progress and educational goals and curriculum. "Standardized tests focus on basic skills, not on critical thinking, reasoning or problem solving. They emphasize the quick recognition of isolated facts, not the integration of information and the generation of ideas" (Neill & Medina, 1989, p. 684). Students do not attend school only to learn basic skills, but also to develop the personal, intellectual, and social skills necessary to enable them to become happy, productive members of a democratic society.

As administrators in schools, the authors witness discussion of student evaluation and standardized and norm-referenced testing among school faculties. Informal research indicates that the general discussion is universal in schools. It is time to pay heed to what teachers and other front line staff are saying and thinking about standardized testing. A principal from Commerce City, Colorado stated, "Dangers outweigh potential usefulness" (K. Braiman, personal communication, April 16, 1990). The following are samples of comments from classroom teachers in Ontario, Colorado, Michigan, and Minnesota:

"Tests do not often relate to student experiences."
"They can be a difficult experience for many students."
"The time spent testing would be better spent teaching."
"Standardized tests tell us that which we already know."
"Students are measured against tests that do not necessarily reflect what has been emphasized in class."
"The learning process is not considered."
"The testing seems to be focusing on things of minimal importance to students' real progress in thinking and problem solving."
"I hate like hell to take the time away from my curriculum to teach to tests."

Finally, as noted by George Flynn (personnal communication, September, 1989), Director of Education, Waterloo Region Catholic School Board:

> Standardized testing is useful only in terms of managing the systems. Clearly established standards with benchmarks along the way make it easier to stand accountable for expenditures. The downside is that the process may have little to do with *student* progress as the criteria are usually narrowly focused and will probably "sort out" any students the historical system has wished to segregate.

Although Flynn's comments may suggest that standardized, norm-referenced testing procedures are ineffective, this is not the authors' contention. Methods and procedures used in the past may become only a portion of consistent educational evaluation that does not place great importance on standardized norm-referenced tests. There are other methods of student evaluation that are more preferable and relevant to learning.

Standardized Testing and Segregated School Placement

A debate that continues in local and state jurisdictions involves the placement of students in programs, schools, and classes based on standardized testing results. This debate has caused and will continue to cause serious concern for students and their families, particularly if the results of these testing programs restrict a student, perhaps indefinitely, to some form of segregated education. As long as school systems believe it is morally, ethically, and educationally right to segregate and exclude students based on test scores, extensive use and misuse of standardized testing will occur. What can happen, unfortunately, is that students can be pigeonholed into a program, class, or facility (usually for the duration of their education) or considerable differences in test scores can appear and the "system" will take months (or years) to decide on its version of a "least restrictive environment." There are some educators, including the authors, who may consider the terms "segregated" and "education" to be mutually exclusive. If evaluation is to help students, test scores should never be used to exclude a student from the mainstream of school and community life. The debate could conclude as soon as local school jurisdictions put the concept of inclusive education into practice; that is, when all students, regardless of ability, are attending their neighborhood schools with appropriate support.

An example of the role that standardized, norm-referenced testing has played in many schools is reflected in the case of Joe. When he was 5 years old, Joe (a pseudonym) entered the school system. His academic performance was seemingly below average; yet, more importantly, his social skills and behavioral peculiarities provided significant concern for his teacher. The basic concerns about Joe were intensified throughout first and second grade. He was, apparently, a student who was "inconveniencing" the traditional system. His academic performance continued to lag and his behavior was violent at times, causing great concern. The school district mobilized itself in an effort to reduce concern and a barrage of tests were administered by the school psychologist. Prior to the testing, the school proposed two possible alternative placements: 1) a behavioral adjustment class, or 2) a class for the trainable retarded. Placement would, however, essentially rest with the test results. After months of scheduling and scoring, the test results were available. The recommendations based on those test results indicated that Joe could not be placed in a behavior adjustment class as he was too "low functioning." It was obvious that the psychometric personnel did not think he would be able to take advantage of the program designed for "brighter" students with behavioral concerns. Conversely, the recommendations also suggested that he would not be placed in a trainable retarded class because of his behavior. The question that school districts and schools must continually face is simple—how many pigeonholes can be created? The authors recommend eliminating the pigeonholes and thus significantly reducing the need for and amount of standardized norm-referenced testing.

The interesting sidelight to this brief case study is that Joe remained in a regular class, with additional support, and is now entering high school. Of further interest, the sometimes violent and supposedly inappropriate behaviors that "inconvenienced" the school system no longer exist. Could being part of an inclusive school have something to do with his personal growth?

The practice of testing students and using the test results to decide who shall be admitted into the typical school classroom or even the typical school is common across North America. Educators, and to a greater extent the public, assume that there is an appropriate placement for students with disabilities that can be determined scientifically by administering tests. An alternative practice, however, would be to view placement as a political, philosophical, or moral decision and to use assessment tests or other measurements as useful tools for determining how best to educate students of diverse ability (Biklen, 1985). The authors recognize that standardized testing is a profitable subindustry of education. They contend that the majority of finances spent by school districts on testing programs should be used instead to facilitate children learning in a more holistic fashion.

THE EVALUATION PROCESS

Evaluation is a collaborative, cyclical process that involves the students and the teacher. The learning objectives and opportunities should determine what is to be evaluated and how it is to be evaluated.

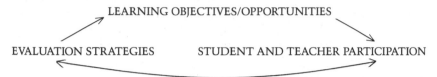

LEARNING OBJECTIVES/OPPORTUNITIES

EVALUATION STRATEGIES   STUDENT AND TEACHER PARTICIPATION

The close relationship between objectives and evaluation is fundamental to any process of student evaluation. A balanced evaluation plan includes many forms of evaluation that are *appropriate to the student's development and level of achievement*. When considering evaluation strategies, a number of factors noted by the Board of Education for the City of Etobicoke (1987) should be kept in mind:

The need to regard evaluation as a positive component of the student's learning experience

The need to relate evaluation activities to the student's level of development

The need to recognize and address the relationship between stated objectives, learning activities, and evaluation activities

The need to develop evaluation practices that support learning-as-process as well as learning-as-product

The need to modify evaluation procedures for exceptional students, and to differentiate for students at different levels of ability

The need continually to re-examine evaluation practices, and to be open to changing them should it prove necessary

The need to determine whether or not we are truly evaluating what we think we are evaluating

USING A DECISION-MAKING MODEL

Within a decision-making model, evaluation involves moving back and forth between data collection and decision making. A decision-making model incorporates not only the assessment of students' abilities and progress, but also the planned interventions and adjusted program. It is the authors' intent to highlight key components of a decision-making model as it is used within their system. Bachor and

Crealock (1986) discuss a similar, but more detailed, model. The basic premise of a decision-making model is one of hypothesis formation and reformation depending upon the information gathered. The model used here has three phases.

Phase One: Information Sharing

A teacher's concern regarding the progress of a student marks the beginning of the decision-making cycle. The teacher gathers and assembles all of the available background information about the particular student. This should involve interviews with parents and previous teachers, an examination of the cumulative record file and health form, and current ongoing observation of the student (see Figure 1). An initial hypothesis is formulated from this information and the teacher needs to link this assessment to curriculum and instruction. For many students, an adjusted or modified instructional plan is prepared from the information gathered. Performance must be continuously monitored in order to evaluate student progress and to make necessary instructional modifications. Some students may require further investigation of their abilities before proceeding to the next phase.

Phase Two: In-School Team Meeting

If a student is displaying complex problems, the teacher may seek assistance from the in-school team consisting of the principal and support facilitator/consultant, as well as other appropriate resource personnel in the problem-solving, decision-making model. Through discussion and collaboration, the initial hypothesis may be confirmed or may be extended or reformulated. Often, at this point, the support facilitator/consultant may become involved through classroom observation, work sample analysis, and other informal or formal testing. Following this inquiry, more specific statements about what the student can and cannot do are possible. Based on the recently gathered information, a student education plan (SEP) may be developed and implemented cooperatively by the classroom teacher and the support facilitator/consultant. However, for some students the hypothesis may prove to be only partially correct or even incorrect and may require further problem solving and decision making. Phase Three of the procedure is then initiated.

Phase Three: Collaborative Team Meeting

To assist the in-school team, resource personnel consisting of a support facilitator/consultant, behavior consultant, speech-language pathologist, and social worker and/or other specialist meet as a collaborative team in the third phase of the procedure. The need and di-

AREAS TO CONSIDER	WHAT DO I ALREADY KNOW ABOUT THE CHILD?	WHAT MORE DO I NEED TO KNOW?	HOW DO I FIND OUT?
Physical			
Behavior Social-Emotional			
Speech & Language • Oral • Written			
Cognitive			
Academics • reading • writing • math • other			

Figure 1. Information gathering guideline.

rection for further assessment, whether informal or formal, is agreed upon by the team. The specific nature of individual team member involvement is case specific and needs driven. The information gathered at this juncture is shared with school personnel and the implications are then translated into the SEP. Although the hypotheses stated at this point have been finalized, it is important to remember that they are hypotheses and are always subject to change.

The philosophy and structure of this model lead to a better understanding of the individual by incorporating a variety of evaluative strategies, and to better instructional planning and evaluation for any student.

EVALUATION STRATEGIES

As suggested earlier, student evaluation should not be the final product of education. Student evaluation must encompass a continual process of observing student growth in many ways. Learning is a complex process that occurs in many ways and at many levels; no single evaluation approach will enable a teacher or student to fully understand the extent of learning. Evaluation should be comprehensive and must take into account the growth and development of individual students so the teacher can determine the suitability of the program and adjust it when necessary. Once the purposes for evaluation have been determined and the objectives of each facet of the curriculum have been identified, then various ways of assessing whether students are meeting the objectives can be considered. Several types of evaluation strategies that can be used are reviewed on the following pages.

Cumulative Record File Review

A review of the cumulative record file (see Figure 2) is often overlooked as a strategy to be incorporated into the evaluation process. A thorough review of reports and records is an excellent way to become familiar with a student's learning needs as well as learning style. By noting teacher comments from reports in a chart organized by subject area (e.g., math, reading, personal interest subjects), patterns of strengths as well as weaknesses often emerge and direct the teacher to formulate an initial hypothesis about the student's needs. Checking the number of days absent (and reasons), noting a decline in performance, or detecting repeated concerns about work habits and organization skills may serve as the impetus for a more detailed investigation.

Student–Teacher Interview

The student–teacher interview, which may be considered a variation of observation, is an important strategy to be used in the evaluation process. The following information may be accumulated in the interview:

Interests, preferences, motivation
Self-concept related to ability and disability
Communication skills
The student's perception of his or her subject or skill strengths and
  needs
Strategies that have or have not been used and the degree of success
An understanding of the student's expectations of the present pro-
  gram.

STUDENT: _____ D.O.B.: _____ REVIEW DATE: _____

LANGUAGE ARTS	
Listening	Speaking
Writing	Reading
Learning Behaviors/Strategies	

MATHEMATICS		
Arithmetic	Geometry	Measurement

CONTENT AREAS		

BEHAVIORS		
Academic	Social	Learning Strategies

Figure 2. Cumulative record file.

Sample items for an interview may include: 1) open-ended statements such as "I learn best when . . .," "I am happiest when . . .," "If
someone makes fun of me . . ."; and 2) questions such as "What do
you like to do after school?", "What subject do you like or dislike the
most?", "How do you study for a history test?"

This strategy is a form of self-report and allows the student to
describe himself or herself to whatever degree he or she feels comfortable. Discussions with several educators revealed that many thought
the student interview strategy is the most revealing and helpful in
the evaluation process. Depending on the student's age of course,
many students can readily verbalize specific areas of concern or
weakness as well as tell what compensatory strategies they have used
or mastered to accommodate for these weaknesses. This very perti-
nent, as well as personal, information cannot be tapped or measured
using tests or examinations as the major means of evaluation.

If the process of education is viewed as a series of partnerships
with the primary goal to foster learning, then the partnership between the student and teacher in terms of student evaluation must be
carefully examined. The old adage "You never will know until you
ask" seems very appropriate here. Although teachers can develop instruments for student evaluation that require written summations, a
complete written report documenting how student knowledge or
skills were gained does not seem congruent with contemporary
teaching methodologies.

Observation

Direct observation of the student provides a wealth of information
about the student's learning both individually and in a group. It
provides an assessment of a range of characteristics—cognitive, affective, and psychomotor. While taking into account evaluation of
certain aspects of student performance or behavior that cannot be
measured using other evaluation techniques, it provides immediate
feedback to the student and the teacher. Observation is not only the
evaluation of a finished product or skill, but perhaps more importantly, it is the evaluation of the student's performance while creating
the product or performing the skill. This simply involves observing a
student when he or she is reading, writing, working math problems,
or engaged in some activity to see what he or she can and cannot do.

It is important to observe the student's performance in a variety
of tasks and settings and then to compare and contrast behavior and
performance variances (see Figure 3).

ACTION

REFLECTION

UNDERSTAND

- child development

- Do I understand the physical, intellectual, social, and emotional characteristics of a child at this age and stage of development?
- Do I need to do some professional reading or consult a colleague to increase my understanding?

PLAN

- what you are looking for
- to create or select an effective record-keeping device
- when and where you will observe

- Will this record-keeping device capture the information I need?
- What situations will most likely yield the information I am looking for?

OBSERVE

- behaviors related to the established criteria
- the student in activities independent of the teacher
- while interacting with the student
- while using a "trial teaching" technique
- what the student is doing and how s/he is doing it

- Am I sure this is what I see and not what I conclude?
- Does the student behave differently when I am working with him/her?
- Does the student's behavior change in different situations?
- Can the student tell me something about his/her behavior?
- Do I need to modify my interactions with the student to increase my understanding?
- Am I sensitive to the student's body language, attention span, stress level, and individual learning profile?

RECORD

- in precise detail the behavior observed
- the circumstance related to the observed behaviors (e.g. environmental conditions, health factors)

- Do I need to see the student in a different situation?
- Is there anything else I need to look for now?
- Have I recorded anecdotal comments relevant to my observations?
- How can I validate any hypothesis I have as a result of this observation?

Figure 3. Steps to purposeful evaluation.

Informal Testing

Informal testing should reflect the content and process of typical learning tasks found in the classroom setting. This can be accomplished by: 1) using materials that the student would normally use in the classroom, 2) finding out what the student can and cannot do with these materials, 3) identifying existing successful learning strategies, 4) identifying strategies that may be helpful, and 5) using trial-teaching techniques to determine the success of these strategies.

Teacher-Made Tests

Tests should be an integral part of the teaching–learning process and should not be separated from the ongoing daily classroom learning. There must be a strong connection among teaching–learning objectives, classroom activities, and testing activities.

Teacher-made tests are based on the content and objectives of a unit or course of study. Such tests assist teachers to clarify and define the educational objectives of a program. They serve to integrate evaluation with teaching and to motivate and direct student learning. Tests can also extend observations of student behavior, making these observations more precise and dependable. A teacher-made test should be relevant to the instruction it is intended to evaluate and should stress comprehension and application rather than trivial details. A lack of planning and structure in designing and utilizing tests effectively is likely to cause students to feel threatened and perceive tests as separate from the learning process. It is essential testing components be balanced and integrated with the rest of the curriculum.

Group Projects

It is becoming obvious that student evaluation is a part of a much larger process of education and that a function of the educational process is to prepare students for the future world of work. As almost everyone in society places some reliance on their work with others, it is essential that group dynamics and group learning occur in all schools. There are many advantages to group projects when cooperative learning principles are used. Whether the project occurs in English, science, drama, or mathematics, students are given the opportunity to be evaluated as a member of a group. The clear advantage to utilizing this form of evaluation is that it allows both teacher and student the opportunity to assess interpersonal skills. It also allows partners to understand and appreciate the contributions of their team members. These might sound or appear incidental if one is strictly evaluating skill development; yet, the process, group dynamics, and skills involved in this area will also be heightened.

Student Contracts

Although individual differences in learning are expected in today's classrooms and teachers have begun to address differences through an increasing variety of instructional methods, various evaluative techniques are also needed to provide more student involvement in the learning process. For this reason, many teachers are now beginning to use contracts for particular students in their classrooms. This is certainly not a new technique as many courses in undergraduate and graduate schools have contracts as a basis for evaluation. The process of negotiating contracts with students can occur in all classrooms as children begin school and continue through high school and college.

There are advantages to this process-oriented technique. The forming of contracts provides a sense of consistency for the student. It assists him or her to understand the instructional goals of a particular subject area and it promotes an increased understanding between student and teacher. Although contracts are seen as valuable, they are not recommended as an exclusive technique for student evaluation. They should, however, be considered an important part of individual student evaluation.

Peer Evaluation

Peer evaluation is directly linked to group project evaluation because what is to be evaluated and the parameters associated with the evaluation are clearly known to the teacher and the students. Peer evaluation can and should be used as an important component in a student's evaluation program. From daily experience in the classroom, teachers suggest that this technique should receive increased attention and credibility after the third grade.

As recommended by the Board of Education for the City of Etobicoke (1987), a peer evaluation component can be developed in every classroom to: 1) provide students with responses to their work other than those of their teacher, 2) to create situations where students can compare their work, and 3) to provide further records to be considered in summative evaluation. As student evaluation is seen as process oriented, peer evaluation is consistent with such concepts as peer tutoring and cooperative learning. Initial research on peer tutoring strongly promotes the value of this activity (Lipsky & Gartner, 1989; Stainback, Stainback, & Forest, 1989); therefore, peer tutors can also be involved in the evaluation of progress. This process will, of course, respect the fact that the skilled teacher and/or observer is essential to the professionalism involved in student evaluation.

Self-Evaluation

Employers are increasingly asking their employees to provide sources of self-evaluation as part of a performance appraisal program. To foster a free and honest partnership between the student and teacher, students generally should be allowed the opportunity to provide a mode of self-evaluation as part of the total evaluative program. This type of evaluation should be used to:

1. Develop students' sense of responsibility for their own learning.
2. Contribute to their awareness for the objectives of the course.
3. Help students evaluate their own work.
4. Inform teachers about student reactions to the program.

The daily interaction between the student and teacher is perhaps the strongest point in an evaluative program. Individual student achievement will prosper when a student can enter into the partnership of education with his or her teacher knowing that performance, grades, and evaluation can somehow be influenced by an honest, reflective self-evaluation that is based on effort.

IMPLICATIONS OF EVALUATION RESULTS

The results of student evaluation should be used as a basis for the reassessment of course objectives, content, and methods. If any student is not successful, the following areas should be re-examined and modified as necessary: 1) the original course or unit objectives for the student, 2) the teaching methods or learning experiences, and 3) the evaluation procedures.

REPORTING STUDENT PROGRESS

The primary forms of reporting student progress are the report card and the parent–teacher conference or interview. The fact that student progress is reported in various ways suggests that there is a need for the reporters and reportees to communicate. These two main strategies for reporting student progress need to be examined in some detail to ensure that student needs are being met.

Student Report Card

All school districts appear to have developed methods that measure student progress. There are no universal forms or report cards, but teachers, and to some extent parents, have concerns about many of the report cards that are presently in use. As schools and/or school districts develop, implement, and review their report cards, some fundamental questions need to be asked about them:

1. Do they allow for positive reinforcement?
2. Do they provide for both summative and formative aspects?
3. Are they consistent with the objectives of the individual students?

4. Are they clear and free of ambiguity?
5. Is the educational jargon kept to a minimum?
6. Do the reports indicate to parents how well the teacher knows the child?
7. Do they allow for modification if a particular student's program has been modified?
8. Are they curriculum based?
9. Is there sufficient opportunity (space) for the teacher to provide anecdotal comment?
10. In their development phases, were the cards designed by a representative committee involving parents, students, teachers, principals, and board members?

Obviously, if the answer to all of the above questions is "yes," then the report card, which is a legal document, will have a needs-based, child-centered philosophy and will provide for continuous growth. Any report card that does not provide for parent reaction and/or discussion either in written or oral form falls short of a good reporting system.

Parent–Teacher Conference or Interview

There is perhaps no better way to successfully report student progress than the parent–teacher conference. Schools and school districts have employed diverse methods for conducting these conferences. Schools and parents have had instances that negate student progress because of ineffective parent–teacher conferences; parents and teachers do not always get along. Teachers sometimes complain that the problem results from too many uninvolved parents who just don't care. However, there is also the complaint that some parents get too involved; they want to control everything. Similarly, parents may express their distrust of teachers and schools. Even if these teachers and parents are not totally representative, it can be assumed that at least some of the time, some parents and teachers are separated by a gulf of mistrust, skepticism, and hostility (Biklen, 1985).

The problem is understandable. Some parents are intimidated by the school for a variety of reasons, perhaps as a result of their view of school when they were students. They can feel left out, undervalued, and relatively powerless in the educational process. Conversely, some teachers have not communicated effectively with parents and when parents place demands or offer advice, they feel that their professionalism has been invaded. A significant yet unfortunate result of these feelings is then brought out by ineffective parent–teacher conferences and ultimately proves detrimental to the progress of the student.

However, the effective parent–teacher conference can provide for incredible student growth and further positive growth in the relationship between home and school. Some fundamental questions can be posed about the parent–teacher conference:

1. Does the school have a policy of promoting parent involvement?
2. Can parents make direct and indirect contact with the school on a needs basis (phone calls, notes)?
3. Is there an ongoing system whereby parents and teachers can communicate with each other?
4. Are there periodic formal parent–teacher conferences?
5. Are parents involved in the decision making of the school (e.g., Parent Advisory Council)?

Again, if "yes" is answered to the above questions, the relationship between the school and home will grow appreciably and parent–teacher conferences will be more effective.

REPORTING STUDENT PROGRESS: BUILDING THE PARTNERSHIP

As students learn and their progress is reported it seems clear that in the future the positive partnerships among schools, students, and parents must be extended. The ways in which schools report progress will then become more critical as the process continues to evolve. Sound, effective reporting could be based on the following components:

1. A planning document that is cooperatively developed for the needs of the child and that clearly defines curriculum, curriculum modification, evaluative methods, and modes of communication is fundamental to optimum student success.
2. Community involvement in and development of a curriculum base should be accentuated. As such, the process becomes more of a shared responsibility.
3. Parent–teacher conferences should be scheduled on a needs-based system and should not be directly tied into formal reporting times. Some students and their parents may have conferences with the school at varying times to allow for more expediency in parent–school communication.

In any productive enterprise that requires significant interpersonal relationships, differences between parents and a teacher may limit student progress. This should be seen as a very rare occurrence. There may be situations where reporting student progress to parents provides for some level of discomfort; yet, far more situations have been observed where parent involvement accentuates student progress and a deeper relationship is fostered between home and school. The key issue at this juncture is for schools and/or school districts to develop planning mechanisms that allow for greater partnership in the reporting of student progress.

CONCLUSION

The current system of measuring and reporting student progress requires further modification in many instances to meet individual student needs. Large scale, norm-referenced testing and grading programs are seen by teachers to be ineffective and of little use in determining the learning patterns and applicable skill development of students. There is an increasing need to develop appropriate curriculum at the local level of education and individualize it to any particular student's needs when necessary. A student evaluation plan should be developed with curriculum as its base.

There is no singular strategy recommended as the exclusive way to measure student progress. A variety of approaches need to be developed to assist the student's learning style. When there is need for modification, parents and students should be fully informed regarding the level of modification and what criteria will be used in the evaluative program.

The development of curriculum modification should rely heavily on partnerships that will be formed in the educational process. As more people become involved in the delivery of a collaborative educational program, partnerships must apply their cooperative efforts to ensure that students are evaluated based on a curriculum and program that fits their needs. Teachers need to be recognized as the prime contributors in student evaluation. Their daily work should encompass numerous strategies to accurately assess student progress in both affective and subjective domains. The teacher must be provided with the skills to assess and report student progress; therefore, a continuum of preservice and inservice training opportunities are suggested.

The methods of reporting student progress vary greatly from school to school and teacher to teacher. A standardized report card and perhaps a formal interview will not necessarily improve learning outcomes. Parents and teachers must further the development of partnerships so that everyone has a valued responsibility in the educational process. Open, two-way communication based on the needs of the child is fundamental to an effective reporting system. Any form of student evaluation that is to be developed by the partners in education must be meaningful for parents, teachers, and students. The data must be relevant to all concerned and must also be clearly classified so that modifications to the program can occur as appropriate.

Schools and school systems have used numerous resources to develop contemporary education practices that reflect current thought and research on child development. Educators are at a juncture in the educational process where they must ensure not only that teaching practices and curriculum are useful and contemporary, but that evaluative and reporting practices are consistent with all other contemporary practices in education.

REFERENCES

Bachor, D., & Crealock, C. (1986). *Instructional strategies for students with special needs*. Englewood Cliffs, NJ: Prentice Hall.

Biklen, D. (1985). *Achieving the complete school*. New York: Teachers College Press.

Board of Education for the City of Etobicoke. (1987). *Making the grade*. Englewood Cliffs, NJ: Prentice Hall.

Deno, S. (1985). Curriculum-based measurement: The emerging alternative. *Exceptional Children, 52*(3), 219–232.

Lipsky, D.K., & Gartner, A. (Eds.). (1989). *Beyond separate education: Quality education for all*. Baltimore: Paul H. Brookes Publishing Co.

Neill, M., & Medina, N. (1989). Standardized testing: Harmful to educational health. *Phi Delta Kappan, 70*, 688–697.

Shanker, A. (1988). Those old–fashioned cures . . . They produce the same old results. *New York Times, 8*.

Stainback, S., Stainback, W., & Forest, M. (Eds.). (1989). *Educating all students in the mainstream of regular education*. Baltimore: Paul H. Brookes Publishing Co.

Stainback, W., & Stainback, S. (Eds.). (1990). *Support networks for inclusive schooling: Interdependent integrated education*. Baltimore: Paul H. Brookes Publishing Co.

Tucker, J. (1985). Curriculum based assessment: An introduction. *Exceptional Children, 52*(3), 199–204.

III

Related Considerations

11

Quality in Our Schools
A Parental Perspective

Jeff Strully, Barb Buswell,
Leslie New, Cindy Strully, and Beth Schaffner

THERE ARE MANY ways to measure quality in schools. Some of the "markers" that have been used include increasing standardized test scores, increasing graduation rates, reducing dropout rates, measuring the percentage of graduates attending postsecondary educational programs, and administering proficiency exams.

Although these "markers" provide one way to determine quality in our schools, they have certain limitations that directly or indirectly have an impact on the children "represented." Many children have been excluded because of these markers. In addition, many of these markers do not take into account the unique needs of diverse learners.

This chapter is not a review of the literature on quality education in our schools; instead the authors use a personal approach—"How does it feel to us and would we want our children in this classroom or school?" Although many people could argue with the authors about the nonscientific approach to measuring the quality of schools, this approach is based on our beliefs as parents and people who support children in obtaining a quality educational experience. It is the authors' belief that this approach is more user friendly than any other.

There are at least three major ways of measuring quality in schools for all children: 1) determining if students are welcomed into the school and class, 2) observing interactions with peers and assessing the nature of these interactions (i.e., Are they voluntary and/or

spontaneous?), and 3) evaluating what is being taught in the classroom (i.e., Are the students learning things that are fun, relevant, useful, and interesting and is attention given to how the curriculum is
being taught?).

It should be noted that quality in education is a very elusive concept. On one occasion a parent may walk into a classroom and see
interaction and inclusion taking place for his or her child; yet, the
next day the parent may walk in and observe a complete change. This
"roller coaster ride" is a wild one with many ups and downs and unexpected turns. Support is found in unexpected places and challenges
are discovered where least expected. Although this ride may seem out
of control, it is worth taking. Parents want to walk into schools that
welcome and want to include their child. Welcoming a child does not
necessarily ensure quality; however, it is a necessary beginning.

Quality education for *all* students is the authors' goal. It is their
firm belief that quality for any student is dependent upon quality for
all. Any school that does not pay attention to all learners and does not
try to meet each of their unique needs cannot be an inclusive school
community. Every learner, including those who have been labeled,
gang members, teenage parents, potential dropouts, delinquents, or
children who simply lack interest must be welcomed and invited in
schools. An effective curriculum must be developed that will challenge and meet each of their unique needs. Schools cannot reject certain students and serve others and still be considered as offering a
quality program. The rejection of any group has a direct impact on the
quality of *all* learners.

As the search continues for quality in schools, it will become
very clear that quality cannot take place without parental and community involvement and active participation. Quality education is
not something that only educators are concerned about or should be
involved in determining. Quality in schools is a responsibility for everyone, including the students. Students must be held responsible for
identifying the problems in schools as well as in helping to create positive change. It is the authors' belief that there are solutions that can
make schools places that welcome diversity and meet the unique educational needs of all learners.

WELCOMING ALL DIVERSE LEARNERS

The most important aspect of a quality education has to do with welcoming all students into the life of the school. It starts when parents
enroll their child in school and the principal and classroom teacher
express excitement about teaching the child. This sincere pleasure in

enrolling a new student is expressed by principals such as Bill Gillen-water in Greeley, Colorado, Jim Jackson in Cedar Falls, Iowa, and Brian Cullen in Kitchener, Ontario. This acceptance should be the experience of every student, new or returning. Each student should be viewed as an integral part of the whole student body.

Unfortunately, many parents with children who have been labeled receive a different message from teachers and administrators. The authors have experienced reactions to their children ranging from "There is a wonderful program just 5 miles away for children like this"; to "Our school is highly competitive and your child just will not feel included"; and "We have only 20 computers, we cannot waste one of these computers for your child when there are children who could really benefit." These or similar responses are obvious messages that some children simply are not welcome.

What really lies behind this message is that the child is a devalued individual. The problem is not that some children are different, but that the differences are negatively perceived and overly emphasized. As parents of children who once were labeled by an educational system, the authors are proud that their children are different. Children are different because of unique personalities, gifts, and talents. Being different is not a characteristic that people should hide from or want to change. The possibilities of learning from different people and viewing differences as a possibility for growth and development should be recognized rather than viewed as an obstacle that must be overcome. Welcoming a person is synonymous with honoring, cherishing, and appreciating that person. All children should experience the true meaning of being welcome and held in high esteem. Welcoming someone is the first step toward accepting a person for his or her unique gifts and talents. It says a lot about the school and what takes place within the school.

In 1963, a young black man, James Meredith, tried to enroll in college. People revolted against his attempts and shouted that he did not belong there. Armed soldiers had to intervene to ensure that people would not harm him as he entered the school. It was clear that the University of Mississippi was not a place that welcomed diversity. It would seem that such an incident would never occur today and that people are more open-minded. Yet, in 1989 a young lady in Ontario who wanted to enroll in her neighborhood school was asked to leave. When she and her family did not leave, the police were called to escort her off the property (Till, 1990). Clearly, many people's attitudes still show signs of not accepting differences.

Quality begins with welcoming *all* students, despite differences. No one should be excluded because he or she is considered different.

Uniqueness is a *quality* to be cherished, not shunned. Welcoming a stranger is an act of hospitality and it means inviting someone to be involved rather than isolated. Welcoming a stranger does not require money, regulations, experience, or even school board policy, it requires that people view others as having potential and the ability to lend something to the whole, to make things better for everyone.

Welcoming must be present for quality education to take place. Otherwise, children are only visitors, strangers in the school with no real connections to the school community. Each student should have the opportunity to attend a school that welcomes him or her and where everyone knows his or her name.

SPENDING TIME WITH PEOPLE

After a child is welcomed into a school and class, the relationships that take place between the child and the other students are the next indicator of the presence of quality. Who spends time with the student in the classroom? What are the interactions like? Do people voluntarily choose the student as a partner in a learning activity, to be a part of a group, or to joke and talk with? These daily interactions can lead to more important relationships, as well as make the classroom experience worthwhile.

Interaction can take place naturally and spontaneously, but sometimes it requires direct involvement and participation from the teacher, facilitator, and other students. It may require organizing activities that bring people together or implementing other methods to increase positive interaction.

Even negative interactions can potentially lead to positive outcomes. For example, if a student expresses a negative reaction about disabilities during class, the teacher should use this opportunity to discuss devaluation, labeling, or the government's role in protecting certain groups of citizens. This is an opportunity to learn about differences, express feelings, and talk about vulnerabilities.

How teachers and facilitators respond to these interactions and how parents help initiate them determines whether students will have the chance to make friends in the classroom. These interactions require viewing every activity as a potential opportunity for forming relationships.

Some methods to help facilitate interactions might include: 1) using cooperative learning groups, 2) using small group discussions, 3) pairing students to work on an assignment, and 4) finding common areas for discussion to take place.

If a student requires some support to increase interaction, then creating a "circle of friends" may be useful. The circle of friends can assist the student to schedule classes and can help introduce the student to other people.

Teachers can use group facilitation skills to acquaint his or her class to the student. Students should have the opportunity to ask the student questions about his or her interests and plans for the future. Learning about common interests is important in establishing relationships. The level, diversity, and intensity of relationships will vary for each student. Interactions in classes, in common areas of the school, after school, on weekends, holidays, and during the summer need to be fostered and supported. These interactions may lead to more permanent and closer relationships that are important to all people.

CURRICULUM AND CLASSROOM EXPERIENCES

The third variable in determining quality involves students' experiences in the classroom and school. After people are welcomed in the school and interactions begin to develop (working on interactions and curriculum can take place at the same time), quality dictates that students will expand their knowledge, skills, and awareness.

The first question that should be asked at this stage is "What outcomes do we expect for any learner and are they applicable to people with very challenging needs?" The outcomes that should be developed for any student include:

1. Increasing self-esteem—how the person feels about himself or herself
2. Concern for others—thinking about the importance of other people
3. Moral education—learning that there is a right and a wrong; that commitment, honesty, and integrity are important
4. Critical thinking skills—learning how to think about a problem and resolve it
5. Process skills—learning how to think about issues
6. Living skills—ability to live a pleasing life in the community

The school reform movement (e.g., Coalition for Essential Schools, Outcome Based Education) is attempting to redefine student outcomes. It has motivated people to look again at what should be required for graduation. Graduation requirements should not be based on the amount of seat time and credit accumulated, but on mastering certain levels of acquisition.

Once students' outcomes have been determined, curriculum decisions can be made. Curriculum can be divided into the following major areas:

1. Functional learning—practical, real-life, useful skills for the present or the future
2. Academic—learning that can be generalized now or in the future; learning that is more global
3. Fun and enjoyment—academic or functional in nature, but the outcome is the enjoyment rather than the event itself

Curriculum is determined in a number of different ways. Parent input is the first method. Parents need to tell the people involved with their child which outcomes they would like to see their child achieve. They should be aware of the importance of certain skills as well as when to stop trying to teach someone a useless skill. Parents typically have appropriate expectations about what they would like to see their child learn and professionals should be attentive to parents' suggestions and concerns. It is better for professionals to attend to the suggestions parents consider important, even if they do not seem very useful, than to disempower a parent and tell him or her what the child needs to learn.

For some parents, meaningful relationships are the most important area for schools to develop. For others, it may be a communication system, reading, or other specific skill. Parents do not always share the same concerns; however, it is agreed that all learning must take place in the context of an inclusive school. Learning that is technically effective can take place in either a segregated, isolated situation (e.g., self-contained school, class) or an integrated classroom, but only in full-time integrated situations can children learn to interact socially, communicate, and care about each other.

Another group of people who understand the needs of students are their friends. Friends can help people think about areas that need attention and educational goals that are not worth the effort.

Community members should also expect school faculty to actively help students learn. It is inappropriate to think that they just teach students. Students are the ones responsible for their learning. Teachers should be helping and coaching students to want to learn and grow. There is a joint responsibility between students and teachers to help all students achieve their desired outcomes. However, students must be part of the process, not quiet members who let other people make decisions about their lives.

Curriculum decisions are made when a group of people who care about a student work together. There are no preset approaches or curricula, and there are no easy shortcuts. When people work together to make decisions about a student's curriculum, it needs to be done with respect and appreciation for everyone's unique perspective and input. The process of working together will lead people in the right direction more times than not.

PARENTAL AND COMMUNITY INVOLVEMENT

Parents and community members can actively ensure a quality education for all learners in schools. They can do this by using the following guidelines:

1. They should share their knowledge of a quality education with teachers and staffing teams, school improvement committees, professional accreditation bodies, and school board members. Once everyone agrees on the meaning of a quality education, they should make it clear to everyone in the school.
2. They should become involved in making quality education a reality for their child and other children. This means not only getting involved with their own child's education, but with larger groups that are concerned about quality education. They should not expect people to understand the interrelationship between the education of a child who is labeled and a quality education for all students—this information has to be learned over time.
3. They should demand outcome-based education for all students —districts should be able to provide information about what their former students do after graduation and what their lives are like. They should also demand a critical analysis of quality indicators in people's lives.
4. They should provide expertise and talent to the school; they should be involved in the school.
5. They should help other parents understand the power of coalitions and the need for everyone to work together for a better school for all children.
6. They should work to ensure that their child's school program is the best that it can be—their efforts will influence others.
7. They should support teachers and administrators to learn more about inclusiveness and quality by taking people to conferences, purchasing books or videos, sharing information, and talking with people about their hopes and dreams.
8. They should advocate for positive change so that their child and the children that their child will meet may have the experience of a quality education in an inclusive school.

9. They should celebrate the victories, learn from things that do not work, and commend the people who are making positive changes for all children.
10. They should believe in a future not only for their child, but for all children. Change happens when people come together and struggle, when everyone works for a better school for all children rather than fighting for a bigger slice of the pie for a specific group or child.

Children who have been labeled and/or previously excluded from neighborhood schools and classrooms as well as many other children need friends who care about them and can provide support. What the authors have learned from their experiences is that no one can make it without these people. Schools need to be made into communities that welcome everyone and understand that each person has some quality he or she can contribute. Quality education is not just about schools, but about communities and how people want to live their lives. It is about children who will grow up in a more understanding and integrated society where *all* children are included and welcome, interactions among children are supported and facilitated, *all* children are expected to learn, *all* adults are excited about their new students each year, and principals say "thank you" for sending a child to his or her school!

When these behaviors are realized, then quality education for all students will become a reality. Until then, there is more work to be done.

REFERENCES

Till, L. (1990, December). Speech given at the annual conference of The Association for Persons with Severe Handicaps.

12

Community-Referenced Learning in Inclusive Schools

Effective Curriculum for All Students

Michael Peterson, Barbara LeRoy,
Sharon Field, and Paula Wood

IN ONE SCHOOL, a bright, articulate middle school student has just completed a full year of geometry, yet he has no idea how to figure out how much wallpaper is needed to cover the walls of his room. Mexican American students attend a school where classes are only taught in English and where their rich cultural and language experiences are essentially ignored. Students with learning difficulties are sent to rooms to repeatedly drill and practice basic math and reading skills, but do not learn how to apply for jobs, maintain their homes, or participate in community elections. Students drop out in this urban school system at alarmingly high rates because they see no relevance of the school program in their daily lives.

In another school, students learn together to identify and work on solutions in interaction with community members, and they engage in individual internships in community agencies. Classes in this school include support for individualized learning for "gifted," disadvantaged, disabled, and "regular" students together. All classes involve applications of skills in meaningful life and community activities, and typical school subjects are often team taught. For example, the history and geography teachers combine their efforts to focus on simulating major political events in the world that involve students from both of their classes. Students of various ability levels work as cooperative teams to deal with real world and community issues. Students like this school and so does the community. A real purpose and excitement about the process of learning occurs and the dropout rate is low.

These two scenarios illustrate what is happening and what is possible in schools. Although schools in the United States implement some innovative educational practices, the curriculum, teaching process, and structure of public schools do not work. Radical restructuring of what and how students learn and how their learning is assessed and evaluated is needed.

There have been significant efforts in recent years to redefine the educational curriculum as well as to enhance teaching and learning practices in all areas of education. Unfortunately, the improvement of these vital elements has often occurred on parallel tracks with little interaction between, for example, regular and special education, and without the mutual benefits that would accrue if such collaboration occurred. In addition, what has developed to this point is generally viewed as inadequate. Many professionals are now calling for a radical reform of what students learn, how they learn, and what kind of support is provided for their learning. The development of community-referenced learning in inclusive schools has the potential to effectively merge important developments in such areas as regular education, special education, compensatory education, and vocational education while also bringing about fundamental, yet practical, changes in how education occurs.

Community-referenced learning involves students in applied, real-world activities to enhance learning of academic, vocational, and social skills. Simultaneously, community-referenced learning ensures that students can apply skills in real-life activities that may range from home management to political activism in the community. This chapter provides a framework for creating an effective curriculum that is meaningful for all students.

TRADITIONAL SCHOOLING:
BASIC SKILLS TAUGHT USING A FACTORY MODEL

Since the opening of public schools in the nineteenth century, curriculum has been largely based on a *basic skills model* that breaks down life skills into discrete units and does not apply them to practical use (Anderson, Hiebert, Scott, & Wilkinson, 1985; Brown, Collins, & Duguid, 1989). This model is based on the theory of scientific reductionism, which formed the basis for the industrial revolution. According to Jones (1990), in this model learning is "essentially a matter of decoding skills in reading, computation skills in mathematics, and memorizing various facts in history and science . . . 'higher order thinking skills' are desirable objectives, but only after students have mastered the basics" (p. 1).

This model of education assumes that there is a finite set of knowledge and that students can acquire that body of information. However, as Johnson and Johnson (1989) point out, there has been more knowledge generated in the past 10 years than in all of civilization. Old models of educating students are inconsistent with the rapidly increasing body of information.

Typically, curricula have been based upon adaptations of this basic skills model. Existing school curricula have been simplified or, in some cases, detailed basic skills have been broken into a typical developmental sequence for instruction.

Unfortunately, this basic skills model does not work effectively in defining content and instruction processes (Jones, 1990). Students memorize isolated facts, but quickly forget them. They do not utilize abstract skills in real-life situations. Increasingly, literature is indicating that learning even basic skills occurs best when they are applied in the context of meaningful life and community activities (Anderson et al., 1985; Brown et al., 1989; Commission on Reading, 1990; Greenberg, 1989; Jones, 1990; Resnick & Klopfer, 1989; Romberg, 1988; Wilcox & Bellamy, 1982).

As curriculum objectives were "scientifically" analyzed into discrete basic skills, the process of instruction was "rationally" designed around economies of scale. According to nineteenth century writers, early public schools were established to prepare people to function well in factories (Berryman, 1988; Jones, 1990). Not surprisingly, then, schools were set up using a factory model—short periods for discrete basic skills subjects, orderly rows of desks, limited student interaction and involvement, and hierarchical management structures. Perhaps this approach was useful in its time; however, today's work force and society demand very different learning objectives, teaching approaches, management structure, and support for students and teachers (Berryman, 1988; Jones, 1990).

EFFECTIVE CURRICULUM:
EXPERIENTIAL LEARNING IN COMMUNITY ACTIVITIES

Research and reform efforts suggest that curriculum for all students should be radically restructured so that it is community-referenced in both content and process of learning. An expanding body of literature indicates the following common themes for school curriculum:

Content of learning: students should learn to perform meaningful activities in areas that are important to their daily lives and apply skills they learn in math, science, language, and other areas.
Process of learning: the most effective method of learning activities and basic skills involves utilizing them in real-life activities.

These themes are consistent with recent efforts by many educators to promote community-referenced instruction (Falvey, 1988; Ford et al., 1989; Wilcox & Bellamy, 1982, 1987). Combined with the increasing use of cooperative learning and other approaches that support a diversity of students learning together, such restructuring of curriculum may provide meaningful activities in integrated and inclusive schools where students are encouraged to work together, support one another, and develop relationships.

CONTENT OF LEARNING: OUTCOMES FOR COMMUNITY LIFE

Schools traditionally have been concerned with academic performance in artificial settings without a focus on future outcomes. Although this approach has been modified with the expansion of vocational education, a variety of elective courses, and extracurricular activities, schools still focus on teaching basic skills in contexts unrelated to how the skills are used in professional and everyday life. This does not imply that history, science, English literature, math, and other school subjects are nonfunctional for students—all students need to learn as much as possible in these subjects. However, these areas need to be learned by all students in ways that are purposeful and meaningful to their lives. The school curriculum should be expanded to include information in daily living, vocational skills, and community problem solving for all students.

Skills for School Curriculum

What should schools teach? What should students learn in school? As it is becoming clear that basic skills are inadequate learning objectives, educators and communities are beginning to carefully examine these important questions. The framework developed will provide the basis for curriculum in schools. The following list provides guidelines for what students should learn in schools based on current research and literature related to effective restructuring of curriculum:

1. Learning in schools must focus on meaningful outcomes for adult life—obtaining satisfying employment, participating in community life, developing and maintaining supportive relationships, obtaining and maintaining a home, and engaging in leisure, recreational, and cultural activities.

2. Learning should provide opportunities for students to identify community, state, national, and world needs and problems and to engage in activities designed to have an impact on solutions to problems (Banks, 1988; Berryman, 1988; Boyer, 1984; Jones, 1990; Wees, 1975).

3. Learning units in schools (courses, classes) must be structured and restructured so that life outcomes are systematically included in the context of the curriculum. This may involve efforts to cross-reference life outcomes to traditional course and learning offerings.

4. Learning must include a strong focus on the process of problem solving and the desire to learn.

Skills for Adult and Community Living

Educators and community members typically believe that schools should equip students with the ability to function as effective adults and community members (Berryman, 1988; Jones, 1990; Michigan Department of Education, 1990). This goal changes the focus of education from isolated academic skills to the use of skills in performing community activities. The Michigan Department of Education (1990), for example, has identified competencies that should be integrated into more traditional "core curriculum" areas. These include life management, vocation, avocation, employability, aesthetic appreciation, and technology. Similarly, Benjamin (1989) has suggested that education that focuses on the whole person should include affective skills, relationships, mental health, and physical health, as well as more traditional academic skills. Gardner (1989) advocates a curriculum that focuses not only on traditional academic skills, but on the multiple skills inherent in people. These include: 1) linguistic, 2) logical-mathematical, 3) spatial, 4) musical, 5) bodily-kinesthetic, 6) interpersonal, and 7) intrapersonal.

Peterson (in press) developed an "Individual Life Profile" that provides the basis for a curriculum structure that was compiled from a variety of adult living skills. The profile identifies competencies for adult living that may form a bank of potential learning objectives based on the interests and needs of the individual student. This framework has been developed based on a comprehensive review and synthesis of studies that identify important outcomes for community life. It includes the following competency areas:

Life choices—Develop life goals based on personal needs, interests, values, and available options in the community.
Relationships and support—Develop relationships, support networks, and resources that have an impact on the quality of life, employment, and community participation.

Foundation skills—Develop cognitive, affective, and psychomotor skills that have an impact on the performance of community activities and the development of relationships.

Work—Develop work skills and obtain and maintain meaningful and satisfying employment.

Home living—Develop family and home life skills and obtain and maintain a personal home.

Community participation—Participate in and contribute to community life.

Recreation and leisure—Develop leisure skills and engage in recreation and leisure activities.

Learning To Think: Critical Thinking Skills   Central to school curriculum reforms is the focus on critical thinking skills. Instead of providing students with predetermined content, teaching them to think involves actively identifying problems, gathering information, and recognizing, testing, and evaluating potential solutions. Such critical thinking and problem-solving skills are intended to be at the base of all learning rather than available to students only after the "basics" have been learned (Berryman, 1988; Jones, 1990; Resnick & Klopfer, 1989). Learning how to solve problems is best accomplished by engaging in actual problem-solving activities rather than viewing it as a separate, abstract subject (Benjamin, 1989). The participation of students in support circles, life planning, curriculum adaptation, and other activities designed to aid fellow students provides an excellent opportunity for the learning and use of critical thinking, problem-solving, teamwork, and even management skills.

Teamwork and Interpersonal Communication   Our society is increasingly dependent upon complex interpersonal relationships; therefore, teamwork and interpersonal communication are increasingly important educational goals (Berryman, 1988). Students need opportunities to engage in teamwork related to a range of activities. Cooperative learning uses teamwork and cooperation as an appropriate learning goal as well as an effective learning strategy for other skills (Johnson & Johnson, 1989). Developing teamwork skills will prove valuable in the workplace, for example, to design and test solutions to technical and social problems (Berryman, 1988).

School Subjects and Learning Goals

As those responsible for structuring school curriculum are designing, implementing, and testing restructuring efforts, professionals in various traditional subject areas are attempting to apply their efforts in community activities. For example, language and reading instruction is placing an emphasis on using language in natural contexts, drawing on the life and language experiences of students, and engaging students in active understanding of reading rather than focusing on the mechanics of the reading process (Commission on Reading, 1990; Weber & Dyasi, 1985). Math educators (National Council of Teachers of Mathematics, 1990) have recommended that students work as teams to learn and apply math skills related to actual problem situations. Romberg (1988), after observing such a team, stated that "in various classrooms, one could expect to see students recording measurements of real objects, collecting information and describing the properties of objects using statistics, or exploring the properties of a function by examining its graph" (p. 16). Yager (1987) described the following key elements of a science curriculum for elementary schools: 1) understanding and experiencing processes of discovery, 2) creativity, 3) positive attitudes toward science, and 4) connections and applications to daily life. An Iowa curriculum (Yager, 1987) involves students in active inquiry and problem solving related to students' real-life activities. The National Council of Social Studies (1990) has demonstrated similar approaches. All of these approaches provide natural opportunities for students with varied levels of ability to learn together in actual community situations. These efforts are important since most schools are making curriculum reforms that maintain existing school subject areas. In the Michigan core curriculum, for example, life competencies are to be incorporated in the core curriculum subject areas of art, health, language, mathematics, science, and world studies (Michigan Department of Education, 1990).

In designing the curriculum of a school system, a matrixing procedure may be used to incorporate life goals and activities into traditional school subjects. Table 1 illustrates the relationships of applied activities in various school subjects. It may be used as part of a formal process of curriculum analysis and planning for the school curriculum development team or by an individual teacher. In addition, it may be used informally as a guide to developing relationships between curriculum goals related to life activities and school subjects. The table is designed for a sixth grade math class, but the process can be applied to other classes as well. Curriculum planners may use such a curriculum matrixing procedure to ensure that applied activities and skills at varying levels of difficulty are available throughout the school. The table may also provide a framework for evaluating the degree to which a particular class or subject is providing opportunities for applying skills in relevant community activities.

Transdisciplinary learning, various school disciplines or "subjects" jointly focusing on related learning goals, has also been espoused in school restructuring literature (Jones, 1990). Community problems

Table 1. Sample format of a mathematics curriculum matrix: Sixth grade

Learning goals	Activity
Life choices	Exploring interest in math and technical processes to solve problems; interest in working as part of a technical team
`Relationships	Work in groups with other students
Foundation skills	
Reasoning	Solving problems using reason and mathematics skills
Reading	Reading technical information
Language	Describing problems and methods of solutions in technical language
Mathematics	Developing and using basic math, simple algebra, and basic statistics to solve technical and social problems
Personal adjustment	Work with others as part of a technical problem-solving team
Learning	Developing learning strategies for applying technical information systematically
Work	Learn to solve problems in a variety of occupations using mathematics (e.g., auto repair, social science, food service)
Home living	Use math at home when measuring for cooking, cleaning, or making home repairs
Teamwork	Working as part of a technical problem-solving team
Critical thinking skills	Developing solutions to technical problems in the community

often require simultaneous application of language, math, science, and interpersonal skills; therefore, as students learn to engage in community activities and apply skills, it is reasonable to expect that teachers from these various classes may work together. The curriculum matrix provides a simple framework for helping teachers and curriculum planners identify such opportunities. For example, several teachers may join to engage in a community project related to environmental problems. In this project, students might apply skills related to math, science, technical use of written language, and other skills.

ASSESSMENT FOR STUDENT
PLANNING AND OUTCOME EVALUATION

As schools restructure their curriculum goals and learning strategies, assessment practices are also being changed. Consistent with the basic skills model, traditional assessment has focused almost exclusively on the measurement of abstract responses. This information generally has minimal value for use in student planning. Some educational approaches attempt to use assessment to prescribe individualized education programs (IEPs). However, such assessment is typically structured on a basic skills model. Consequently, educational prescriptions tend to follow this model.

Recent efforts have been made to incorporate functional and applied vocational and life skills assessment into secondary curriculum (Albright & Cobb, 1986; Peterson, 1986). However, this focus on life and vocational domains is not widely accepted at this point in time. The following are guidelines for student assessment and evaluation:

1. Students are provided assessment and planning guidance that is focused on desired life and work outcomes.
2. Students are actively involved in self-evaluation and planning.
3. Assessment for planning and evaluation is curriculum- and activity-based (based on activities and skills assessed by observing student performance in meaningful activities).
4. Students are evaluated by demonstrating their application of abilities in critical life activities. Outcome evaluation expands beyond traditional academic achievement to focus on relevant educational outcomes.

In an effective curriculum, assessment involves a dynamic, comprehensive system in which similar activities are used for multiple purposes. Students demonstrate interests and skills through involvement in activities. Documented results are used to: 1) assist students in planning for their future, 2) provide teachers and related services personnel with helpful information about the skills and learning style of the student, and 3) provide administrators and teachers with information regarding student performance and interests.

The assessment approach is similar to that of school curriculum—meaningful outcomes in life and work activities. A variety of efforts are underway to include a wider range of focus for student assessment; some of these are based on the changing content of standard curriculum subjects that incorporate life activities. For example, the National Writing Project has piloted hands-on tests that apply reading skills in graphics, small engines, and science (Wiggins, 1989). Gardner (1989) has developed approaches to assessment for a range of student "intelligences" related to a variety of community activities.

In an effective curriculum, assessment and learning occur simultaneously and observation and evaluation of student performance becomes very natural (Bloom, Madaus, & Hastings, 1981; Sizer, 1986). Activity and task analysis (Berk, 1986; Browder, 1991; Peterson, 1986), utilization of behaviorally based rating scales of critical skills (critical thinking, teamwork) (Stiggins, 1987, 1988), qualitative assessment of demonstrations (Gardner, 1989; Wiggins, 1989), observation of activities and simulations (Berk, 1986), and portfolios of student-produced work (Wolf, 1989) may all replace standardized tests for a more natural assessment.

These approaches are used to track life and community skills of varying degrees of sophistication across grades and subjects. They may also provide a format that can be used for a district-wide evaluation of the school. Students would have an ongoing record that demonstrates achievement of life and activity skills across subjects. Rather than reporting to the community about standardized academic achievement test scores, administrators would report types of community skills demonstrated by students. Such community skills would vary in degrees of complexity to accommodate learning objectives.

In this model, teachers are central to the assessment of students as they observe and evaluate them. They complete assessments of student performance and document demonstrated student life and community skills. As some educators provide support in the classroom as "instructional support specialists," they can also provide assistance in planning and conducting effective assessment of students who have more intense learning needs (Peterson, 1990).

Additional support is needed to develop and implement this comprehensive assessment and planning process. Various teacher evaluations of life and community performance would be synthesized into a comprehensive portrait of the individual that can be used as the basis for developing IEPs and service plans. Psychologists, vocational assessment specialists, and others involved in student assessment would adopt new roles providing support and assistance in organizing and implementing the assessment process. Such roles include providing assistance in organizing the student assessment and planning process, engaging in consultation with teachers regarding methods of curriculum-based assessment that also focuses on life skills and activities, participating in more intensive curriculum and community-based observations, and coordinating individualized planning meetings (Peterson, 1990, in press). Such ongoing, curriculum-based assessment of student life skills is used as a basis for individual planning in the school curriculum and in community activities (Gardner, 1987).

PROCESS OF LEARNING:
ACTIVE LEARNING IN APPLIED ACTIVITIES

In an effective curriculum, many instructional and support techniques promote and encourage diverse students in learning together and supporting one another in the learning process. These strategies include cooperative learning (Johnson & Johnson, 1989), peer tutoring (York, Vandercook, Macdonald, & Wolff, 1989), support circles (Forest, 1984, 1987), and structuring "schools within schools" (Johnson & Johnson, 1989). These efforts establish a supportive environment for learning through teamwork and development of interpersonal relationships.

For students to learn community-referenced content, they must be involved in active learning in which they explore problems and actively engage in inquiry to reach solutions. Extracurricular activities such as Olympics of the Mind, drama clubs, and service clubs fulfill these functions that the factory model used in typical public schools cannot. The following are guidelines based on current research for the process of effective learning:

1. Students learn most effectively when their education is individualized and they have opportunities to learn in a heterogeneous group of learners.
2. Students learn best in an atmostphere of support, cooperation, and encouragement in which all students are welcome rather than an atmosphere of competition and exclusion.
3. All students benefit from peer support.
4. Students have the opportunity to learn and use skills in meaningful applied activities related to the community and home life.
5. Students are involved in active learning. Such learning is most effective when it occurs in the community.

Structuring a Supportive Learning Environment

A number of teaching and organizational strategies may be used to structure the learning environment to encourage learning and accommodate diverse abilities and styles. Large school buildings can be made into smaller, cohesive communities through a "schools within schools" approach. In this design, a core group of teachers and students join together for all instructional activities. Often, these "schools" establish identities by choosing a name or mascot, going on retreats, and planning schoolwide learning experiences around specific themes (ecology, civil war, a multicultural fair). Classrooms choose various themes and children mingle throughout the school. Teachers may also structure classrooms and other settings in the school to encourage support and cooperative learning. Classrooms that establish cozy, inviting, quiet spaces encourage children to come together in small groups or pairs to share reading or problem-solving activities. Inclusive classrooms often have small couches, rugs, floor pillows, or beanbag chairs. A break from the institutional classroom furniture communicates that this is not a factory, learning can occur in comfort, and not everyone likes the same type of seating. A student who uses a wheelchair, mats, or wedges is more comfortable and included in a classroom where diverse seating arrangements are welcomed.

Seating arrangements can also encourage learning in applied activities. For example, seating within a room can be arranged in pairs or groups of four to facilitate cooperative learning activities. Johnson and Johnson (1989) suggest that these seating arrangements can develop base groups, which are stable, long-term units of support, encouragement, and assistance. These base groups can personalize academic work and the school experience, resulting in higher quality and quantity of performance.

Aside from establishing environments that welcome students as active learners, instructional techniques also can communicate to students that they are at the center of their education. Techniques such as cooperative learning, demonstrations or role plays, multimedia projects and productions, games, and community experiences and mentorships accommodate a range of interests and styles.

Johnson and Johnson (1989) suggest that a minimum of 60% of classroom instruction should be used for cooperative learning activities. Cooperative learning allows a class to address goals in both academic and affective skill areas. Students learn and practice academic skills at the same time that they develop small group social skills and refine their own process for learning. Johnson and Johnson (1989) challenge old instructional paradigms by contending that all academic content can be taught in a cooperative format. For example, students in an eighth grade algebra class work in groups of four to identify prime numbers from 1 to 100. They challenge each other to apply the rules for prime numbers by analyzing the numbers and generating a list. In a second grade class, student groups work together on spelling words (writing definitions, opposites, and sentences). They use a jigsaw strategy to divide the assignment among the group members. In both of these examples, students with diverse skills and abilities participated to complete the tasks. In algebra, one student used a calculator to divide numbers to test a theory while another student thought of word opposites as a peer read the definition of the spelling word from the dictionary.

Active Learning Through Community-Referenced Applications

After schools establish environments and cooperative learning strategies, they must focus on the curriculum. Current research on effective curricula indicates that all students learn how to participate and contribute to community life by engaging in applied learning activities. A range of techniques and approaches can be used to involve students in real-life learning activities in which they explore and apply skills. These are described on the following pages.

Simulations   In simulations, essential elements of community activities may be "acted out" or replicated in the school. They may involve relatively short activities with a few students or engage an entire class (or even a school) in a project. Berryman (1988) described a fifth grade teacher in Virginia who ran a simulation of a small economy in her classroom. " 'Taxation' means much more when another seatmate who represented government has bought the classroom door, forcing everyone to pay taxes every time they need to go in or out of the room" (p. 8).

Applied Learning Stations   A classroom can be structured to communicate that it is a fun place to learn. Learning stations around the parameter of the classroom encourage children to become active in their education and each station can be structured for independent activity (accommodating a range of ability levels). They can be established for every academic content area with challenging activities changing on a weekly or biweekly basis. For example, in a third grade classroom the math station focused on measurement for 2 weeks in the fall. At the station, students were encouraged to complete at least five measurement activities. They had a checklist for recording their answers and responses to each activity and at the bottom of the checklist were two blanks encouraging students to create their own measurement activities and to "test" those activities with other students. All activities at the station required teamwork; partners were assigned by the teacher to avoid concerns about favoritism and rejection. For each activity, various levels of performance were permitted to encourage students with diverse interests and abilities to participate. Examples of activities at the measurement station were: 1) measuring quantities of ingredients to make popcorn, salad, or cookies; 2) measuring heights of students in the classroom and graphing the heights by sex and age; 3) measuring the parameter of the classroom and making a scale drawing; 4) measuring the temperature of various liquids and charting them; 5) guessing the weights of various objects and then measuring their weights; and 6) calculating the mileage for a family trip using a map and scale measurement.

Role Play and Demonstrations   Demonstrations and role play are a valuable technique for students to learn basic knowledge and concepts as well as providing an opportunity for developing higher order thinking skills. Research (Johnson & Johnson, 1989) has demonstrated that people who teach a body of knowledge retain 90% of what they teach; therefore, students absorb the majority of what they teach in demonstrations or role play. In a tenth grade television production class, groups of students used demonstration techniques to learn television production. They were required to work in small groups to develop a format for teaching ninth grade students how to operate a camera and recorder. In a similar situation, a fifth grade class demonstrated how to structure a cooperative group activity for their second grade peers and then assisted them in a pizza making project.

Community-Referenced Projects Community-referenced projects can turn routine learning into an active process for all students. In a seventh grade social studies class, for example, students are required to complete state reports. Two students are allowed to work as partners and the project has to contain the following components: a written report, a travel poster, an oral report to the class and/or to another class in the building, and one of four optional activities—a play about an interesting historical event or person in that state, a food festival related to local cuisine, a video simulation of an interview with the governor of the state, or a student-generated activity. Student teams contract with their teacher for how they will complete the project and develop their timeline for activities.

In a high school law class, student teams take turns throughout the semester serving on juvenile juries in the local court system. Through this experience, they gain direct knowledge of the judicial process. They hear testimony on actual juvenile court cases (based on an agreement between the judge and the defendant), assign verdicts, and recommend punishments. After their rotation in court, the students return to the classroom to share their experiences by reenactments and written briefs.

Community-Based Learning Students may also be involved in community activities as part of the learning process. Benjamin (1989), for example, describes "service learning" that engages students in actual problem-solving and work activities in their community. Shuman (1984) and Toffler (1981) suggest that learning should focus on real problems in which students provide services to the community and then discuss and analyze them in the school. Service experiences may include assistance in hospitals, museums, community agencies, and schools through internships, and mentorships. While vocational education has prompted cooperative education for many years, the difference is that these activities are central to the educational process in the total curriculum of the school.

The typical procedure in public schools is to first teach students the "basic skills." They can then apply those basic skills in real-world activities. They can also engage in learning critical thinking and higher order cognitive skills. However, research indicates that skill development occurs best in the context of applied activities that make sense to the student. Disadvantaged and poor students need to see a purpose in learning and a connection between school, community, and home (Comer, 1988; Denton, 1989; Greenberg, 1989).

Yager (1987) suggests that, in science, learning does not come from applying knowledge to solve problems; rather, if students identify real-world problems that they want to solve, they will seek to acquire knowledge. For example, in a ninth grade biology class, a teacher engaged students in learning about ecology, scientific inquiry, and scientific measurement. In this activity, the students formed learning teams who were assigned the responsibility of testing the local river's water quality on a biweekly basis. The teams gathered samples of the water, cultured the organisms, and measured the levels of various chemicals in the water. One student classified as having a severe mental disability assisted in the experiments and had the opportunity to work on some other goals, such as street crossing, acquainting himself with the community, and walking on uneven terrain.

A group of four students in a fifth grade class visit community businesses each week as part of a journalism assignment. They return to the class to write an article for the school newspaper about the local business. There are two students in this group who are focusing on gaining skills in community mobility, community awareness, communication, and story writing. Two other students who accompany the group each week are working on interviewing skills, newspaper production, and theme writing. The four students work together to complete all individual goals and practice their skills.

Students in a third grade class are divided into small groups for trips to the city library. Parents and local neighborhood volunteers assist the groups on each visit. Students are learning to cross streets, identify landmarks, utilize the library resources, find books, and check out books related to a specific topic and project they must complete. If a student requires additional practice to master these skills, he or she may accompany several groups on the library visits.

In another sixth grade class, a partnership between a classroom and a branch of a local bank allowed students to practice several academic, community, and vocational interest activities during the year. Small groups of students travel by city bus to spend a day at the bank several times during the year. The students learn about banking functions and personnel roles, develop social skills, and learn about handling money. In addition, they eat lunch with the bankers and follow them on their routines. Different students engage in learning based on their own need—one learns about loans, another helps a teller, and another student counts money in the vault.

Community-referenced experiences abound at local high schools that are committed to fostering active, inclusive learning for all students. In a physics class, teams of students work with a local bioengineering firm to develop adaptive equipment for their classmate. In the home economics class, teams of students rotate once a week at a local church to prepare food for the shelter's breakfast program. For art and business classes, teams of students complete internships at one of four local art centers developing practical knowledge and skills in marketing, selecting and booking art events, and business management.

One Michigan high school program has created an open cooperative campus between the community and the school. In each academic and nonacademic class, four to five community references for student skill enhancement have been developed. Each student is required to complete a community experience in at least 50% of his classes (they choose the classes). The students receive academic credit for each learning experience. For example, students in an English class can complete community experiences in journalistic writing at the local newspaper, radio writing at one of three radio stations, television script writing at the local television station, writing for a church newsletter, writing for nonprofit organization newsletters, writing advertising copy at one of three advertising companies, or learning editorial skills at a local book publishing company.

CHANGING ROLES FOR TEACHERS
AND SUPPORT SERVICE PERSONNEL

As schools become inclusive communities where all students are welcomed and supported in learning together, the role of support services changes dramatically. Special education teachers, Chapter 1 teachers (funded by federal money allocated for disadvantaged students), and other specialized personnel funded to assist students with special needs will become instructional support specialists in regular education classes. This staff will provide resources and assistance for adapting curriculum involving school and community activities for students with varying abilities.

Similarly, other support personnel roles in this approach will also change. School psychologists will focus less on diagnoses of students and will use functional assessment based on observations in school and community activities to aid students in identifying and achieving life goals. Related services personnel (speech therapists, occupational therapists, physical therapists, counselors) will provide assistance to teachers. Such related services will occur primarily in the context of the regular educational curriculum. In a restructured, effective curriculum these services occur as part of the activities in the classroom, school, or community.

STEPS IN DEVELOPING COMMUNITY-REFERENCED INSTRUCTION: A GUIDE FOR TEACHERS

School systems need to make fundamental changes in the content and delivery of curriculum if all students are to learn more effectively. The total curriculum and activity of the school needs to be carefully studied to incorporate these changes. That is, these changes need to occur in history, science, English literature, and other subject areas as well as in vocational subjects. Individual teachers can do a lot to incorporate community-referenced learning into instruction. This requires effort and work; however, the result will be more effective learning for all students. Teachers may even enjoy teaching more as they become involved in a process of learning with their students through meaningful activities. The following guidelines provide a summary of steps for developing community-referenced instruction for all students. These steps are designed to be used by teachers to facilitate the development of community-referenced curricula in traditional subject areas.

1. A variety of everyday life and professional activities in which the subject area is likely to be used by the students should be identified.
2. Activities should be selected that are appropriate for the students' age levels.
3. Simulations, activities, and situations in the school and community should be identified that may be used for learning.
4. Teachers should identify skills that they must (want to) teach during the year. If needed, skills should be added that relate to team work, problem solving, critical thinking, and other important areas identified for student outcomes.
5. Teachers should develop a curriculum matrix of skills (step 4) and applied activities (step 3). This can be used as the basis for structuring class activities.
6. This information should be used with the assistance of support personnel to develop applied learning activities that fit the individual learning needs and interests of each student.
7. In implementing step 6, learners should be placed in diversified

groups where they can help each other. Students may provide assistance to one another in higher level learning tasks, students working on simpler tasks may be assisted by other students, and learning circles may be used involving students of all levels to solve problems together. This diversified learning approach gives all students opportunities to pursue their individual learning goals while participating in a diverse group.

CONCLUSION

Community-based instruction and learning as a result of functional life and community activities is critical to an effective curriculum for all students. Research and school restructuring literature suggest important changes in the content of instruction, assessment practices, and process of instruction—all of which promise to assist schools to provide a supportive learning environment. In this context, all students may be included in regular education and benefit from the development of friends and relationships while learning skills and participating in community activities.

There is still a lot to learn as restructured curriculum for community-referenced learning is developed and implemented. Several areas require ongoing exploration, demonstration, and research such as the range of learning objectives, models of support and learning, and the degree of heterogeneity in classes.

The challenge to create effective curricula for all students is great. Educators are called to work together in this important process; they must actively participate in improving the total school. Similarly, educators are challenged to develop a team with fellow educators and other support personnel to obtain assistance. The challenge is great, but possible.

The outcomes of creating effective curriculum and supports in schools is dramatic. All students, as well as the educators who support them, engage in new and exciting methods of learning in meaningful situations. In addition, students learn more and they learn to support and accommodate each other outside of the school. With effective community-referenced learning in inclusive, supportive schools, educators can begin the important process of creating better communities and better lives for all people. If the challenge is great, the potential benefits make the process exciting and worth the effort.

REFERENCES

Albright, L., & Cobb, B. (1986). *Curriculum-based assessment and program planning for handicapped students in secondary vocational education programs*. Long Beach: Bureau of Employment-Related Education and Training for Special Populations, California State University-Long Beach.

Anderson, R., Hiebert, E., Scott, J., & Wilkinson, I. (1985). *Becoming a nation of readers: The report of the commission on reading.* Urbana: University of Illinois.

Banks, J. (1988). Education, citizenship, and cultural options. *Education and Society, 1*(1), 19–22.

Benjamin, S. (1989). An ideascape for education: What futurists recommend. *Educational Leadership, 7*(1), 8–14.

Berk, R.A. (Ed.). (1986). *Performance assessment: Methods and applications.* Baltimore: Johns Hopkins University Press.

Berryman, S.E. (1988, October). *The educational challenge of the American economy.* Paper prepared for a forum of the National Education Association, Washington, DC.

Bloom, B., Madaus, G., & Hastings, J. (1981). *Evaluation to improve learning.* New York: McGraw-Hill.

Boyer, E. (1984). A critical examination of American education. In J. Surwill (Ed.), *A critical examination of American education: A time for action.* Billings: Conference sponsored by Eastern Montana College (ERIC Document Reproduction Service No. 269 357).

Browder, D. (1991). *Assessment of individuals with severe disabilities: An applied behavior approach to life skills assessment* (2nd ed.). Baltimore: Paul H. Brookes Publishing Co.

Brown, J., Collins, A., & Duguid, P. (1989). Debating the situation. *Educational Researcher, 18*(4), 10–12.

Comer, J. (1988, November). Educating poor minority children. *Scientific American*, 42–48.

Commission on Reading (1990). What is reading? In D. Ogle, W. Pink, & B.F. Jones (Eds.), *Restructuring to promote learning in America's schools* (pp. 137–148). Columbus, OH: Zaner Bloser.

Denton, W.H. (1989). The next educational reform: Family support system. *Community Education Journal, XIV*(4), 4–10.

Falvey, M. (1980). *Changes in academic and social competence of kindergarten aged handicapped children as a result of integrated classrooms.* Unpublished doctoral dissertation, University of Wisconsin, Madison.

Falvey, M. (1989). *Community-based curriculum: Instructional strategies for students with severe handicaps.* Baltimore: Paul H. Brookes Publishing Co.

Ford, A., & Black, J. (1989). The community-referenced curriculum for students with moderate and severe disabilities. In D. Biklen, D. Ferguson, & A. Ford (Eds.), *Schooling and disability* (pp. 91–119). Chicago: University of Chicago Press.

Ford, A., Schnorr, R., Meyer, L., Davern, L., Black, J., & Dempsey, P. (1989). *The Syracuse community-referenced curriculum guide for students with moderate and severe disabilities.* Baltimore: Paul H. Brookes Publishing Co.

Forest, M. (Ed.). (1984). *Education/integration: A collection of readings on the integration of children with mental handicaps into regular school systems.* Downsview, Ontario: G. Allan Roeher Institute.

Forest, M. (1987). *More education/integration.* Downsview, Ontario: G. Allan Roeher Institute.

Gardner, H. (1987). Developing the spectrum of human intelligences. *Harvard Educational Review, 57*(2), 187–193.

Gardner, J. (1989). Building community. In W. Pink (Ed.), *Restructuring to promote learning in American schools.* Elmhurst, IL: North Central Regional Educational Laboratory.

Greenberg, J.B. (1989, April). *Funds of knowledge: Historical constitution, social distribution, and transmission.* Paper presented at the session on Collaborative Research: Combining Community and Social Resources to Improve the Education of Hispanics in Tucson, Society for Applied Anthropology, Annual Meeting, Santa Fe, NM.

Johnson, D.W., & Johnson, R.T. (1989). *Leading the cooperative school.* Edira, MN: Interaction Books.

Jones, B.F. (1990). The importance of restructuring schools to promote learning. In Ogle, D., Pink, W., & Jones, B.F. (Eds.), *Restructuring to promote learning in America's schools* (pp. 13–34). Columbus, OH: Zaner Bloser.

Michigan Department of Education. (1990). *Proposed position statement on core curriculum.* Lansing: Michigan Department of Education.

National Council of Social Studies. (1989). Essentials of social studies. In D. Ogle (Ed.), *Restructuring to promote learning in America's schools* (pp. 52–69). Columbus, OH: Zaner Bloser.

National Council of Teachers of Mathematics. (1990). *Curriculum and evaluation standards for school mathematics.* Reston, VA: Author.

Peterson, M. (1986). *Vocational assessment of special students: a procedural guide.* Lathrup Village, MI: VOC-AIM.

Peterson, M. (1990). *Vocational and life assessment and planning: Recommendations to the Kent Intermediate School District.* Detroit, MI: Developmental Disabilities Institute, Wayne State University.

Peterson, M. (in press). *Life assessment and planning for persons with special needs.* Newton, MA: Allyn & Bacon.

Resnick, L.B., & Klopfer, L.E. (1989). Toward the thinking curriculum: An overview. In L.B. Resnick & L.E. Klopfer (Eds.), *Toward the thinking curriculum: Current cognitive research: 1989 ASCD Yearbook* (pp. 3–20). Washington, DC: Assocation for Supervision and Curriculum Development.

Romberg, T.A. (1988, November). *Principles for an elementary mathematics program for the 1990's.* Paper prepared for the California Invitational Symposium on Elementary Mathematics Education, San Francisco, CA.

Shuman, R. (1984). Education, society, and the second millennium. *NASSP Bulletin, 68*(474), 95–103.

Sizer, T. (1986). Changing schools and testing: An uneasy proposal. *The redesign of testing for the 21st century.* Princeton, NJ: 1985 ETS Invitational Conference Proceedings.

Stiggins, R. (1987). Design and development of performance assessments. *Educational Measurement: Issues and Practices, 6*(3), 33–42.

Stiggins, R. (January, 1988). Revitalizing classroom assessment. *Phi Delta Kappan, 69,* 5.

Toffler, A. (1981). Education and the future. *Social Education, 45*(6), 422–426.

Weber, L., & Dyasi, H. (1985). Language development and observation of a local environment: First steps in providing primary-school science education for non-dominant groups. *Prospectus, XV*(4), 665–676.

Wees, G., & Leu, J. (1975). A skinny dip into the future of education. *The National Elementary Principal, 55*(1), 24–28.

Wiggins, G. (1989). Teaching to the authentic test. *Educational Leadership, 46*(7), 41–47.

Wilcox, B., & Bellamy, G.T. (1982). *Design of high school programs for severely handicapped students.* Baltimore: Paul H. Brookes Publishing Co.

Wilcox, B., & Bellamy, G.T. (1987). *A comprehensive guide to The Activities catalog: An alternative curriculum for youth and adults with severe disabilities.* Baltimore: Paul Brookes Publishing Co..

Wolf, D. (1989). Portfolio assessment: Sampling student work. *Educational Leadership, 46*(7), 35–39.

Yager, R. (1987). Assess all five domains of science. *The Science Teacher, 54*(7), 33–37.

York, J., & Vandercook, T. (1988). *Strategies for achieving an integrated education for middle school learners with severe disabilities.* Minneapolis: Institute on Community Integration, University of Minnesota.

York, J., Vandercook, T., Macdonald, C., & Wolff, S. (1989). *Strategies for full inclusion.* Minneapolis: Institute on Community Integration, University of Minnesota.

13

Extracurricular Activities

Mary Falvey,
Jennifer Coots,
and Susann Terry-Gage

HISTORICALLY, THE ROLE of schools has been to develop a literate citizenry (Bastian, Fruchter, Gittel, Greer, & Haskins, 1988; Ravich, 1983). The objective has been to develop academic skills that foster an effective, productive citizenship. However, an increasing number of parents, educators, and community members have been concerned with both the school's ability to meet this objective and how well this limited academic focus has adequately prepared students for life outside of the school environment.

SHORTCOMINGS OF EDUCATIONAL PROGRAMS AND SERVICES

The existing practices and organizational structures of schools have been criticized in several ways, particularly by the educational community. First, schools are often organized with the assumption that the student population is homogencous even though students with a diversity of skills, interests, strengths, and needs are present in to-day's classrooms. The limited focus of the curriculum is not always appropriate for this diverse student population. Second, the creativity of teachers and administrators is often stifled due to bureaucratic procedures. Existing rules and procedures often inhibit rather than facilitate change and improvement. Third, schools often seek universal solutions rather than attempt to identify strategies that are effective for individual students. These universal solutions to specific challenges are not always appropriate for the increasingly diverse population of students. Fourth, teaching students to compete against one another is emphasized rather than teaching cooperation, collaboration, and interdependence. This focus has been criticized because it limits applicability and utility outside of school. Fifth, teachers and administrators often have "boundary restrictions," particularly with regard to categorical programs. These categorical territories inhibit teachers and administrators from developing relationships, sharing expertise, and educating students in a comprehensive manner (A. Lieberman, personal communication, September 25, 1990).

In addition to the concern expressed by educators about educational services and programs, many parents have also expressed concern about their children's limited opportunities to develop meaningful and supportive friendships with their peers (Grenot-Scheyer, Coots, & Falvey, 1989). Friendship is a difficult concept to define. It is elusive and often awkward; however, it is also very familiar and important to a person's quality of life (Perske, 1988). An extensive body of literature exists describing the characteristics of and strategies for facilitating friendships. Within this literature, a prerequisite condition identified for children and adolescents to develop friendships is to have close proximity and frequent opportunity with peers who are prospective friends. Schools, especially those in children's neighborhoods, are places where children have frequent opportunity to interact with one another and form friendships. For many children, developing friendships is a comfortable and easy process. Their home and school situations allow for and facilitate the development and maintenance of friendships. However, for other children, schools are not facilitating students' friendships with a variety of peers. Parents and community members contend that in some cases schools are even inhibiting friendship development, particularly when students are forced to attend categorical and centralized programs rather than their neighborhood schools.

One of the most frequently acquired skills children learn when they have friends is the ability to interact and cooperate with others. Extensive research has focused on developing skills of cooperation (Johnson & Johnson, 1981). However, schools have a tendency to stress competition rather than cooperation by emphasizing test scores and academic achievement. A number of educators, parents, and community members are expressing an increased interest in the ability of school personnel to assist students to develop skills other than academics (e.g., skills necessary to cooperate with peers, develop relationships and friendships with peers, and to better assume their responsibility as caring and participating citizens).

SCHOOL-BASED EXTRACURRICULAR ACTIVITIES

Although schools have traditionally not emphasized the development of nonacademic skills, they have sponsored extracurricular activities that provide the setting and context for students to develop social skills, such as cooperation and friendship. These extracurricular activities have often been funded by volunteer or auxiliary groups such as parent/ teacher associations or organizations. When these activities are sponsored by the schools, they are usually the first item to be eliminated when budgets are reduced. Since extracurricular activities are not well funded, they are often supported, facilitated, and sponsored by volunteer school personnel, parents, and/or community members.

Extracurricular activities include those activities that students participate in during and after school that are not considered the major emphasis of the school program (e.g., lunch, recess, scouting, clubs, teams). These activities can be sponsored by the school, local parks and recreation departments, private organizations, or other community and neighborhood groups. These activities can be oriented toward academics, sports, service to the community, and/or just having fun. In addition, extracurricular activities can facilitate career exploration and/or development, particularly for junior and senior high school students.

Importance of Extracurricular Activities

Typically, school personnel have not viewed the development of friendships as part of their overall mission, even though they generally consider social skills development a part of it. In spite of the lack of emphasis on fostering friendships, most children and adolescents develop peer friendships with those who attend the same school and/or live in the same neighborhood. Friendships and the opportunity to develop friendships are often a result of students participating in extracurricular activities. Many of these friendships become important, lifelong relationships. When adults recall positive, happy experiences from their years in elementary and secondary schools, it is often the friendships with their peers that made the events and experiences so important and memorable (Ford & Davern, 1989). Opportunities to participate in extracurricular activities during school years often result in new or stronger friendships with peers. Participation in extracurricular activities can provide students with a context for what to share and how to interact with each other.

In addition, extracurricular activities are important for teaching essential citizenry skills. "Our failure (referring to the school system) to create an informed and thoughtful citizenry will also have continuing impact on our quality of life as a culture and as a society that aspires toward democratic pluralism" (Bastian et al., 1988, p. 25). Extracurricular activities allow students to develop skills that go beyond the rise or fall of test scores by encouraging critical thinking, observation, problem-solving, and interaction skills—all of which are generally identified as good citizenship skills within a democratic, pluralistic society.

Participation of All Students in Extracurricular Activities

Extracurricular activities are often flexible in nature and thereby attract students with many different interests, talents, and methods of performing skills. Extracurricular activities can provide an opportunity to respect and rejoice in the diversity of society rather than to discriminate against individual differences. They can also allow and encourage students to participate to the greatest extent possible, rather than requiring everyone to do the same thing, at the same time, and in the same way. This allows for a variety of students with different strengths to participate, including students who might not excel academically at the same rate as the majority of their peers.

Students with different strengths and abilities can be facilitated to participate in extracurricular activities through the use of a variety of supports and adaptations. These supports and adaptations do not necessarily require additional or new funds, but rather a reorganization of existing resources. Traditionally, children and adolescents have been required to participate in specialized programs in order to receive extra and individualized supports (e.g., Special Olympics, government funded after-school programs for low income families). The resulting value of including all children and adolescents regardless of their race, sex, ability levels, and income levels should determine how and where individualized supports are provided, as opposed to the use of categorical funding and provision of services characteristic of many communities.

Supports for Extracurricular Activities

Supports should be made available to students to facilitate their participation in activities and interactions with peers. Supports may be provided in at least two different forms—people supports and information. People supports include the formation of a buddy system when one student is unsure of the requirements and is unable to participate in activities independently (e.g., a student who is unable to talk, read, or write is able to participate in the high school newspaper club with the help of a "buddy" who will write the student's thoughts and feelings dictated by his or her eye gaze and body language). In some cases, older peers might be recruited and trained to provide support for younger students needing assistance. For example, a bilingual fourth grader might accompany a monolingual first grader to Cub Scouts to interpret for the peers and scout leader as well as to teach English to the first grader and the student's native language to everyone else.

Information supports involve providing information to the staff who can adopt the activity to be accessible to all students. For example, adapting rules might involve allowing a student to hit a baseball off a "tee" instead of hitting a pitched ball because the student is capable of hitting a stable ball, but not a moving one. Another example is providing information about student characteristics and needs to the staff supervising the extracurricular activities. The student who has frequent seizures must be supervised by people who have been informed of the type of seizures he or she generally has and the proper procedures to follow if a seizure occurs.

EXTRACURRICULAR ACTIVITIES ACROSS AGES

Students of all ages generally have access to a variety of extracurricular activities within their communities, including their schools. The nature and type of activities vary according to the ages of the students. This section provides a rationale for offering extracurricular activities to children and adolescents of various ages, identifies common extracurricular activities, and identifies and describes strategies for including all students in these activities.

Preschool

Recently, recreation and educational programs have been placing a greater emphasis on peer interactions and relationships (Leach, 1983). Research has demonstrated that preschoolers who have opportunities to interact with one another and develop relationships are better prepared for kindergarten (Safford, 1989). In addition, school districts in various parts of the country have developed and are offering preschool programs for children under 5 years of age (e.g., Head Start, prekindergarten programs). Although Head Start and other government funded and subsidized programs have provided access to educational and related services for many children whose families cannot afford tuition at private preschool programs, these children are segregated and forced to attend different programs. That is, preschoolers requiring financial assistance are relegated to the state operated, subsidized, and/or controlled preschools, while middle and upper class preschoolers attend private, tuition paid preschools. Preschoolers with disabilities are often in the same situation when they are forced to attend centralized, segregated programs. In order for children to appreciate the pluralism of society, school districts must develop school and extracurricular activities that are accessible to all preschoolers within that community.

The types of extracurricular activities available in many communities for preschoolers include the following:

Music lessons
Dance lessons
Computer lessons
Swim lessons
Gymnastics, such as "Gymboree" programs
Cooking lessons
Classes in music and art at the local museum
Church sponsored activities and lessons
Arts and crafts
Neighborhood playgroups, such as "Mommy/Daddy and Me" groups
Day care and after-school programs

There are several strategies that educators, parents, and members of the community can use to facilitate activities for preschoolers. First, activities that the preschooler enjoys are more likely to be successful than those they do not like. Second, they can become involved in the same activities as the child's neighbors and friends. This allows neighborhood families to share responsibilities such as car pooling and babysitting while they participate in the same activities. Third, they can support and show gratitude toward the teacher or leader of the activity (this would be appreciated since they may be volunteering or receiving minimal compensation). Fourth, if a student needs extra assistance in order to participate, a support group can be formed of children and adults responsible for identifying where and how to obtain the needed assistance, considering the use of informal supports whenever possible. Fifth, parents should make friends with other parents so that their children might have more opportunities to get together. Sixth, parents might plan separate activities at local parks or at home to help foster additional opportunities for children to play together. Finally, parents, if possible, might volunteer to drive in a car pool, prepare snacks, or provide other needed assistance.

Elementary

During the elementary years, children are beginning to explore their unique abilities, including talents, gifts, and strengths. Extracurricular activities can provide extra support for children to discover and develop their unique talents. In addition, children in elementary school are forming relationships and friendships that will last a long time, perhaps a lifetime. Extracurricular activities can provide an opportunity to facilitate the development and maintenance of those relationships and friendships. Finally, due to thc large number of working families, many elementary children participate in child care or after-school programs and services. These can be considered extracurricular activities and can provide the child with numerous opportunities to facilitate friendships, acquire skills not typically taught in school, and/or obtain extra assistance in completing homework assignments.

The following are various types of extracurricular activities available to elementary age children:

Scouts (Brownies, Girl, Cub, Boy, Campfire)
Indian Princess/Indian Guides "Y" programs
Sports (e.g., Pop Warner football, Little League baseball, soccer, hockey, basketball, gymnastics, dance)
Swim or skating (ice or roller) clubs and teams
Church and synagogue activities for children (e.g., religious instruction, choir, play groups)
Park and recreation programs
Boys' and girls' clubs
Summer enrichment and/or school
Summer camps
Special interest lessons (e.g., ballet, music, jazz, computer)
After school programs and/or camps

Educators, parents, and community members can use various methods to facilitate extracurricular activities for elementary age children. First, students should have the opportunity to attend their neighborhood school so that after-school and neighborhood activities are accessible to them. Second, they should be encouraged and assisted to participate in activities that are consistent with their strengths, preferences, and talents. Third, students should not be excluded from activities due to skill limitations; instead, adaptations should be developed that can enhance the child's participation. For example, a child who is unable to see could participate in softball using a ball that "beeps." Fourth, after-school programs should not separate children based on arbitrary criteria such as funding (government funded or subsidized after-school programs that are separate from family funded programs). Fifth, parents could become involved in the Parent/Teacher Association and other community activities that help facilitate their child's involvement. Finally, parents should support and encourage their child's participation in extracurricular activities.

Secondary

Secondary students are at an age where they begin to develop a substantial amount of independence from their families. They also become concerned about their future careers, jobs, and postsecondary education as well as their peer networks and relationships. Extracurricular activities can provide opportunities for students to develop independence from their families, explore career opportunities, and develop friendship networks.

There are many extracurricular activities available to secondary students, including the following:

School clubs and organizations (e.g., Spanish, chess, Peace and Freedom, social, pep, environmentalist, Students Against Drunk Drivers, computer, ski and hiking, drama, service)
Other activities within the school (e.g., Girls' League, debate team, band, chorus, publicity committee, color guard, school mascot, student council and/or government, cheerleading, drill and flag team, pep rallies,)
School team sports (e.g., football, baseball, soccer, hockey, cross country/track, swim, basketball, gymnastics, tennis, softball, golf)
Attending school functions (e.g., sporting events, dances, balls)
Scouting (e.g., Eagle Scouts, cadets)
Church and synagogue activities (e.g., religious instruction, teen groups)
Teams, classes, city sport leagues and groups at health clubs, local park and recreation centers, and teen centers (e.g., aerobics, tennis, gymnastics)
Teen camps and retreats

Educators, parents, and members of the community can still have an active role in facilitating secondary students' active involvement in extracurricular activities. For example, at Napa High School in Napa, California, several members of the community and faculty were concerned about the lack of clubs that emphasized and facilitated friendships, did not focus on competition, and were accessible to *all* students. Therefore, they developed the Friendship Club. The club was advertised as an opportunity to explore issues related to friendships and to develop friendships. More students joined the club than any other on campus that year (P. Saunders, personal communication, October 17, 1989). Using the work of Marsha Forest and Evelyn Lusthaus (1989), the students developed a circle of friends for themselves and their peers. The Friendship Club remains one of the most popular clubs on campus.

Parents or other people involved with secondary students could also organize neighborhood car pools to get to and from school, sporting events, dances, and other school and community activities. In addition, faculty and parents should make sure that students purchase student identification cards, which will allow them access to high school sponsored events and activities; sign up for clubs; and know when and where to be for club meetings and events.

CONCLUSION

Participation in extracurricular activities can provide opportunities to develop citizenship skills by promoting inclusive participation of students with a diverse set of strengths, abilities, talents, and needs. Extracurricular activities are important to the personal growth and development of all students. They are an opportunity to engage in special interest areas and to expand and refine unique talents. They are also occasions for students to develop and strengthen friendships and learn a range of social skills. Parents and teachers need to actively promote the involvement of all students in extracurricular activities. These activities can be an opportunity for students to understand and value all people as unique and contributing members of society.

REFERENCES

Bastian, A., Fruchter, N., Gittel, M., Greer, C., & Haskins, K. (1988). *Choosing equality: The case for democratic schooling.* Philadelphia: Temple University Press.

Ford, A., & Davern, L. (1989). Moving forward with school integration: Strategies for involving students with severe handicaps in the life of the school. In R. Gaylord-Ross (Ed.), *Integration strategies for students with handicaps* (pp. 11–31). Baltimore: Paul H. Brookes Publishing Co.

Forest, M., & Lusthaus, E. (1989). Promoting educational equality for all students: Circles and maps. In S. Stainback, W. Stainback, & M. Forest (Eds.), *Educating all students in the mainstream of regular education* (pp. 43–57). Baltimore: Paul H. Brookes Publishing Co.

Grenot-Scheyer, M., Coots, J., & Falvey, M.A. (1989). Developing and fostering friendships. In M. Falvey, *Community-based curriculum: Instructional strategies for students with severe handicaps* (pp. 345–358). Baltimore: Paul H. Brookes Publishing Co.

Johnson, R.T., & Johnson, D.W. (1981). Building friendships between handicapped and nonhandicapped students: Effects of cooperative and individualistic instruction. *American Educational Research Journal, 18,* 415–423.

Leach, P. (1983). *Babyhood* (2nd ed.). New York: Alfred A. Knopf.

Perske, R. (1988). *Circle of friends.* Nashville: Abingdon Press.

Ravich, D. (1983). *The troubled crusade: American education 1945–1980.* New York: Basic Books.

Safford, P.L. (1989). *Integrating teaching in early childhood: Starting in the mainstream.* White Plains, NY: Longman, Inc.

14

Curriculum in Inclusion-Oriented Schools

Trends, Issues, Challenges, and Potential Solutions

Michael F. Giangreco

A TEACHER IN one classroom gives instructions to 23 students seated at desks arranged in the shape of a horseshoe. In other classrooms, students are working in small groups on a social studies assignment or taking a weekly quiz. While these and similar scenes may seem ordinary based on outward appearances, these particular classrooms are anything but ordinary. What makes them unique is that the adults responsible for designing the educational experiences in these classrooms have purposefully included students with a range of learning characteristics much wider than traditionally found in schools. The people associated with these classrooms have made a commitment to include *all* the children who live in their community in general education classes with the supports they need to

The author conducted a series of seven semistructured interviews with Ann Nevin, Professor of Special Education at the University of Vermont, ranging in length from 1½ to 2½ hours. Questions regarding her searches of the ERIC system and resources used in educational methods courses were asked. I wish to extend my appreciation to Ann for her written input, editing feedback, and perspectives regarding trends, issues, challenges, and potential solutions for facilitating the adoption of curriculum for inclusive schooling. Thanks are also extended to my colleague Chigee Cloninger for her helpful and often amusing editing suggestions. Finally, I wish to express sincere thanks to the many people at Charleston Elementary, Irasburg Elementary, Park Street Elementary (Springfield), Sheldon Elementary, and St. Alban's Bay Elementary for providing me with the opportunity to learn from their inclusion-oriented efforts.

learn. Ordinary classrooms have been rearranged to create a new educational experience that seeks the extraordinary in each member of the classroom community.

This chapter offers perspectives based on a review of literature of selected educational issues and the author's work in schools with people who are striving toward full inclusion, hereafter referred to as *inclusion oriented*. The term *inclusion oriented* is offered not as a descriptor of programs that are necessarily fully inclusive at the moment or models to be emulated and exactly replicated. Rather, inclusion-oriented people seek to establish an inclusionary ethic that welcomes all children into their local schools and simultaneously pursues a range of individually meaningful learning outcomes through effective instructional practices. The purpose here is to present ideas to encourage the reader to question the way schools currently do business. Similar to the introduction, the focus in this chapter is on the overall context for decision making about curriculum. The chapter is organized in five sections. First, common features of inclusion-oriented education are described based on observations and discussions with educators at schools where inclusive practices are being implemented.[1] Second, an overview of selected societal and educational trends that affect inclusion-oriented schooling efforts are discussed. Third, some major challenges and opportunities facing the development of inclusion-oriented curricula in schools are described. Fourth, potential courses of action people might take at both "macro" and "micro" levels are suggested to facilitate inclusion-oriented schooling now. The chapter concludes by encouraging the pursuit of the vision of inclusion-oriented curriculum in all community schools.

FEATURES OF INCLUSION-ORIENTED SCHOOLING

To claim that general education classes in neighborhood schools welcome and provide meaningful learning experiences for *all* students, regardless of their characteristics, would be to ignore the obvious. As the inequities of separate and unequal education continue to be debated and analyzed, a growing number of parents and professionals are making efforts to do something about it.

During visits with some inclusion-oriented people who work in

---

[1]Semistructured interviews were conducted with individuals who work in or with inclusion-oriented schools. These interviews ranged in length from 30 to 60 minutes each. Questions regarding the features of the school or personnel that make them inclusive were asked. Thanks are extended to Michael Collins, Richard DeYoung, Laurie LaPlant, George Salambier, and Richard Villa for their input regarding a variety of Vermont schools, and to Gordon Porter for his insights regarding inclusion in New Brunswick, Canada.

Vermont schools, the author observed a number of similarities among the schools and the people who work in them. The majority of these people place a balanced emphasis on both the academic/functional achievement of their students as well as the social/personal aspects of schooling.

In contrast, some people in traditional schools de-emphasize the social/personal aspects of the school experience. In some cases, tracking, segregation, and homogeneous grouping of students are rationalized by a claim of academic integrity. Programs with an exclusively academic/functional focus may graduate students who have basic literacy or survival skills, but who lack the social networks and life experiences to apply these skills in ways that facilitate their ongoing development and participation in personally and societally valued activities. A more likely outcome of separate schooling rationalized by academic integrity is a widening equity gap between the "haves" and "have nots" (Lipsky & Gartner, 1989).

Earlier attempts at heterogeneous groupings of students focused exclusively on the social/personal benefits of inclusion (e.g., affiliation, friendship). Academic/functional achievement was de-emphasized, resulting in wasted human potential. Such practices call into question the interdependencies between participation in shared instruction, student self-image, and social acceptance/affiliation. How students perceive themselves and each other as belonging may be affected, in part, by their presence in the same locations and their shared learning experiences (Schnorr, 1991). Inclusion-oriented advocates seem unwilling to sacrifice either the social/personal or academic/functional aspects of students' educational programs.

In the process of identifying a variety of social/personal and academic/functional outcomes for their students, inclusion-oriented school personnel attempt to establish a clear link between the school's educational program and students' quality of life. They seek to ensure that students' lives are improved as a result of being in school. Learning opportunities are created to achieve outcomes and then evaluated to determine if they are producing the intended results. Evaluation of a student's success in school does not need to be limited to narrowly defined target behaviors, but extended to include measures of meaningful outcomes that directly or indirectly relate to the quality of a person's life (Meyer & Janney, 1989).

In each of the inclusion-oriented schools that the author visited, at least one leader was identified who spearheaded inclusive reforms. As part of their ongoing school responsibilities, inclusion-oriented leaders emphasized the value of quality education for *all* youngsters, provided varying types of supports to facilitate inclusion on a practical level, and promoted inclusion-oriented activities by collaborating with members of the school community.

The nature and quality of education is primarily dependent upon people. People who work in inclusion-oriented schools seem to approach the challenges of school restructuring with optimism. These individuals are problem solvers who focus on how to make education better for all students rather than on enumerating a myriad of reasons for inaction. Making an attempt at a task, whether successful or not, is admirable. Hearing someone say, "Well, at least she tried," suggests that while trying and succeeding may be most valued, trying and only partially succeeding or even failing is more highly valued than not trying at all. Regardless of the level of perceived success, inclusion-oriented advocates actively try to improve education for all students.

Inclusion-oriented personnel tend to be flexible and individualize their approaches to both students and colleagues. They tend to reject highly standardized approaches to curriculum and instruction where students with particular characteristics are offered educational "one size fits all" programs. Their willingness to learn, ability to critically self-evaluate, and propensity for action have led to constructive school improvement. The presence of inclusion-oriented people can, and usually does, positively affect the status of inclusion and curriculum in schools.

INFLUENCE OF SOCIETAL AND EDUCATIONAL TRENDS ON CURRICULUM

Societal Trends

As social institutions, schools cannot be fully understood outside the context of societal and cultural influences. Regardless of whether one believes that schools reflect society, respond to societal needs, or exist to provide a model for society, schools are undeniably linked to multiple features of culture and society. Contemporary domestic issues such as fundamental changes in the configuration of families (e.g., single parent families), homelessness, hunger, immigration of people who speak a variety of languages, unemployment, teen pregnancy, and substance abuse challenge urban, suburban, and rural schools to adapt to meet and/or influence student and societal needs. In the face of these issues, clinging to traditional bureaucratic patterns of school organization that attempt to standardize complex work and reduce it to an assembly line model has exacerbated the challenge of providing appropriate education to a variety of students (Skrtic, 1987, 1989, 1991).

It is clear that the challenges faced in the United States and Canada are not completely influenced by factors within our exclusive control. We are part of an interdependent global economy, characterized by Naisbitt (1989) as "world free trade" and an "era of globalization." As Benjamin (1989) states in his comprehensive summary of societal and educational futures literature, "Our world is shrinking for several reasons. For example, advances in communications, microelectronics, and transportation have made it physically easier and more enjoyable for people to travel about the globe" (p. 8). Moreover, major economic trends such as: 1) a shift to an information/service-based economy, 2) the influence of high technology industries, 3) the need to shift jobs frequently, and 4) the so-called "short half-life" of knowledge will strain beliefs regarding many aspects of the information used by scientists, business people, teachers, and the graduates of our schools (Alley, 1985; Benjamin, 1989). Our graduates must be prepared to learn new information while on the job and be prepared to change jobs frequently.

Collectively, these trends mean that an increasing proportion of our students and their teachers will come from and be required to interact with people of different family structures, cultures, languages, and personal characteristics. This increased heterogeneity will naturally result in increased demands for graduates to value and cooperate with people who have diverse characteristics. Some local public school systems, in their attempts to meet these challenges, may see the demands as reasons to exclude or separate certain students from being served by the public school. Others will capitalize on the same demands by utilizing them as resources to assist students in developing solutions to pursue a better life through inclusion-oriented models of education. The abilities of people with diverse backgrounds and characteristics to live harmoniously in an increasingly interdependent world will be influenced by society's decision to pursue inclusion-oriented or separate schooling for various groups.

Educational Trends

Until recently, the vast majority of school reform initiatives pertained exclusively to students served within the general education system. Minimal national attention was directed toward educational reform for students with a range of educational needs. Recent literature suggests that the issues of school reform cannot be separated from educational equity for all types of students (Biklen, Ferguson, & Ford, 1989; Gartner & Lipsky, 1987; Graden, Zins, & Curtis, 1988; Lezotte, 1989; Lipsky & Gartner, 1989). In part, widening the scope of students included in reform efforts has meant extending research on "effective schools" (Bickel & Bickel, 1986; Lezotte, 1989) and "selected best practices" (Fox & Williams, 1990) to include *all* types of students.

Educational trends such as the impact of new technology (Dede, 1989; Levin & Rumberger, 1987; Warren, Horn, & Hill, 1987), global education (Kniep, 1989), advancements in staff development (Showers, 1990; Villa, 1989), teaching strategies for learning (Deschler & Schumaker, 1988), and teachers and teams as decision makers have clear implications for inclusion-oriented curriculum and instruction. The focus here is on two trends having an impact on inclusion-oriented curricular efforts.

Strategies for Learning   A resurgent interest in strategies and processes to encourage learning has been spawned by societal changes, particularly the information explosion, the pace of change, and increasing global interdependence. Trends are shifting toward teaching both students and teachers ways to learn. Structural arrangements provided through cooperative learning models have been advocated to facilitate student academic and social learning as well as adult group interaction ("Cooperative Learning," 1990; Johnson & Johnson, 1987; Johnson, Johnson, & Holubec, 1986; Johnson, Johnson, & Maruyama, 1983). Problem solving is increasingly recommended to assist students, teachers, and teams in generating creative alternatives to a range of challenges (Crabbe, 1989; Eberle & Stanish, 1985; Giangreco, 1990; Parnes, 1981, 1988; Torrance & Goff, 1989). Teachers are encouraged to assist students in learning how to learn through approaches such as the "Strategies Intervention Model" (Deschler & Schumaker, 1988). Deschler and Schumaker (1988) describe the five key components of the Strategies Intervention Model as: 1) instructional interventions take place in multiple settings, 2) roles of all those involved in instruction need to be clearly specified, 3) cooperative planning and feedback among team members, 4) retention and generalization of targeted learning strategies in the settings where they will be used (e.g., general education classrooms), and 5) support systems including families, school staff, and relevant nonschool agencies.

Emphasis has been shifting from a focus on content toward a focus on learning strategies such as teaching skills, processes, and practices that allow learners of all ages to sustain and update their acquisition and application of specific knowledge as it continues to change and expand. Rather than homogeneous student grouping based on content-oriented performance levels, the shift toward learning strategies presents opportunities for instruction within heterogeneous groups.

Teachers and Teams as Decision Makers   Teacher and student participation in curricular and instructional decision making is a growing trend. Now and in the recent past, teaching basic skills (e.g., reading, writing, mathematics) and subject content (e.g., science, social studies) has been dominated by materials developed by curriculum designers. The teacher's role ranged from using readings and suggested activities that guide instruction to explicitly following highly standardized, scripted lessons. The students had virtually no role. In such cases, decisions about what and how to teach are removed partially or completely from the people most directly involved in the instruction.

While commercially developed curricular materials will probably continue to have a place in public schools, trends are shifting toward approaches that allow for and encourage decision making at the school and classroom level. While the valuable work done by curriculum designers is acknowledged, educators have recognized for many years how unlikely it is that any standardized materials will address the learning needs of all the students in a class or school. Strict adherence to rigid curricular sequences of questionable validity and generic instructional methods may contribute to the exclusion of some students from general classrooms because they do not readily fit into the standard program. The whole language perspective to teaching reading and language arts (Hierbert & Fisher, 1990; Watson, 1989) is one example of a current viewpoint that reestablishes the teacher as a primary decision maker. In doing so, teachers and teams are empowered to individualize instruction to match students' needs, interests, and learning styles.

Shifting away from predominantly textbook approaches has encouraged many teachers to design active learning experiences for students in classrooms, labs, and real-world settings. These motivating learning experiences may be designed not only by teachers, but by teams that include students, parents, and other professionals (see Villa & Thousand, chap. 7, this volume). There is growing recognition that school personnel, with the help of students, parents, and community members, can develop meaningful educational programs that accommodate a range of individual differences. This provides students and parents with opportunities to participate in the design of local education ("Strengthening Partnerships," 1989). Educational trends that rely on learning strategies and encourage classroom level decision making are congruent with inclusion-oriented curricular restructuring because they allow for heterogeneous grouping, encourage individualization, and base methods on situational variables affecting education. While several of the approaches discussed in this section were not introduced into general education as methods to facilitate inclusion of all students, their compatibility with inclusion-oriented restructuring suggests that many general and special educators are pursuing similar approaches to educational improvement. This proposition provides encouragement that parallel systems of education (general and special) can be merged to provide appropriate education to students without the need to label, sort, and separate.

CHALLENGES AND OPPORTUNITIES
FACING INCLUSION-ORIENTED SCHOOLS

Curricular Relevance

Ensuring the relevance of curricular content is a challenge that will continually face schools since it is determined, in part, by the ever-changing characteristics of the environment and culture, as well as the needs and perceptions of consumers. While climate, culture, population, technology, and economy vary from one place to another, certain broad goals of education remain relevant across time and settings. Some goals of inclusion-oriented curriculum that can be actualized individually for students with varying characteristics and needs (Dewey, 1897; Goodlad, 1979; Minnesota State Board of Education, 1990; Ysseldyke & Algozzine, 1982) are listed below:

1. Acquire basic competencies to participate effectively in current and life-long learning.
2. Develop basic competencies in personal management.
3. Develop a positive self-image.
4. Increase the numbers of environments and personally satisfying activities.
5. Develop, maintain, and expand mutually meaningful relationships with others.
6. Acquire and apply knowledge to community membership and citizenship.
7. Solve problems that are personally and/or societally meaningful.
8. Develop creative and aesthetic appreciation and abilities.
9. Value, accept, and understand human diversity and interdependence.
10. Address human needs through collaborative effort.
11. Cope with change that is self-initiated or initiated by others.
12. Use leisure time in personally and societally valued ways.
13. Acquire competencies that will maintain and enhance personal health.
14. Acquire home living skills.

15. Be vocationally productive (contribute fully or partially to one's own support).

As stated earlier, people in inclusion-oriented schools seek to ensure that all students' lives are improved as a result of having been in school. Therefore, the goals of inclusion-oriented curriculum reflect what society has historically considered desirable outcomes for many students and challenge that these same outcomes be extended to *all* students.

As one examines the goals of inclusion-oriented curriculum, it is difficult to take exception to such pragmatic and philosophically desirable outcomes. Yet, there are arguments that such optimistic outcomes are unrealistic or unattainable for some children, necessitating exclusion of some students. Rationalizing the exclusion of individual students based on certain personal characteristics to serve the majority is inherently detrimental to educational improvement. As Donald Baer (1981) wrote in his essay on educability:

> I will proceed as if all children are capable of learning under instruction. Note that this is a very comfortable statement at the level of policy. If I proceed in this way, sometimes—perhaps often—I will be right, and that will be good for children, good for society, and good for behavioral science. What will be good is not that I will have been right (much as I enjoy that), but rather that some children who we otherwise might have thought could not learn now will learn at least something useful to them, and that will be good for them. To the extent that such efforts make it manifest that this society means to do its best for even the least of its children, that is good for society's ethos and therefore for all of its children, even if *these* children progress only one response toward better self-help in their whole lives. And to the extent that we sometimes finally succeed in teaching a child whom we have consistently failed to teach in many previous efforts, we may learn something about teaching technique and about the nature of behavioral prerequisites to behavior changes . . . If we declare only a very few children to be incapable of learning, then we risk a correspondingly small amount of the first two outcomes—but we risk an exceptionally important part of the third: We risk perhaps the best encounters we could have with the nature of behavior. Too often, in my opinion, we teach children who are not only capable of teaching themselves, but eager to do so; in their wisdom, they cheat us of learning completely how the trick is done because they do some of it for us and do it privately. It is when they cannot do much if any of it for us that we get to find out how to do all of it ourselves, as teachers. (pp. 93–94)

In the early 1980s when Baer wrote these passages he was speaking primarily to psychologists and special educators who worked with children and youth labeled "profoundly mentally retarded." The children were typically taught in homogeneous special classes, special schools serving only children with disabilities, or institutions.

Although his ideas were originally intended for this audience of specialists, his message has renewed meaning for today's educators as inclusion-oriented advocates are exploring ways for all children to be part of the mainstream of school and community life and no one is designated "the least of society's children."

Instructional Practices

Pursuing the goals of inclusion-oriented curriculum offers educators significant opportunity to learn and improve. When education in the mainstream was only available for students considered easy to teach, educators could violate almost every known precept of good teaching and students would learn anyway. Teachers knew that if students failed they would become someone else's responsibility. Fortunately, there were enough educators committed to educational improvement that the trend shifted with exciting results, not just for the previously excluded students, but for all students.

Today's inclusion-oriented classrooms are stimulating learning environments for students and adults where active learning is stressed, students work in cooperative groups, and problem solving results in a variety of new solutions rather than a single correct answer. Trying to maintain the status quo of lectures, workbooks, and worksheets will not work in heterogeneous classes if educators seek a range of meaningful outcomes for students. The pressures of heterogeneous grouping on instructional design forces teachers to either exclude students (within or from the classroom) or meet the challenge to accommodate them. Delayed academic progress, low self-esteem, school misbehavior, substance abuse, and dropouts are a few of the major problems that have been associated with tracking and other artificial social constructions that separate children based on varying student characteristics (Natriello, 1987; Oakes, 1985).

Conversely, educators have only scratched the surface of opportunities available for teachers to learn and grow along with their students. The link drawn between the relevance of curricular outcomes sought for students in inclusion-oriented schools and the manner in which they are taught is simple: Instructional practices must match desired curricular outcomes. For students to establish a positive self-image, learning experiences must be designed to combine challenge and success. If students are to value, accept, and understand human diversity and interdependence, they must learn together with students who have different characteristics so they can draw upon the abilities of each other. For students to collaborate and solve problems, educators must design collaborative learning experiences and teach problem-solving skills to address personally and societally relevant problems. For students to cope effectively with change, educators must allow change to occur and model positive coping strategies. Today's emerging emphasis on cooperative learning, whole language, peer tutoring, active learning, problem solving, and learning strategies match the goals of inclusion-oriented curriculum. Instructional practices that are congruent with inclusion-oriented curriculum can facilitate the kinds of skills that children will increasingly need as the world becomes more complex and interdependent.

Leadership in Schools

Curricular and instructional changes can be influenced significantly by the relative presence or absence of leadership in schools. Today, on the brink of an inclusionary explosion, educators are in desperate need of leaders to step forward and facilitate the process. In times of change, leadership often comes from multiple and sometimes unexpected sources. The standard belief that leadership is the exclusive dominion of administrators is antiquated in inclusion-oriented schools (Villa & Thousand, 1990). People were once considered leaders because it was believed that they had innate skills, knowledge, insight, vision, and/or charisma (Johnson & Johnson, 1987). These and other leadership qualities may be possessed by administrators as well as teachers, support personnel, parents, community members, and students. More recent perspectives suggest that leaders are people capable of engendering leadership qualities and a propensity for action in others. This highlights the need to combine effectively the skills and qualities of group members rather than consolidating leadership in one person or a select group with vested authority (Johnson & Johnson, 1987; Peters & Waterman, 1982).

Just as instruction must be congruent with the goals of inclusion-oriented curriculum, so must leadership approaches be consistent with both inclusion-oriented goals and instructional practices. It is virtually inconceivable that inclusion-oriented curriculum and instruction could be initiated, sustained, or appropriately modified given incongruent leadership models (e.g., autocratic, laissez faire). Alternative forms of *collaborative leadership* (Johnson & Johnson, 1987), *value-added leadership* (Sergiovanni, 1990a, 1990b), *facilitating leadership* based on group problem solving (Parnes, 1985), and *adhocratic leadership* (Skrtic, 1991, 1987; Thousand, 1990) may be used or combined to form organizational patterns congruent with inclusion-oriented education. These process-referenced approaches seek to strike a "delicate balance" (Parnes, 1988). "How loose can a person stay before falling apart, and conversely, how tight can one remain before freezing up?" (Parnes, 1988, p. 319). Many of the processes inherent in collaborative, problem-solving, and adhocratic approaches attempt to balance openness with structure. The goals of inclusion-oriented curriculum also provide a framework for leadership and organization. School personnel can benefit from a positive self-image, collaboration with colleagues, problem-solving methods, valuing differences, and building upon interdependencies. In fact, the challenges faced by educators today are so complex and massive that faithfully practicing the ideas and strategies is essential.

Diffusion of Innovations

Widespread adoption of an inclusion-oriented curriculum as described in this book would be a significant departure from the status quo in public schools. As an educational innovation, there is much to learn about how inclusion-oriented curriculum can work to effectively serve students with diverse needs. At the same time, many advocates of inclusion-oriented schooling believe there is sufficient knowledge and skill to begin the process of change now. In his book, *Diffusion of Innovations*, E. Rogers (1983) wrote:

> An *innovation* is an idea, practice, or object that is perceived as new by an individual or other unit of adoption. It matters little, so far as human behavior is concerned, whether or not an idea is *objectively* new as measured by the lapse of time since its first use or discovery. The perceived newness of the idea for the individual determines his or her reaction to it. If the idea seems new to the individual, it is an innovation. (p. 11)
> *Diffusion* is the process by which an innovation is communicated through certain channels over time among the members of a social system. It is a special type of communication, in that the messages are concerned with new ideas. It is the newness of the idea in the message content of communication that gives diffusion its special character. (p. 5)
> The newness means that some degree of uncertainty is involved. (p. 6)

Whether the innovation is inclusion-oriented curriculum, magnet schools, sex education, or AIDS education, change in today's schools is inescapable and occurring with an increasing frequency that parallels societal change. This highlights the rationale for one goal of inclusion-oriented curriculum, "cope with change that is self-initiated or initiated by others" (see p. 246, this chapter). Diffusion for the purpose of adopting and sustaining an innovation is a major challenge facing inclusion-oriented advocates. Given the scope of inclusion-oriented education, understanding the extensive and complex nature of diffusion becomes imperative.

Change can be facilitated through any combination of structural, political, human resource, and symbolic actions (Bolman & Deal, 1984; Fullan, 1982). Having a framework to conceptualize change can reduce people's anxiety and thus advance their potential for meaningful participation in the process (Giangreco, 1989). The potential contributions by members of the immediate or extended school community could be too valuable to prevent anyone from active participation in the change process. Chastising others for their "behind the times" thinking is likely to perpetuate defensiveness among group members and impede desired changes. Therefore, initiators of inclusion-oriented curricular changes must actively listen to and consider the perspectives of those with whom he or she disagrees. By deferring judgment regarding the ideas of others while simultaneously building on shared beliefs and goals, inclusion-oriented advocates can facilitate change in ways more likely to be adopted and sustained over time.

Diffusion of innovations including inclusion-oriented curriculum typically advance via standard sources such as preservice preparation, inservice staff development, media resources (e.g., books, journals, videos), and people-to-people contacts (e.g., presentations, technical assistance, collaborative consultation). Initiators of innovation seeking the scope of change required to implement inclusion-oriented curricula use these standard sources in addition to developing new ones, such as the involvement of class peers in joint problem solving (Giangreco, 1990; Giangreco & Cloninger, 1990) or "circles of friends" (Snow & Forest, 1987). Currently, people-to-people contacts and an emerging body of inclusion-oriented media resources (Biklen, 1988; Lipsky & Gartner, 1989; Stainback & Stainback, 1990b; Stainback, Stainback, & Forest, 1989; Vandercook, Wolff, & York, 1989; York, Vandercook, MacDonald, Heise-Neff, & Caughey, 1989; York, Vandercook, MacDonald, & Wolff, 1989) are the primary sources of diffusion. While the emergence of inservice staff development approaches offers initial ways to promote diffusion (Showers, 1990; Villa, 1989), preservice preparation for teachers, administrators, and other school-related professionals lags far behind. In part, this may account for the significant time period between the initiation and widespread adoption of educational innovations. Few educators or support personnel (e.g., speech-language pathologists, school psychologists, occupational therapists, physical therapists) enter their profession with an inclusion-oriented ethic or with the competencies and supervised practice required for success in inclusion-oriented schools. Relaying the message about what inclusion-oriented curriculum is, why it is beneficial for students, and how it can be done effectively remains a challenge.

This section identified four major challenges facing the move toward inclusion-oriented schooling: 1) ensuring curricular relevance for all students, 2) matching instructional practices to the curricular content, 3) establishing leadership and organizational perspectives congruent with inclusion-oriented curriculum and instruction, and 4) diffusing inclusion-oriented innovations through standard and emerging sources. While these and other challenges present formidable obstacles, they also provide sterling opportunities for the rejuvenation and growth of our field. In the next two sections potential courses of action are offered to facilitate inclusion-oriented schooling on both macro and micro levels.

POTENTIAL ACTIONS TO FACILITATE INCLUSION-ORIENTED SCHOOLING (MACRO)

Adhocracy

School administrators are poised to take one of the first courses of action to promote inclusion-oriented school environments, curricula, and instruction. Changes in how school personnel interact with each other seem to be a key ingredient of success for inclusion-oriented schools. Skrtic (1987) articulated the consequences of "machine and professional bureaucracies" (p. 4) on the ability of school personnel to meet the needs of individual learners. Skrtic recommends the development of an *adhocracy*, meaning that "teams of professionals mutually adjust their collective skills and knowledge to invent unique, personalized programs for each student" (Thousand, 1990, p. 32). Given the changing nature of knowledge as well as the unpredictable, and thus nonstandardizable needs of individual learners with educational challenges, an adhocratic model of organization allows invention to occur, in contrast to bureaucracies that standardize production.

One adhocratic example described by Thousand and Villa (1990) as a "teaching team" approach is successfully operating in some inclusion-oriented schools.

> A teaching team is an organizational and instructional arrangement of two or more members of the school and greater community who distribute among themselves planning, instructional, and evaluation responsibilities for the same students on a regular basis for an extended period of time. Teams can vary in size from two to six or seven people. They can vary in composition as well, involving any possible combination of classroom teachers, specialized personnel (e.g., special educators, speech and language pathologists, guidance counselors, health professionals, employment specialists), instructional assistants, student teachers, community volunteers (e.g, parents, members of the local 'foster grandparent' program), and students, themselves. (pp. 152–153)

The result, according to Thousand and Villa (1989), is that any student may receive intensive instructional support within the classroom if the existing staff is reassigned to result in a lower instructor–learner ratio. This redistribution of resources capitalizes on the diverse knowledge and instructional styles of the team members. As Skrtic (1989, 1991) notes, adhocracies can promote successful accomplishment of complex work, coordination through mutual adaptation of skills, and novel services that meet unique client needs in a dynamic, fluid, and changing environment.

Research and practice literature clearly indicate that administrators *can* address several variables associated with successful implementation of inclusion-oriented curricula. Some of these variables, shown in Table 1, include: 1) establishing and building consensus, 2) expecting and creating opportunities for collaboration, 3) expanding the curriculum, 4) redefining roles, and 5) creating common conceptual frameworks through staff development (Thousand et al., 1986; Thousand & Villa, 1990; Villa & Thousand, 1990).

Integrating Existing Innovations

Integrating innovations, although a challenging endeavor, is both necessary and encouraging. It is necessary because innovations must be conceptualized and implemented within the context of an overall school plan if they are to lead to constructive, coherent improvement. It is encouraging because it appears that sufficient knowledge exists to achieve many more inclusion-oriented schools than presently exist. More than 10 years ago, based on a review of effective schools, Edmonds (1979) concluded:

> We can, whenever and wherever we choose, successfully teach all children whose schooling is of interest to us. We already know more than we need in order to do this. Whether we do it must finally depend on how we feel about the fact that we haven't done it so far. (p. 29)

Table 1. Organizational strategies for promoting inclusion-oriented schools

Strategy	Outcomes
Establishing and building consensus	Common assumptions and beliefs
Expecting and creating opportunities for collaboration	Flexible and fluid teaching assignments
Expanding the curriculum	Increased variety, options, and responsiveness to student needs
Redefining roles	Acquisition of new job functions and knowledge due to shared expertise
Creating common conceptual frameworks through staff development	Acquisition of best practices and curriculum development

Source: Adapted from Villa and Thousand (1990).

In his summary article on integrating innovations, Guskey (1990) offers five guidelines to assist school leaders in their efforts to synthesize various innovations within the context of overall school improvement plans:

1. All innovative strategies in the improvement program should share common goals and premises.
2. No single innovative strategy can do everything.
3. The innovative strategies in the improvement program should complement each other.
4. All innovative strategies need to be adapted to individual classroom and building conditions.
5. When a well conceived combination of innovative strategies is used, the results are likely to be greater than those attained using any single strategy.

These guidelines represent common sense ideas for selecting and evaluating innovations being considered for adoption in schools. They also presume that schools have articulated a clear mission so they can judge innovations based on their congruence with the goals they seek for students.

Research demonstrating the effectiveness of any particular strategy or innovation is appealing, yet it also has potential drawbacks. Innovations must first be congruent with values embedded in the school philosophy and have a logical basis. While efficacy research is desirable, a congruent value base and underlying logic are sufficient for initial adoption. Evaluation of initiated innovations is then needed to assess the impact of the change. Educators must avoid being enticed by the appeal of efficacy data without corresponding values and logic congruent with the school mission. The following story exemplifies such a situation:

> Three coals miners are working in an underground tunnel when they hear an unusual sound and the lights go out. The miners smell what they believe is a gas leak. Without fully considering the situation, one miner struck a match to shed some light on the situation. Luckily for the miners, the ensuing explosion was minor, resulting only in a few scrapes. The other two miners, who were understandably upset by their coworker's lack of good judgment, asked him why he lit the match. He explained, "We needed light and I knew it would work. It seemed like a good idea at the time."

We have years of data indicating that matches work to produce light and heat. However, just because something works to produce a particular effect does not mean it should be used in all circumstances; other factors must also be considered. If research data supporting the efficacy of a particular innovation lead to its adoption, an educational explosion and potential destruction may occur if it is incongruent with the school's values and logic. Although there may be hundreds of research studies demonstrating the efficacy of a particular approach to teaching basic literacy skills, the approach is unlikely to facilitate inclusion-oriented schooling if it is based on homogeneous grouping and a "one size fits all" approach to instruction. If a particular "discipline" program with impressive efficacy data is aversive (e.g., subjects students to physical or psychological pain) or includes procedures that may constitute public humiliation (e.g., ridicule of a student in the presence of classmates), it would be an incompatible choice since such approaches violate inclusion-oriented goals sought for children. Guskey's (1990) guidelines for evaluating innovations may provide opportunities for members of the school community to clarify their mission and take steps to implement it.

POTENTIAL ACTIONS TO FACILITATE
INCLUSION-ORIENTED SCHOOLING (MICRO)

While educational philosophers and scholars struggle with the challenges associated with integrating macrolevel innovations, many educators wonder what they can do to facilitate inclusion-oriented environments, curriculum, and instruction in the meantime. Like any grassroots movement, the collective power of individuals cannot be underestimated. The small changes implemented by individuals and groups can have significant cumulative effects (Carnoy & Levin, 1985; Giangreco, 1989). The ideas presented in Tables 2 and 3 represent two categories for educators to use as guidelines, General Inclusion-Oriented Actions and Curricular/Instructional Inclusion-Oriented Actions. Although these categories are presented separately, they need not be considered consecutively. Many of the suggestions can be addressed simultaneously and in any variety of combinations. The ideas in Tables 2 and 3 are not comprehensive or prescriptive in nature; they are suggestions for educators to initiate or continue inclusion with instructional integrity in schools and communities.

These microlevel actions can be summed up as the four "Ps": *personal, political, professional,* and *practice* (A. Nevin, personal communication, May 24, 1990). Personal actions include expanding personal boundaries at every opportunity and reaching out and interacting on personal, social, and professional levels with people who have a range of individual differences. Educators should find out first hand how these people cope, contribute, and celebrate their differ-

Table 2.   Potential actions for facilitating inclusive education: General inclusion-oriented actions

Find out where inclusion-oriented programs are going on and learn more about them.

Plan a conference or workshop for your school on inclusive education.

Establish transition policies and procedures to create the opportunity for all students recently referred for special education and existing students to receive special education and/or related services in general education classes (Thousand et al., 1986).

Establish prereferral procedures to strengthen general education and avoid unnecessary referral, labeling, and placement of students in special education (Graden, Casey, & Bronstrom, 1985).

Design a staff development plan to provide school faculty and staff with information, shared language, skills, and experiences that will allow them to be increasingly successful in teaching heterogeneous groups of students (Villa, 1989).

Establish peer support networks (Stainback & Stainback, 1990a).

Establish policies only to serve students from one district, thus creating the need for neighboring districts to serve their own students.

Present information to the school board regarding the potential benefits to all students by pursuing inclusion-oriented schools.

Ask elected officials (school, local, state, national) what their views are regarding inclusion-oriented schooling; inform them of your views and vote accordingly.

Learn another language (e.g., American Sign Language, Spanish, Russian).

Arrange for people who are pursuing inclusion-oriented schooling in your community to be recognized locally, regionally, and nationally for their exemplary work.

Lobby for reallocation of school budget to support inclusion-oriented schooling.

ences. Political actions include becoming involved in the organizations and systems that can create change in communities. Professional actions include being aware of current trends, research, and literature within and outside the field of education. Some of the best ideas to improve curriculum and instruction may be the result of implementing ideas from other fields. Educators should take steps to ensure that they actively continue their learning. Finally, as educators practice their personal, political, and professional actions, they will create opportunities to take risks and set an example that may inspire others to act with them. In these ways one person *can* make a difference.

Actions for change are often initiated with a "best guess" in an experimental and evaluative mode. This does not mean that initiating change is so haphazard that it does not matter what is done first. Change may start in any variety of ways or places based on many factors unique to a situation. The need for more inclusive schools and

Table 3.   Potential actions for facilitating inclusive education: Curricular/instructional inclusion-oriented actions

Converse with a colleague from a different discipline (administration, regular education, special education, psychology, physical therapy, occupational therapy, speech pathology) to learn more about what they do.

Take a course to increase teaching skills for learners who have a range of individual differences and learn how to adapt curriculum.

Read literature on innovations that are congruent with inclusive education such as cooperative learning (Johnson & Johnson, 1987; Johnson, Johnson, & Holubec, 1986), whole language (Watson, 1989), multilevel instruction (Campbell, Campbell, Collicott, Perner, & Stone, 1988), curriculum overlapping (Giangreco & Meyer, 1988; Giangreco & Putnam, 1991), peer tutoring (Pierce, Stahlbrand, & Armstrong, 1984), and creative problem solving (Parnes, 1981, 1985, 1988).

Establish a school-level or district-level task force to determine if curricular innovations are consistent with each other (Guskey, 1990; Olson, 1989).

Talk to graduates of your school's special education programs to determine what was positive about your services and what could be improved.

Talk to employers and business people in the community to find out what kinds of skills, attitudes, and characteristics they value and consider when hiring employees.

Establish a regular item on the faculty meeting agenda to discuss curricular issues.

Use instructional approaches and inclusive curricular content that potentiate each other (e.g., cooperative group learning promoting collaborative skills).

Photocopy the tables of contents from regular and special education journals and send to faculty members so they can be aware of recent developments and read articles of interest.

Critique recent literature on curriculum/instruction with colleagues on a regular basis.

Establish individual student planning teams.

Develop a peer support group among faculty; teach and coach each other regarding curricular/instructional innovations.

educational programs requires action, regardless of its perceived magnitude. As Alex Osborn, who coined the term *brainstorming* said, "A fair idea put to use is better than a good idea kept on the polishing wheel" (Parnes, 1988, p. 37).

CONCLUSION

The fact that the world is changing is unavoidable. Educators have choices to make about how education can improve the lives of students as a result of having been in school. A good start may be to join with other members of school communities to determine what children should learn. Once that is accomplished in at least an initial way (it is always changing), the next tasks are to design instructional practices that will assist in achieving student goals and to select forms of school organization that support curriculum and instruction.

Inclusion-oriented schools exist, yet diffusing them remains a challenge. All inclusion-oriented schools may not be models of excellence for curriculum and instruction. The quality of education in inclusion-oriented schools varies dramatically. Continued efforts to restructure schools and integrate innovations should lead to further school improvements and more widely available models of inclusion with instructional integrity.

Although this chapter has suggested methods for individuals and groups to facilitate inclusion-oriented schooling through curriculum and instruction, the true challenge is not whether educators *can* develop inclusive schools, it is whether educators *will* develop inclusive schools. Do educators think it is worth doing? Can they afford to do it? Can they afford not to do it?

A few cost-analysis studies have documented the economic advantages of including people with significant disabilities in more integrated activities and environments (Hill, Wehman, Kregel, Banks, & Metzler, 1987; Piuma, 1989). It is encouraging that extending new opportunities to previously excluded people is considered money well spent and good news for taxpayers. Yet, the author hesitates to embrace cost-benefit analysis as a criterion to provide or not provide inclusion-oriented education for children in the United States. In Donald Baer's (1981) essay on educability, he symbolically dedicated one of his points to the federal Office of Management and Budget (OMB). He wrote:

> The amount we spend on even unnecessarily expensive attempts to teach the most profoundly retarded can always be compared to the amount that we spend on unnecessarily designed jeans, photographs of Saturn's rings, ballistic and antiballistic missiles of unknown necessity, nonfunctional tanks, skirts of a yearly-different length, lapels of a yearly-different width, nuclear alternatives to oil, and Southeast Asian wars. The essence of the OMB-like point is that how much we spend on anything is not determined by its necessity, its value, its frivolity, or even its price, so much as it is determined by behavior modification (most often in the form called politics). Thus, it is always open to re-modification. If NARC (formerly the National Association for Retarded Citizens) and its allies think they can move sufficient representatives and senators into investing another millipercentage of the gross national product into the teaching of the most profoundly retarded, the point is either to help them, hinder them, or watch them, but hardly to suggest that they are flying in the face of natural law. Indeed, they are merely acting as if politicians are capable of learning under instruction; they are trying to develop the most effective techniques of that instruction. (p. 95)

Although there is hope that inclusion-oriented efforts can be cost-effective, whether the United States pursues this course of action on behalf of children will probably depend less on cost and more on politics, and whether, collectively, educators are willing to take the risks involved in change.

In closing this book, this author shares a hopeful observation about a phenomenon observed in inclusion-oriented classrooms—an "upward spiraling effect." If people preparing for a career in teaching are asked why they want to be teachers, it is rare that someone would describe their dream as "giving straightforward lectures and having kids complete ditto sheets and fill in workbooks." No, most of the people this author has met during the last 15 years who want to be teachers have a vision to teach relevant content through stimulating activities. They picture themselves designing experiments, real-world field study, provocative discussions, and a multitude of variations that make learning enjoyable and motivating. Yet, somewhere along the way many teachers lose that dream. For whatever reasons, many may realize that after 10 or 15 years they have resorted to giving lectures and using workbooks and ditto sheets. Whether by choice or not, some of the teachers who find themselves faced with inclusion-oriented change have experienced a rejuvenation in their excitement about teaching. That enthusiasm, combined with their skill, has encouraged students to become more excited about learning. This response encourages teachers and the spiral continues upward at varying speeds for different people. The energy inherent in these collaborative and mutually beneficial interactions among adults and students is the fuel that fires the engine of inclusion-oriented schools. Inclusion-oriented people have a vision of schools where all children are welcomed and where teachers design educational experiences to meet student needs and, at the same time, some of their own. To paraphrase Baer (1981), you can help them, you can hinder them, or you can watch them. Your decision, whatever it is, *will* matter.

REFERENCES

Alley, J. (1985, April–May). *Future research data and general education reform.* Paper presented at the annual forum of the Association for Institutional Research, Portland, OR. (ERIC Document Reproduction Service No. ED 259 674)

Baer, D. (1981). A hung jury and a Scottish verdict: "Not proven." *Analysis and Intervention in Developmental Disabilities, 1*(1), 91–98.

Benjamin, S. (1989, September). An ideascape for education: What futurists recommend. *Educational Leadership,* 8–14.

Bickel, W.E., & Bickel, D.D. (1986). Effective schools, classrooms, and instruction: Implications for special education. *Exceptional Children, 52*(6), 489–500.

Biklen, D. (Producer). (1988). *Regular lives* [Video]. Washington, DC: State of the Art Productions.

Biklen, D., Ferguson, D., & Ford. A. (Eds.). (1989). *Schooling and disability: 88th yearbook of the National Society for the Study of Education, Part 2.* Chicago: University of Chicago Press.

Bolman, L.G., & Deal, T.E. (1984). *Modem approaches to understanding and managing organizations.* San Francisco: Jossey-Bass.

Campbell, C., Campbell, S., Collicott, J., Perner, D., & Stone, J. (1988). Individualizing instruction. *Education New Brunswick—Journal Edition, 3,* 17–20.

Carnoy, M.M., & Levin, H. (1985). *Schooling and work in the democratic state.* Palo Alto, CA: Stanford University Press.

Conn-Powers, M., Ross-Allen, J., & Holburn, S. (1990). Transition of young children into the elementary education mainstream. *Topics in Early Childhood Special Education, 9*(4), 91–105.

Cooperative learning. (1990). *Educational Leadership, 47*(4).

Crabbe, A.B. (1989). The future problem solving program. *Educational Leadership, 47*(1), 27–29.

Dede, C.J. (1989). The evolution of information technology: Implications for curriculum. *Educational Leadership, 47*(1), 23–27.

Deschler, D., & Schumaker, J.B. (1988). An instructional model for teaching students how to learn. In J. Graden, J. Zins, & M. Curtis (Eds.), *Alternative educational delivery systems: Enhancing instructional options for all students* (pp. 391–411). Washington, DC: National Association for School Psychologists.

Dewey, J. (1897). My pedagogic creed. *The School Journal, 54*(3), 77–80.

Eberle, B., & Stanish, B. (1985). *CPS for kids: A resource book for teaching creative problem-solving to children.* East Aurora, NY: D.O.K. Publishers.

Edmonds, R. (1979). Some schools work and more can. *Social Policy, 9*(5), 25–29.

Fox, T., & Williams, W. (1990). *Selected best practices for meeting the special needs of all students in their local school and community.* Burlington: University of Vermont, Center for Developmental Disabilities.

Fullan, M. (1982). *The meaning of educational change.* New York: Teacher's College Press.

Gartner, A., & Lipsky, D. (1987). Beyond special education: Toward a quality system for all students. *Harvard Educational Review, 57,* 367–395.

Giangreco, M.F. (1989). Facilitating integration of students with disabilities: Implications of "planned change" for teacher preparation programs. *Teacher Education and Special Education, 12*(4), 139–147.

Giangreco, M.F. (1990). *Using creative problem solving methods to include students with severe disabilities in general education activities.* Manuscript submitted for publication review. Burlington: University of Vermont, Center for Developmental Disabilities.

Giangreco, M.F., & Cloninger, C.J. (1990). Educational program development for children and youth with dual sensory impairments: Facilitating inclusion through problem-solving methods. *The TASH Newsletter, 16*(5), 10.

Giangreco, M.F., & Meyer, L.H. (1988). Expanding service delivery options in regular schools and classrooms for students with severe disabilities. In J. Graden, J. Zins, & M. Curtis (Eds.), *Alternative educational delivery sys-*

tems: Enhancing instructional options for all students (pp. 241–267). Washington, DC: National Association for School Psychologists.

Giangreco, M.F., & Putnam, J.W. (1991). Supporting the education of students with severe disabilities in regular education environments. In L.H. Meyer, C.A. Peck, & L. Brown (Eds.), *Critical issues in the lives of people with severe disabilities* (pp. 245–270). Baltimore: Paul H. Brookes Publishing Co.

Goodlad, J. (1979). *What are schools for?* New York: Phi Delta Kappa Educational Foundation.

Graden, J., Casey, A., & Bronstrom, 0. (1985). Implementing a prereferral intervention system: Part I. The Model. *Exceptional Children. 51*, 377–384.

Graden, J., Zins, J., & Curtis, M. (Eds.). (1988). *Alternative educational delivery systems: Enhancing instructional options for all students.* Washington, DC: National Association for School Psychologists.

Guskey, T.R. (1990). Integrating innovations. *Educational Leadership, 47*(5),11–15.

Hierbert, E.H., & Fisher, C.W. (1990). Whole language: Three themes for the future. *Educational Leadership, 47*(6), 62–64.

Hill, M.L., Wehman, P.H., Kregel, J., Banks, P.D., & Metzler, J. (1987). Employment outcomes for people with moderate and severe disabilities: An eight-year longitudinal analysis of supported competitive employment. *Journal of The Association for Persons with Severe Handicaps, 12*(3), 182–189.

Johnson, D.W., & Johnson, F. P. (1987). *Joining together: Group theory and group skills* (3rd ed.). Englewood Cliffs, NJ: Prentice-Hall.

Johnson, D.W., Johnson, R.T., & Holubec, E.J. (1986). *Circles of learning: Cooperation in the classroom,* (rev. ed.). Edina, MN: Interaction Book Co.

Johnson, D.W., Johnson, R.T., & Maruyama, G. (1983). Interdependence and interpersonal attraction among heterogeneous and homogeneous individuals: A theoretical formulation and a meta-analysis of the research. *Review of Educational Research, 3*(1), 5–54.

Kniep, W.M. (1989). Global education as school reform. *Educational Leadership, 47*(1), 43–46.

Levin, H.M., & Rumberger (1987). Educational requirements for new technologies: Visions, possibilities, and current realities. *Educational Policy, 1*(3), 333–354.

Lezotte, L. (1989). School improvement based on the effective schools research. In D.K. Lipsky & A. Gartner (Eds.), *Beyond separate education: Quality education for all* (pp. 25–37). Baltimore: Paul H. Brookes Publishing Co.

Lipsky, D.K., & Gartner, A. (Eds.). (1989). *Beyond separate education: Quality education for all.* Baltimore: Paul H. Brookes Publishing Co.

Meyer, L.H., & Janney, R. (1989). User friendly measures of meaningful outcomes: Evaluating behavioral interventions. *Journal of The Association for Persons with Severe Handicaps. 14*(4), 263–270.

Minnesota State Board of Education. (1990, February). *State board of education curriculum rules: 3500.1060, Learner goals.* St. Paul: Author.

Naisbitt, J. (1989, April). *Millenium trends.* Presentation at the Illinois Association of School Boards, Chicago. As quoted by Adkins, G. (1989), "*Megatrends" author foresees the millenium. Educational Leadership, 47,*(1) 16–17.

Natriello, G. (Ed.). (1987). *School dropouts: Patterns and policies.* New York: Teacher's College Press.

Oakes, J. (1985). *Keeping track.* New Haven, CT: Yale University Press.

Olson, J. (1989). Surviving innovation: Reflection on the pitfalls of practice. *Journal of Curriculum Studies, 21*(6), 503–508.

Parnes, S.J. (1981). *The magic of your mind.* Buffalo, NY: Creative Education Foundation, Inc.

Parnes, S.J. (1985). *A facilitating style of leadership.* East Aurora, NY: D.O.K. Publishers.

Parnes, S.J. (1988). *Visionizing: State of the art processes for encouraging innovative excellence.* East Aurora, NY: D.O.K. Publishers.

Peters, T.J., & Waterman, R.H. (1982). *In search of excellence: Lessons from America's best-run companies.* New York: Harper & Row.

Pierce, M., Stahlbrand, K., & Armstrong, S. (1984). *Increasing student productivity through peer tutoring programs.* Austin, TX: PRO-ED.

Piuma, M.F. (1989). *Benefits and costs of integrating students with severe disabilities into regular public school programs: A study of money well spent.* San Francisco: San Francisco State University, Department of Special Education.

Rogers, E. (1983). *Diffusion of innovations* (3rd ed.). New York: Macmillan.

Schnorr, R. (1991). "Peter? He comes and goes . . .": First graders perspectives of a part-time mainstream student. *Journal of The Association for Persons with Severe Handicaps, 15,* 231–240.

Sergiovanni, T. (1990a). Adding value to leadership gets extraordinary results. *Educational Leadership, 47*(8), 23–27.

Sergiovanni, T. (1990b). *Value-added leadership: How to get extraordinary performance in schools.* San Diego: Harcourt Brace Jovanovich.

Showers, B. (1990). Aiming for superior classroom instruction for all children: A comprehensive staff development model. *Remedial and Special Education, 11*(3), 35–39.

Skrtic, T. (1987). An organizational analysis of special education reform. *Counterpoint, 8*(2), 15–19.

Skrtic, T. (1989, May). *School organization and service delivery: Are schools capable of change?* Paper presented at the Vermont Association of Special Education Administrators Conference, Stowe, VT.

Skrtic, T. (1991). *Behind special education: A critical analysis of professional knowledge in school organization.* Denver, CO: Love Publishing.

Snow, J., & Forest, M. (1987). Circles. In M. Forest (Ed.), *More education integration: A further collection of readings on the integration of children with mental handicaps into regular school systems.* Downsview, Ontario: G. Allan Roeher Institute.

Stainback, S., Stainback, W., & Forest, M. (1989). *Educating all students in the mainstream of regular education.* Baltimore: Paul H. Brookes Publishing Co.

Stainback, W., & Stainback, S. (1990a). Facilitating peer supports and friendships. In W. Stainback & S. Stainback (Eds.), *Support networks for inclusive schooling: Interdependent integrated education* (pp. 51–63). Baltimore: Paul H. Brookes Publishing Co.

Stainback, W., & Stainback, S. (1990b). *Support networks for inclusive schooling: Interdependent integrated education.* Baltimore: Paul H. Brookes Publishing Co.

Strengthening partnerships with parents and community. (1989). *Educational Leadership, 47*(2).

Thousand, J. (1990). Organizational perspectives in teacher education and renewal: A conversation with Tom Skrtic. *Teacher Education and Special Education, 13*(1), 30–35.

Thousand, J., Fox, T., Reid, R., Godek, J., Williams, W., & Fox, T. (1986). *The homecoming model: Educating students who present intensive educational challenges within regular education environments.* Burlington: University of Vermont, Center for Developmental Disabilities.

Thousand, J.S., & Villa, R.A. (1989). Enhancing success in heterogeneous schools. In S. Stainback, W. Stainback, & M. Forest (Eds.), *Educating all students in the mainstream of regular education* (pp. 89–103). Baltimore: Paul H. Brookes Publishing Co.

Thousand, J., & Villa, R. (1990). Sharing expertise and responsibilities through teaching teams. In W. Stainback & S. Stainback (Eds.), *Support networks for inclusive schooling: Interdependent integrated education* (pp. 151–166). Baltimore: Paul H. Brookes Publishing Co.

Torrance, E.P., & Goff, K. (1989). A quiet revolution. *Journal of Creative Behavior, 23*(2), 136–145.

Vandercook, T., Wolff, S., & York, J. (1989). *Learning together: Stories and strategies.* Minneapolis: University of Minnesota, Institute on Community Integration.

Villa, R. (1989). Model public school inservice programs: Do they exist? *Teacher Education and Special Education, 12*(4), 173–176.

Villa, R.A., & Thousand, J.S. (1990). Administrative supports to promote inclusive schooling. In W. Stainback & S. Stainback (Eds.), *Support networks for inclusive schooling: Interdependent integrated education* (pp. 201–218). Baltimore: Paul H. Brookes Publishing Co.

Warren, S.F., Horn, E.H., & Hill, E.W. (1987). Some innovative educational applications of advanced technologies. In L. Goetz, D. Guess, & K. Stremel-Campbell (Eds.), *Innovative program design for individuals with dual sensory impairments* (pp. 283–309). Baltimore: Paul H. Brookes Publishing Co.

Watson, D. (1989). Defining and describing whole language. *The Elementary School Journal, 90*(2), 129–141.

York, J., Vandercook, T., MacDonald, C., Heise-Neff, C., & Caughey, E. (1989). *Regular class integration: Feedback from teachers and classmates.* Minneapolis: University of Minnesota, Institute on Community Integration.

York, J., Vandercook, T., MacDonald, C., & Wolff, S. (1989). *Strategies for full inclusion.* Minneapolis: University of Minnesota, Institute on Community Integration.

Ysseldyke, J., & Algozzine, R. (1982). *Critical issues in special and remedial education.* Boston: Houghton Mifflin.

Index